KU-470-222

Strategic Marketing Management

Alexander Chernev

Kellogg School of Management

Northwestern University

Third Edition

No part of this publication may be reported, stored in a retrieval system, or transmitted in any form or by any means electronic, mechanical, photocopying, recording, scanning, or otherwise, except as permitted under Section 107 or 108 of the United States Copyright Act, without the prior written permission of the publisher. Requests to the publisher for permission should be addressed to Brightstar Media, Inc., at permissions@brightstarmedia.com.

While the publisher and the author have used their best efforts in preparing this book, they make no representations or warranties with respect to the accuracy or completeness of the contents of this book and specifically disclaim any implied warranties of merchantability or fitness for a particular purpose. The advice and strategies contained herein may not be suitable for your situation. Neither the publisher nor the author shall be liable for any loss of profit or any other commercial damages, including but not limited to special, incidental, consequential, or other damages.

Strategic Marketing Management

Third Edition | July 2008

ISBN-10: 0-9790039-2-X

ISBN-13: 978-0-9790039-2-9

(First Edition ISBN-10: 0-9763061-5-8)

(Second Edition ISBN-10: 0-9790039-1-1)

Copyright © 2006–2008 by Alexander Chernev. All rights reserved.

Published by Brightstar Media, Inc., Chicago, IL.

Table of Contents

About the Author

Alexander Chernev is an associate professor of marketing at the Kellogg School of Management, Northwestern University. He holds a Ph.D. in Psychology from Sofia University and a Ph.D. in Business Administration from Duke University.

Dr. Chernev's research applies theories and concepts related to consumer behavior and managerial decision making to develop successful marketing strategies. He serves on the editorial boards of top research journals, including *Journal of Marketing, Journal of Marketing Research, Journal of Consumer Research, Journal of Consumer Psychology,* and *International Journal of Research in Marketing.* Dr. Chernev's research has been published in leading marketing journals and has been quoted in business and popular press, including *Business Week, Wall Street Journal, Forbes, Newsweek,* and *New York Times.* He has written numerous teaching cases focused on corporate planning, marketing strategy, and brand and customer management.

At Kellogg, Dr. Chernev teaches marketing management, strategic marketing, marketing research, and behavioral decision theory in the MBA, Ph.D., and executive education programs. In addition to teaching, he advises companies around the world on issues of strategic marketing planning and analysis, brand and customer equity, new product development, and customer management.

Foreword

Marketing is both an art and a science. Many of its practitioners view marketing as an art, in which both intuition and creativity play a major role—a popular view, particularly in the advertising and sales spheres. Yet, if marketing plans were to be based primarily on intuition and creativity, they would be less effective and less credible to senior management and the company's stakeholders and collaborators. What gives marketing its growing respect and impact is the development and use of a broad range of scientific and analytic tools.

Over the past decades, the field of marketing has accumulated numerous tools. They help define goals and target markets, and facilitate positioning, differentiation, and branding. These tools, however, are usually scattered within marketing textbooks and fail to come together in a clear framework. Here lies the unique contribution of *Strategic Marketing Management*. This concise book presents the major tools and decision processes involved in planning and controlling marketing.

The theory presented in this book is based on three cornerstone ideas:

The first idea is that an offering's ultimate success is determined by the soundness of the five key components of its business model: goal, strategy, tactics, implementation, and control, or the G-STIC framework. This framework is used to streamline a company's marketing analyses and deliver an integrative approach to marketing planning.

The second idea is that when developing its offerings, a company should strive to create value to three key market entities: target customers, the company, and its collaborators. An offering's value proposition, therefore, should be optimized to deliver superior value to target customers in a way that enables the company and its collaborators to reach their strategic goals. These three types of value—customer value, collaborator value, and company value—comprise the 3-V framework, which is the foundation of strategic marketing analysis.

The third idea is that a company's marketing activities can be represented through the process of creating, communicating, and delivering value to its key constituencies, or the C-C-D framework. This framework offers a novel interpretation of the traditional 4-P approach to capture the dynamic nature of the value-management process.

The second part of the book applies these ideas to common business problems, such as increasing profits and sales revenues, developing new products, extending product lines, and managing product portfolios. By linking the theory to practical applications, this book offers a structured approach to analyzing and solving business problems and delineates a set of methodologies to ensure a company's success in the market.

Student testimonies are evidence that this book is very helpful for analyzing marketing cases in the classroom. This book is also very helpful to managers involved in the development and implementation of marketing plans. I further recommend it to senior executives to improve their understanding of what constitutes great marketing analysis and planning.

A company's main focus should be on maximizing value to the customer, the company, and its collaborators. This can be achieved by applying the strategic marketing framework outlined in this book.

Philip Kotler
S. C. Johnson Distinguished Professor of International Marketing
Kellogg School of Management
Northwestern University

Acknowledgments

This book has benefited from the wisdom of my current and former colleagues at the Kellogg School of Management at Northwestern University: Nidhi Agrawal, Eric Anderson, James Anderson, Robert Blattberg, Miguel Brendl, Bobby Calder, Timothy Calkins, Gregory Carpenter, Anne Coughlan, Patrick Duparcq, David Gal, Kent Grayson, Karsten Hansen, Julie Hennessy, Dawn Iacobucci, Robert Kozinets, Lakshman Krishnamurthi, Angela Lee, Sidney Levy, Eyal Maoz, Vikas Mittal, Vincent Nijs, Christie Nordhielm, Yi Qian, Mohan Sawhney, John Sherry Jr., Louis Stern, Brian Sternthal, Alice Tybout, Phillip Zerrillo, and Andris Zoltners. I would like to acknowledge the help of Pierre Chandon (INSEAD) and Ryan Hamilton (Emory) for their valuable comments.

I am indebted to Jim Bettman, Julie Edell Britton, Joel Huber, John Lynch, John Payne, and Rick Staelin at Duke University for their advice and support at the outset of my academic career.

I owe a considerable debt of gratitude to Philip Kotler, one of the leading thinkers in the field of marketing, who through his insightful writings sparked my interest in marketing. I would also like to thank the administration of the Kellogg School of Management and its dean, Dipak Jain, for providing support for my research and teaching activities.

Part One

The Framework

Marketing as a Business Discipline

There is a great deal of confusion about the essence of marketing. This confusion stems from a more general misunderstanding of marketing as a core discipline. Managers often think of marketing in terms of tactical activities, such as sales, advertising, and promotions. In fact, within many organizations, marketing is thought of as an activity designed to support sales by helping managers "sell more of the company's products to more people for more money."

Marketing is far more than tactics. In addition to specialized tactical activities, such as sales and advertising, marketing also involves strategic analysis, the foundation for the success of its tactical elements. This view of the role of marketing as an activity that permeates all areas of an enterprise is underscored by Peter Drucker in his seminal book, *The Practice of Management*:

> *Marketing is not only much broader than selling, it is not a specialized activity at all. It encompasses the entire business... Marketing is the unique, central function of the business enterprise.*[1]

This broad view of marketing as a company's central business function is the foundation of the strategic marketing theory outlined in this book. Marketing as a business discipline is conceptualized in the context of a company's ability to create and manage a leadership position in its markets. This view of marketing can be articulated as follows.

Marketing is the art and science of creating and managing successful exchanges.

An important aspect of marketing is that it is both an art and a science. Marketing is an art because it is driven by managers' creativity and imagination. At the same time, marketing is a science because it represents a body of knowledge that offers a systematic analysis of marketing phenomena. The scientific aspect of marketing that focuses on the logic underlying the process of creating and managing successful exchanges is the essence of strategic marketing.

The term "exchange" is key to understanding the essence of marketing. The core activity of a market is the exchange of goods and services among market participants. Consequently, the role of marketing is to create new exchanges by developing new products and services and to manage the existing exchanges by building sustainable relationships between the company, its customers, and its collaborators.

The ultimate goal of marketing is to ensure the long-term success of an exchange. This success can be defined by financial performance factors, such as net income, shareholder value, and market share, as well as by nonmonetary factors such as customer satisfaction, technology development, and social welfare.

For an exchange to be successful, it should deliver value to all relevant participants. Because the main function of the marketing exchange is to create value, the concept of value is central to marketing. The goal of marketing, therefore, is to ensure that the company's offerings deliver superior value to target customers in a way that enables the company and its collaborators to achieve their strategic goals.

The central role of marketing in a company's business activities and the increasing complexity of these activities call for the development of a systematic approach to analyzing and managing the different aspects of the marketing process. Such a systematic approach to providing a logical structure for organizing complex information can be achieved by using frameworks.

Frameworks are the cornerstones of marketing analysis because they offer a simplified description of complex processes and provide a general solution to a variety of industry-specific problems. Frameworks streamline the decision process by providing managers with a common view of how to frame the problem, a universal approach to identifying alternative solutions, and a shared vocabulary with which to discuss the issues. Because of their level of generality, frameworks rarely offer solutions to specific marketing problems. Instead, they provide a general algorithm that, when applied to a specific scenario, allows managers to identify the optimal solution. Using a framework calls for abstracting the problem at hand to a more general scenario for which the framework offers a predefined solution, and then applying this solution to solve the specific problem (Figure 1). Thus, by relying on the abstract knowledge captured in frameworks, a manager may effectively sidestep the trial-and-error-based learning process.

Figure 1. Using Frameworks in Marketing Management

The marketing framework advanced in this book reflects the process by which a company develops and manages its offerings. It outlines a generalized approach to analyzing and managing different aspects of the marketing process and delineates a set of methodologies to identify and solve specific marketing problems.

Note

[1] Drucker, Peter (1954), *The Practice of Management*. New York, NY: HarperCollins.

Chapter One

The Big Picture

Marketing management involves making a series of decisions aimed at ensuring the market success of a given offering (or a set of offerings). The key aspects of the marketing management process are the focus of this chapter.

Marketing Management as a Process

On the most general level, marketing management can be represented as a process involving four key steps: analyzing the situation in which the company operates, developing an action plan, implementing this plan, and evaluating the outcome (Figure 1).

Figure 1. Marketing Management as a Process

Situation analysis involves evaluating the market in which a company operates and the company's competitive position in this market. Situation analysis is followed by an action plan that outlines a course of action designed to take advantage of an identified opportunity and/or respond to an impending threat. Action planning is followed by the implementation of this action plan, which involves the development and launch of new offering(s), as well as management of existing offering(s). Finally, performance evaluation involves evaluating the outcomes of the company's actions vis-à-vis its plan. These steps are discussed in more detail below.

Situation Analysis

Marketing analysis typically starts with evaluating the market in which a company operates, as well as the company's competitive position in this market. This process usually entails analyzing two key sets of factors: (1) the company's *strengths* and *weaknesses* and (2) the *opportunities* and *threats* presented to the company by the environment in which it operates. A formalized approach to marketing analysis that relies on evaluating these four factors is often referred to as the SWOT framework (an acronym for strengths, weaknesses, opportunities, and threats).

The four factors comprising the SWOT framework can be organized along two dimensions: (1) whether they are internal or external to the company, and (2) whether they are favorable or unfavorable from the company's standpoint (Figure 2). To illustrate, factors such as loyal customers, strong brand name(s), strategically important patents and trademarks, know-how, experienced personnel, and access to scarce resources are classified as strengths. In contrast, factors such as disloyal customers, diluted brand name(s), and lack of technological expertise are classified as weaknesses. Similarly, factors such as emergence of a new, underserved customer segment and a favorable economic environment are classified as opportunities. In contrast, factors such as a new competitive entry into the category, increased product commoditization, and increased buyer and/or supplier power are classified as threats.

Figure 2. The SWOT Framework

	Favorable factors	Unfavorable factors
Internal factors	Strengths	Weaknesses
External factors	Opportunities	Threats

Situation analysis is usually followed by developing a plan to take advantage of the identified opportunity (or, alternatively, defend against an impending threat). This action plan typically details the process of developing and managing the company's offering(s) aimed at fulfilling the need identified by the opportunity analysis. Depending on the situation, a company may decide to pursue either a single opportunity or multiple opportunities. In cases where a company decides to take advantage of multiple market opportunities and develop offerings targeting diverse customer needs, each individual offering requires the development of its own action plan. Because of the importance of the action plan to the ultimate success of an offering, the rest of this chapter focuses on the process of developing such an action plan.

Action Planning

A typical action plan involves five key elements: goal, strategy, tactics, implementation, and control. These five elements comprise the G-STIC framework. The G-STIC framework implies that the actions a manager takes on a day-to-day basis (e.g., product and service design, branding, pricing, managing sales promotions and communications, and setting up a distribution network), should follow directly from the company's overall strategy, which, in turn, should enable the company to achieve its goal. In this context, developing and/or analyzing an action plan involves the following five steps: set a *goal*, develop the *strategy*, design the *tactics*, develop the *implementation* plan, and identify the *control* metrics to measure the proposed action's success (Figure 3).

Figure 3. The G-STIC Framework for Action Planning

The five components of the G-STIC approach to action planning are outlined in more detail below.

Goal

Every action that a company undertakes should be consistent with a well-defined goal. Setting a goal involves two decisions: identifying the focus of the company's actions and defining the specific performance benchmarks to be achieved.

- The *focus* identifies the ultimate criterion for a company's success (e.g., net income, profit margins, sales revenues, and market share).
- *Benchmarks* define the quantitative and temporal aspects of the goal.

For example, a goal may involve increasing earnings per share (focus) by five percent (quantitative benchmark) by the end of the fiscal year (temporal benchmark). The process of setting strategic goals is discussed in more detail in Chapter 5.

Strategy

Strategy outlines the master plan of actions aimed at achieving the company goal. Strategy development involves three key components: identifying target customers, defining the market structure, and designing the offering's value proposition.

- *Target customers* are the potential buyers for whom the company will tailor its offering.
- The *market structure* describes the key aspects of the market in which the company's offerings are presented to target customers. The market structure builds on the selected target customers and is further defined by the following factors: (1) the *company* introducing and managing the offering, (2) *collaborators* working with the company on this offering, (3) *competitors* with offerings that provide similar benefits to the target customers, and (4) the social, technological, economic, political, legal, and physical *context* in which the company operates. The five factors describing market structure (customers, company, collaborators, competitors, and context) are often referred to as the "Five Cs."
- The *value proposition* describes an offering's ability to create value for all relevant market participants—target customers, the company, and its collaborators. Because of its crucial role in ensuring the market success of an

offering, optimizing these three aspects of the value proposition is the key aspect of an offering's strategy.

The processes of identifying target customers, defining the market structure, and designing the offering's value proposition are discussed in more detail in Chapter 2.

Tactics

Tactics identify how the desired strategy is translated into a set of specific actions. Marketing tactics are defined by seven key elements, often referred to as the marketing mix variables: product, service, brand, price, incentives, communications, and distribution. These marketing mix variables are summarized below.

- The *product* aspect of the offering captures its key functional characteristics. Products typically change ownership during purchase; once created, they can be physically separated from the manufacturer and distributed to end-users via multiple channels.

- The *service* aspect of the offering is in many respects similar to the product aspect. However, unlike products, services do not necessarily imply a change in ownership of the offering; instead, the customer acquires the right to use the service within a given timeframe.

- The *brand* serves two key functions: creating an *identity* for the offering that differentiates it from the competition, and creating *value* beyond the product and service characteristics of the offering.

- The *price* reflects the monetary aspect of the offering; it refers to the amount of money the company charges for the benefits provided by its offering.

- *Incentives* offer solutions, typically short term, aimed at enhancing the value of the offering by providing additional benefits and/or reducing costs.

- *Communications* aim to inform target customers about the availability of the offering and highlight its particular characteristics.

- *Distribution* captures the channel through which the offering is delivered to customers.

The tactical aspect of an offering can be represented by the processes of *creating*, *communicating*, and *delivering* value. The processes of creating, communicating, and delivering value can be related to the seven marketing mix variables discussed above, such that the product, service, brand, price, and incentives comprise the value-creation aspect of the offering; communication captures the value-communication aspect; and distribution reflects the value-delivery aspect of the value management process. The tactical aspect of managing an offering's value proposition is discussed in more detail in Chapter 3.

Implementation

The implementation component of market planning outlines the timeline and the logistics of executing an offering's strategy and tactics. Developing an implementation plan involves two key components:

- Defining the *processes* that enable the company to implement its strategy and tactics (e.g., product development practices, service-delivery infrastructure, brand-building mechanisms, and distribution channel structure).

- Identifying the *people* managing the implementation processes (e.g., the core skills and knowledge of the company personnel).

Control

The control aspect of managing an offering aims to ensure adequate progress toward the set goal; it encompasses two key activities: evaluating the company's performance and monitoring the environment in which it operates.

- *Performance evaluation* involves evaluating the outcomes of the company's actions relative to its goals. Performance evaluation can lead to one of two outcomes: (1) success, which indicates adequate progress toward the established goal or (2) a performance gap that represents a discrepancy between a company's desired and actual performance on a key metric (e.g., net income, sales revenues, market share, profit margins, earnings per share, and return on investment).

- *Monitoring the environment* enables the company to identify changes in the environment in which it operates and, when necessary, adjust its business activities to better reflect the new environment. Most changes in the environment are classified into one of two categories: (1) opportunities, which involve a favorable set of circumstances (e.g., favorable government regulations, decreased competition, or an increase in consumer demand) or (2) threats, which involve an unfavorable set of circumstances (e.g., unfavorable government regulations, increased competition, or a decrease in consumer demand).

The key elements of the control aspect of managing an offering are discussed in more detail in Chapter 4.

The Big Picture

The five components of the G-STIC framework and their key aspects can be represented in the form of a pyramid, as shown in Figure 4.

The action-planning process represented by the G-STIC pyramid begins with an outline of the goals that identify the company's focus and the performance benchmarks to be achieved. The goal analysis is followed by a description of the company's strategy, which involves identifying target customers and the other aspects of market structure—collaborators, competitors, the company, and the context in which they operate—as well as outlining the offering's value proposition to the company, its customers, and collaborators. The strategy analysis is followed by a description of marketing tactics, which involve the processes of creating, communicating, and delivering value. The tactical analysis is followed by an implementation plan that identifies the processes and people involved in translating the planned strategy and tactics into reality. The control aspect of action planning outlines a policy for evaluating the company's performance and monitoring the market environment to ensure adequate progress toward the set goal.

Figure 4: The G-STIC Action-Planning Pyramid

Summary

The central role of marketing in a company's business activities and the increasing complexity of these activities call for the development of a systematic approach to analyzing and managing the various aspects of the marketing process. Such a systematic approach to providing a logical structure for organizing complex information can be achieved by using the framework introduced in this chapter.

On the most general level, marketing management can be represented as a process involving four key steps: analyzing the situation in which the company operates, developing an action plan, managing the offering, and evaluating the offering's performance (Figure 1). The focus of this chapter is the development of an action plan, a process captured by the G-STIC (Goal, Strategy, Tactics, Implementation, and Control) framework (Figure 3).

In addition, the key aspects of the G-STIC framework are discussed in more detail in other chapters. The process of setting strategic goals is discussed as an aspect of managing company value in Chapter 6; the development of marketing strategy is outlined in Chapter 2 and addressed in more detail in Part II (Chapters 5–9); marketing tactics are summarized in Chapter 3 and discussed in more detail in Part III (Chapters 10–15); and performance evaluation and control are discussed in Chapter 4.

Chapter Two
Marketing Strategy

Marketing strategy is an integral component of a company's action plan; it outlines the main aspects of the value created by an offering or a product line. Strategy involves three key components: identifying target customers, defining the relevant market structure, and developing the offering's value proposition. These three aspects of marketing strategy are the focus of this chapter.

Overview

The various aspects of an offering's strategy are logically connected. Delineating an offering's strategy begins with identifying target customers, followed by defining the other relevant aspects of the offering's market structure (company, collaborators, competitors, and context), and then by developing the offering's value proposition (Figure 1).

Figure 1. Marketing Strategy: The Big Picture

It is important to note that the development of a marketing strategy is not always a linear process, as implied by Figure 1. Indeed, the selection of target customers is contingent on the offering's ability to deliver superior value (relative to the competition) to these customers in a way that enables the company and its collaborators to reach their strategic goals. This process requires understanding the key aspects of the market structure (company, collaborators, competitors, and context) as well as identifying the value proposition of the offering to target customers, collaborators, and the company. Therefore, developing a marketing strategy should be viewed as an iterative process that simultaneously considers all three steps in order to optimize the value of the offering to target customers, collaborators, and the company. In this context, the linear representation of the three strategic aspects of an offering illustrated in Figure 1 is typically used to structure the presentation of a readily developed strategy (e.g., when writing a marketing plan), whereas the development of the strategy follows an iterative pattern as illustrated in Figure 2.

Figure 2. The Process of Developing a Marketing Strategy

Identify
target
customers

Develop
a value
proposition

Define
the market
structure

The three components of developing an offering's strategy—identifying target customers, defining the relevant market structure, and developing the offering's value proposition—are discussed in more detail below.

Identifying Target Customers

The process of identifying target customers, commonly referred to as targeting, involves identifying potential buyers for whom the company will tailor its offering. Identifying target customers typically involves two decisions: (1) selecting which customers to serve and which to ignore and (2) identifying actionable strategies to reach these customers.

Selecting target customers (also referred to as strategic targeting) is guided by the company's ability to fulfill customer needs better than the competition in a way that creates value for the company and its collaborators. Because fulfilling customer needs is central to the success of an offering, target customers are typically identified through their underlying needs. Selecting target customers through their needs, however, makes it difficult to identify these customers because their needs are, in most cases, not readily observable. Thus, identifying observable (actionable) characteristics that will enable the company to reach customers with these needs (also referred to as tactical targeting) is essential for developing an effective and cost-efficient targeting strategy. Typical actionable characteristics involve demographic (e.g., age, gender, income), geographic (e.g., country, region, and postal codes), psychographic (e.g., personality, moral values, and lifestyle), and behavioral characteristics (user status, purchase frequency, and price sensitivity).

The process of identifying target customers often involves grouping customers into segments, such that customers within each segment are likely to respond in a similar fashion to the company's offerings. This process of dividing customers into groups, commonly referred to as *segmentation*, aims to improve the effectiveness and efficiency of a company's marketing activities by ignoring the nonessential differences among customers within each segment and treating these customers as if they were a single entity.

The process of identifying target customers can yield one or multiple target segments. Because an offering's ability to deliver superior customer value is a function of the underlying customer needs, a company must develop distinct strategies for serving each target segment it decides to pursue.

Defining the Market Structure

The market structure describes the key aspects of the market in which the company's products and services are offered to target customers. Market structure builds on the selected target *customers* to include the following factors: the *company*, its *collaborators* and *competitors*, and the social, technological, economic, political, legal, and physical *context* in which the company operates. An offering's market structure, often referred to as the "Five Cs," can be represented as shown in Figure 3.

Figure 3. The 5-C Framework for Market Structure Analysis

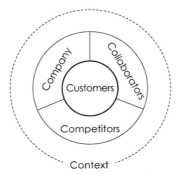

The key factors comprising the market structure of an offering with respect to a given customer segment—company, collaborators, competitors, and context—are summarized in more detail below.

- *Company.* Company analysis involves identifying the business unit (e.g., a department, division, branch, or the entire company) in charge of the offering, defining its strategic goals, and identifying resources (e.g., core competencies and strategic assets) that will enable this unit to deliver superior value to target customers in a way that benefits the company and its collaborators.

- *Collaborators.* Collaborator analysis involves identifying the key collaborators, along with their goals and resources. Collaborators are entities that work with the company to analyze, create, communicate, and deliver value to target customers. Collaboration can occur in several areas: product, service, brand, price, incentives, communications, and distribution. For example, companies can collaborate to develop a product (research and development collaboration), to create a customer incentive (promotional collaboration), and/or to deliver the offering to the customer (channel collaboration).

- *Competitors.* Competitive analysis involves identifying the key current and potential competitors, as well as their goals and resources. Competitors are entities with offerings that aim to fulfill the same needs of the same target customers as the company's offering. Because competitors are defined relative to the needs of the target segment, the competition often goes beyond the traditional industry-defined categories. For instance, Coca-Cola competes not only with other cola producers such as Pepsi, but also with producers of all products that could potentially fulfill the same need, such as juice, bottled water, and milk. In this context, juice, bottled water, and milk are not just substitute products but rather cross-category competitors because they compete to satisfy the same need of the same target customers.

- *Context.* Context includes factors that describe the relevant aspects of the environment in which the company delivers its offering to customers. Typical context factors include the social, technological, economic, political, legal, and physical environment in which the marketing exchange takes place.

  - The social context involves demographic factors, such as race, age, income, education, and employment.

  - The technological context concerns the technologies that are either directly related to the offering or can result in substitute products.

  - The economic context involves factors such as general economic conditions, inflation, interest, and unemployment rates.

  - The political context concerns issues such as political stability of the government, the country and the region; the general business and political orientation of the government; and the role of the government in supporting/protecting specific industries.

  - The legal context involves the legal and regulatory factors that either directly or indirectly affect the offering. For example, the demand for hands-free mobile phone devices is affected by legislation in many cities requiring the use of hands-free phones while driving.

  - The physical context concerns issues such as the overall climate, geographic, and health factors. For instance, the demand for a cold medicine is likely to be affected by the flu season, and ice cream consumption is likely to be affected by the weather.

Note that identifying target customers is crucial for defining the corresponding market structure. By definition, customers in different target segments vary in their needs and are likely to respond in a different fashion to the company's offering; thus, each target segment requires its own market structure analysis. To illustrate, different target customers might be served by different competitors, require a different set of collaborators (e.g., different distribution channels), be managed by different business units of the company, and/or operate in a different social, technological, economic, political, legal, and physical context.

Developing a Value Proposition

An offering's success is ultimately determined by its ability to create value to the relevant market participants: target customers, the company, and its collaborators. The three types of value—customer value, collaborator value, and company value—comprise the 3-V framework and can be visually represented in a Venn diagram (Figure 4). The optimal value proposition is given by the overlap of the three value aspects: value to the customer, value to the company, and value to collaborators. The optimal value proposition reflects the core marketing principle, which asserts that to achieve success, an offering should deliver superior (relative to the competition) value to target customers and collaborators in a way that enables the company to reach its strategic goals. Marketing success can be achieved only when the offering's value is optimized to its target customers, collaborators, and the company; failure to create value for any one of the relevant market participants will inevitably lead to an inefficient marketing exchange and market failure.

Figure 4. The 3-V Framework

Because different target segments vary in their needs, they often have a different set of competitors and collaborators, rely on different core competencies and strategic assets of the company, and are influenced by different aspects of the overall context in which the company operates. This requires that an offering's value proposition be defined for each target segment. Therefore, an offering that targets multiple customer segments must have distinct value propositions tailored to each segment.

The process of creating an optimal value proposition can be better understood when considered as a function of the underlying target market and the corresponding market structure. This approach, illustrated in Figure 5, depicts the three types of value that are crucial to the ultimate success of the offering: customer value, company value, and collaborator value.

Figure 5. Defining the Value Exchange

The concept of creating an optimal value proposition in a competitive context can be illustrated using the example of the iPod, the digital music player from Apple. The key aspects of the iPod's strategy are summarized below.

- The iPod's primary target *customers* are individuals with a need for mobile access to music and video recordings. Most of these customers are teenagers and young adults able to afford the iPod's price tag. For these customers, the iPod offers a revolutionary digital music player that lets them store music and video content in their pocket and listen to/view it wherever they go.

- Apple's *collaborators* include companies like PortalPlayer, which provided the firmware and software platform for the iPod, and Pixo, which was contracted to develop the design and the user interface. These collaborators have benefited from Apple's technological and marketing expertise, as well as from its financial backing. Apple's collaborators also include content providers, such as Sony, EMI, Universal, and Warner record labels. For these collaborators, iPod and iTunes offer an alternative distribution channel to reach a desirable target audience. Apple's collaborators also include a diverse set of retailers: mass merchandisers such as Wal-Mart and Costco, consumer electronics retailers such as Circuit City and Best Buy, and specialized Apple resellers. The iPod creates value for its distributors by attracting customers to their stores and helping them increase their sales revenues and net income.

- From a *company* perspective, the iPod builds on Apple's core competency of customer-focused product development and strategic assets, which include technological, design, and marketing expertise, its existing customer base, and the power of its brand. For Apple, the iPod delivers value by offering a steady stream of revenues and net income, and by providing a platform for product development that enabled Apple to extend its digital player product line (e.g., iPod Shuffle and iPod Nano) and launch revolutionary new products such as the iPhone.

- iPod *competitors* include Zune (Microsoft), Zen (Creative Labs), Sansa (Sandisk), and Insignia (Best Buy), which offer similar benefits and target the same customers. In this context, the success of the iPod is determined by its ability to deliver superior value (relative to these competitors) to its target customers and collaborators.

- The iPod's success is also a function of the *context* in which it is being sold and used. Among the relevant context factors for the iPod are the changes in the overall economy (which affect consumers' disposable income), technological developments (e.g., the development of alternative data compression technologies and their compatibility with Apple's proprietary AAC and Apple Lossless formats), and regulatory factors (e.g., regulations guiding the copyright and licensing of digital content).

Summary

Strategy outlines the master plan of actions aimed at achieving the company goal. Strategy development involves three key components: (1) identifying target customers, (2) defining the market structure, and (3) designing the offering's value proposition for the company, its customers, and collaborators.

Identifying target customers involves identifying potential buyers for whom the company will tailor its offering. The process of identifying target customers typically involves two decisions: selecting which customers to serve (also referred to as strategic targeting) and which to ignore, and identifying actionable strategies to reach these customers (also referred to as tactical targeting). The process of identifying target customers is discussed in more detail in Chapter 9.

The market structure describes the key aspects of the market in which the company's offerings are presented to target customers. Market structure builds on the selected target customers to encompass the following factors: the company, its collaborators and competitors, and the context in which the company operates. Market structure analysis is captured by the 5-C framework (Figure 3).

The value proposition is the key aspect of an offering's strategy; it reflects an offering's ability to create value for the relevant market participants—target customers, the company, and its collaborators. The key principle in developing a value proposition is that it should be optimized to deliver superior value to target customers in a way that enables the company and its collaborators to reach their strategic goals—a concept captured by the 3-V framework (Figure 4). The process of developing and managing a successful value proposition is discussed in more detail in Chapters 5, 6, and 7.

Relevant Frameworks: The 3-C Framework

The 3-C framework, advanced by the Japanese strategist Kenichi Ohmae, suggests that a manager should focus on three key factors for success: the company, the customer, and the competition.[1] By understanding these three factors and integrating them into a strategic framework (or, to use Ohmae's terminology, a strategic triangle), the company can achieve a sustainable competitive advantage. The 3-C framework suggests that managers need to evaluate the business environment in which they operate: the strengths and weaknesses of their own company, the needs of their customers, and the strengths and weaknesses of their competitors. The 3-C framework is simple, intuitive, and easy to understand and use—factors that have contributed to its popularity.

Despite its simplicity, the 3-C framework is often misconstrued. One of the most common misinterpretations of the 3-C framework occurs when unrelated factors also starting with "c," such as capacity and cost, are included in the 3-C model. The problem with this approach is that the Cs describe the key market entities (i.e., company, customers, and competitors), whereas capacity and cost are characteristics of the company and are not independent market entities. Note that the issue here is not whether cost and capacity are important factors in marketing analysis but whether they conform to the logic used to identify the Cs as the main factors that need to be taken into account when designing a company's business strategy. The same logic applies to other potential Cs, such as category, complexity, core competencies, and creativity.

An important limitation of the 3-C framework is that it does not explicitly account for two important market factors: collaborators and context. Despite the important role collaborators (e.g., suppliers and distributors) play in developing and delivering a company's offerings, they are not part of the 3-C model. Furthermore, the 3-C framework does not explicitly account for the variety of economic, regulatory, technological, and political factors that comprise the context in which the company operates. Because of these limitations, marketing analysis can be better served by the more comprehensive and up-to-date 5-C framework (customers, company, collaborators, competitors, and context).

Additional Readings

Aaker, David A. (2007), *Strategic Market Management* (8th ed.). New York, NY: John Wiley & Sons.

Kotler, Philip and Kevin Lane Keller (2008), *Marketing Management* (13th ed.). Upper Saddle River, NJ: Prentice Hall.

Kotler, Philip (1999), *Kotler on Marketing: How to Create, Win, and Dominate Markets*. New York, NY: Free Press.

Lehmann, Donald R. and Russell S. Winer (2007), *Analysis for Marketing Planning* (7th ed.). Boston, MA: McGraw-Hill/Irvin.

Walker, Orville C., Harper W. Boyd, and Jean-Claude Larrâechâe (2007), *Marketing Strategy: A Decision-Focused Approach* (6th ed.). London: McGraw-Hill.

Note

[1] Ohmae, Kenichi (1982), *The Mind of the Strategist: The Art of Japanese Business*. New York, NY: McGraw-Hill.

Chapter Three

Marketing Tactics

Marketing tactics, also referred to as the marketing mix, are a key element of a company's action plan. Unlike strategy, which outlines the main aspects of a company's value proposition, tactics identify a set of specific activities employed to execute a given strategy. The key aspects of developing marketing tactics are the focus of this chapter.

The Key Tactical Elements

An offering's tactics involve a set of specific activities employed to execute a given strategy. Through tactical elements, customers receive an offering's value proposition. Indeed, customers are typically unfamiliar with an offering's strategy; they can only infer strategy by observing the tactical aspects of the offering. Marketing tactics are defined by seven key factors, often referred to as marketing mix variables: product, service, brand, price, incentives, communications, and distribution. A more simplistic, but outdated, interpretation of the marketing mix, commonly referred to as "Four Ps," is discussed in more detail at the end of this chapter.

The seven key marketing mix variables comprising the tactical aspects of an offering are summarized below.

- The *product* aspect of the offering captures some of its key functional characteristics. Products typically change ownership during purchase; once created, they can be physically separated from the manufacturer and distributed to end users via multiple channels.

- The *service* aspect of the offering is in many respects similar to the product aspect, with two main exceptions: change of ownership and separability. Unlike products, which typically change ownership at purchase, services do not necessarily imply a change in ownership; instead, the customer acquires the right to use the service within a given timeframe. Furthermore, unlike products, which can be physically separated from the manufacturer, services are usually delivered and consumed at the same time; as a result, they cannot be inventoried or distributed through multiple channels.

- The *brand* serves two key functions: creating an *identity* for the offering that differentiates it from competitive products and services, and creating *value* beyond the product and service characteristics of the offering. Brand identity differentiates the offering from the competition and is typically achieved on dimensions such as name, logo, symbol, character, slogan, jin-

gle, and packaging. Brand value is typically achieved by creating meaningful brand associations.

- The *price* reflects the monetary aspect of the offering; it refers to the amount
  of money the company charges for the benefits provided by its offering. In dynamic markets, the monetary value of the offering is determined not by price
  alone; it is also a function of various monetary incentives, such as volume discounts, price reductions, coupons, and rebates. Even though from a company's viewpoint, monetary incentives are typically considered part of a
  company's promotional activity, from a customer's perspective, many of these
  incentives are viewed as an integral component of an offering's price.

- *Incentives* enhance the value of the offering by providing additional, typically short-term, benefits and/or reducing costs. Incentives may be divided
  into two categories: monetary, such as volume discounts, price reductions,
  coupons, and rebates; and nonmonetary, such as premiums, contests, and
  rewards. In contrast to monetary incentives, which typically aim to reduce
  an offering's costs, nonmonetary incentives typically aim to enhance the offering's benefits.

- *Communications* aim to inform target customers about the availability of the
  offering and highlight its particular characteristics. The message may involve
  any of the five value-creation marketing mix variables: product, service,
  brand, price, and incentives. For example, a company may choose to promote
  the benefits of its product and service, communicate the meaning of its brand,
  publicize its price, and inform customers about its current incentives.

- *Distribution* captures the channel through which the offering is delivered to
  customers. Distribution is not limited to delivering the company's products
  and services to customers; it can involve the other marketing mix variables
  as well. To illustrate, brand-delivery involves enabling customers to experience the brand (e.g., Disney World theme parks and Nike Town retail stores
  function as channels delivering Disney and Nike brands to customers). Similarly, price-delivery involves the channels for collecting customer payments,
  as well as for processing reverse payments (e.g., refunds). In the same vein,
  incentive delivery involves the mechanisms for distributing and implementing incentives (e.g., processing coupons and rebates).

Marketing Tactics as a Value-Management Process

The tactical aspect of an offering may be represented by the processes of *creating*,
communicating, and *delivering* value (referred to as the C-C-D framework). The processes of creating, communicating, and delivering value may be related to the seven
marketing mix variables—product, service, brand, price, incentives, communication,
and distribution—as shown in Figure 1. Here, product, service, brand, price, and
incentives comprise the value-creation aspect of the offering; communication captures the value-communication aspect; and distribution reflects the value-delivery
aspect of the value management process.

Figure 1. The C-C-D Value Management Framework

The key aspects of the process of creating, communicating, and delivering value are outlined in more detail below.

- *Creating value.* The value-creation aspect of the marketing mix involves five key components: product, service, brand, price, and incentives. For example, the product aspect of the iPod reflects the functionality offered by the digital player, such as hard drive capacity, display, battery life, design, and user-friendly interface. The service aspect of the offering involves the service and technical support that come with the product, as well as augmented services such as iTunes. The brand aspect is defined by the Apple and iPod brands, which differentiate this offering from other functionally similar offerings by Microsoft, Dell, and Sony. The price reflects the retail price at which the iPod is being sold to customers. Incentives include monetary rewards, such as price reductions, coupons, and educational discounts, as well as nonmonetary rewards, such as free music/video downloads.

- *Communicating value.* To illustrate, in the case of the iPod, communications aim to inform target customers about the benefits of iPod and iTunes, enhance the iPod and Apple brands, and inform customers about the price of the iPod and the relevant incentives. This information is conveyed to target customers through various media formats, such as advertising, public relations, personal selling, and product placement in newscasts, movies, and talk shows.

- *Delivering value.* To illustrate, in the case of the iPod, the distribution component encompasses the channels used to deliver the offering to end users. Thus, the iPod product is delivered though various direct and indirect channels, such as Apple's online store, its brick-and-mortar retail stores, and other retailers such as Best Buy and Circuit City. The music download service is delivered through Apple's iTunes website, and diagnostic and repair service is delivered though its brick-and-mortar stores, as well as through various resellers. The Apple brand is delivered through its website and its brick-and-mortar retail stores, which enable customers to experience the essence of the Apple brand. The price is delivered through the retailers, who collect payments from customers and, when necessary, make adjustments to payments made (e.g., price-matching adjustments and refunds). Finally, incentives such as free music downloads are delivered through the iTunes website.

Summary

Tactics identify how an offering's strategy is translated into a set of specific actions. Marketing tactics are defined by seven key elements, often referred to as the marketing mix variables: product, service, brand, price, incentives, communications, and distribution. A more simplistic, but outdated, interpretation of the marketing mix is commonly referred to as the "Four Ps" (product, price, promotion, place).

Conceptually, the tactical aspect of an offering can be represented by the processes of creating, communicating, and delivering value (referred to as the C-C-D framework). The processes of creating, communicating, and delivering value may be related to the seven marketing mix variables, such that product, service, brand, price, and incentives comprise the value-creation aspect of the offering; communication captures the value-communication aspect; and distribution reflects the value-delivery aspect of the value management process.

Relevant Frameworks: The 4-P Framework

The 4-P framework offers a tool for planning and analyzing the execution of a given marketing strategy.[1] According to this model, there are four key decisions that managers must make with respect to a given offering: (1) what features to include in the product, (2) how to price the product, (3) how to promote the product, and (4) in which distribution channels to "place" the product. These four decisions, often referred to as the marketing mix, are captured by the four Ps: product, price, promotion, and place.

The 4-P framework is often misconstrued by managers who try to fit in other factors starting with "p," rather than focus on the underlying logic. For example, a common misinterpretation of the four Ps involves including concepts such as positioning, people, personnel, processes, and productivity as one of the marketing mix variables. Positioning is not a marketing mix variable; rather, it is part of a company's overall strategy, which is then implemented through a particular combination of the marketing mix variables. In the same vein, people are typically viewed as an integral part of the company, rather than as part of an offering's marketing mix. Another common misinterpretation of the 4-P framework concerns the use of "placement" instead of "place." Note that the term "placement" refers to a promotional strategy that involves embedding a product in various forms of entertainment.

The 4-P framework has a number of important limitations. The most obvious is the absence of separate service and brand components. Because it was developed to explain the process involved in marketing consumer-packaged goods, the 4-P framework does not explicitly account for the service element of the offering—a key drawback in today's service-oriented business environment. Furthermore, the brand is not explicitly considered as a separate marketing mix variable and is, instead, viewed as part of a company's product and/or promotion decisions.

Another potential limitation of the 4-P framework concerns the term "promotion." Promotion is a very broad term that includes two distinct types of marketing variables: incentives (e.g., price promotions, coupons, and trade promotions) and communication (e.g., advertising, public relations, and personal selling). While it is a common accounting practice to combine these factors, they each have a distinct impact on business processes. Thus, incentives tend to enhance the offering's value, whereas the primary role of communications is to inform customers about the offering. Therefore, for the purposes of marketing analysis, incentives and communications should be considered separately.

Finally, the use of the term "place" as an element of the marketing mix may be questioned, as well. As the process of delivering the company's offering to customers becomes increasingly complex, it is more accurate to refer to this process as "distribution" or "channel" rather than simply as "place," a term rarely used in contemporary marketing analysis.

Because of the limitations of the 4-P framework, marketing analysis is better served by the more comprehensive and up-to-date C-C-D framework. In fact, the 4-P approach may be interpreted in the context of the C-C-D value-management framework, such that product and price represent the processes of creating value, promotion represents both the value-creation and value-communication aspects of the offering, and place represents the value-delivery aspect of the offering (Figure 2).

Figure 2. Reconceptualizing the 4-P Framework

Additional Readings

Aaker, David A. (2007), *Strategic Market Management* (8th ed.). New York, NY: John Wiley & Sons.

Kotler, Philip and Kevin Lane Keller (2008), *Marketing Management* (13th ed.). Upper Saddle River, NJ: Prentice Hall.

Kotler, Philip (1999), *Kotler on Marketing: How to Create, Win, and Dominate Markets*. New York, NY: Free Press.

Lehmann, Donald R. and Russell S. Winer (2007), *Analysis for Marketing Planning* (7th ed.). Boston, MA: McGraw-Hill/Irvin.

Walker, Orville C., Harper W. Boyd, and Jean-Claude Larrâechâe (2007), *Marketing Strategy: A Decision-Focused Approach* (6th ed.). London: McGraw-Hill.

Note

[1] McCarthy, E. Jerome and William D. Perreault (1996), *Basic Marketing: A Managerial Approach* (12th ed.). Homewood, IL: Irwin.

Chapter Four

Performance Evaluation and Control

To ensure successful implementation of its marketing plan, a company must monitor the progress toward its strategic goals. Performance monitoring involves evaluating the situation in which the company operates and, when necessary, developing a new plan that accounts for the changes in the environment. Conceptually, a company's performance evaluation and control process can be illustrated as shown in Figure 1.

Figure 1. Performance Evaluation and Control

The control aspect of managing an offering involves two activities: (1) evaluating the company's current performance relative to its marketing plan and (2) monitoring the environment in which the company operates for potential opportunities and threats. These two aspects of situation analysis are summarized below.

- *Performance evaluation* involves evaluating the outcomes of the company's actions vis-à-vis its goals. Performance evaluation can lead to one of two outcomes: successes or performance gaps.

  - *Successes* indicate that the company is adequately progressing toward its established goals.

  - *Performance gaps* signify a discrepancy between the desired and actual performance on a key metric (e.g., net income, sales revenues, market share, profit margins, earnings per share, and return on investment). To illustrate, a decline in an offering's market share reflects a performance gap between the company's desire to strengthen its market position and the actual decrease in market share. Other examples of performance gaps include discrepancies between desired and actual net income, profit margins, and revenues. A list of some of the most popular marketing metrics is offered in Chapter 23.

- *Monitoring the environment* enables the company to identify changes in the environment in which it operates and, when necessary, adjust its business activities to better reflect the new environment. Depending on their impact on the company, most environmental factors can be viewed as either opportunities or threats.[1]

- *Opportunities* are factors that are likely to have a favorable impact on the company's offering. Factors typically considered as opportunities involve the introduction of new, favorable government regulations, a decrease in competition, or an increase in consumer demand.

- *Threats* are factors that are likely to have an unfavorable impact on the company's offering. Factors typically considered as threats involve the introduction of new, unfavorable government regulations, an increase in competition, or a decline in consumer demand.

Control analysis is typically followed by a change in the company's existing plan. A notable exception is the scenario in which a company's performance is viewed as a success and neither opportunities nor threats are identified by the environmental analysis.

In cases when performance evaluation reveals a *performance gap*, the first step involves identifying its primary actionable cause—a cause that the company can act on and devise a solution to remove. Because most performance gaps are related to profitability, performance gap analysis typically involves identifying the causes for profitability decline. Once the primary actionable cause has been identified, the next step involves developing a solution that removes the cause and puts the company back on track toward achieving its goal. The key principle in identifying a solution is that it should directly follow from the already identified primary actionable cause of the problem. To illustrate, if a decline in sales volume has been determined to stem from deteriorating product quality resulting from inferior raw materials, then the logical solution is to improve product quality by identifying alternative sources of raw materials (e.g., replacing suppliers).

The process of an offering's performance evaluation and control can be summarized as shown in Figure 2. The company's current and new marketing plans are organized using the G-STIC (goal, strategy, tactics, implementation, and control) framework, and the situation analysis involves evaluating the offering's current performance (success or performance gap) and monitoring the environment for changes (i.e., identifying new opportunities and/or threats).

Figure 2. Control Analysis: The Big Picture

The key principle in developing a new marketing plan is that it should be directly linked to the already identified primary actionable cause of the problem (in the case of performance gaps) and/or to the identified opportunities and threats.

Thus, if the primary cause of the company's inability to meet its benchmarks is that its goals are unrealistic, then the solution is to revise those goals and set new and more realistic ones. In the same vein, if the primary cause is inefficient strategy, then the solution will involve redesigning the existing strategy in a way that maximizes value for all relevant market participants (e.g., identifying new target markets; modifying the overall value proposition of the offering to customers, company, and/or its collaborators; and launching a new product). Similarly, if the problem has been attributed to suboptimal tactics, then the solution needs to focus on optimizing the marketing mix variables. If the cause of the problem is poor implementation, then the solution needs to focus on improving the processes underlying the implementation and training or replacing the people managing these processes. Finally, if the cause of the problem is using inadequate controls, then the solution should focus on developing adequate measurements to evaluate the company's progress towards its goals.

Summary

The control aspect of managing an offering aims to ensure adequate progress toward the set goal. It encompasses two key activities: (1) evaluating the company's performance and (2) monitoring the environment in which it operates.

Performance evaluation involves evaluating the outcomes of the company's actions vis-à-vis its goals and can lead to one of two outcomes: (1) success, which indicates adequate progress toward the established goal or (2) a performance gap that represents a discrepancy between a company's desired and actual performance on a key metric (e.g., net income, sales revenues, or market share).

Monitoring the environment enables the company to identify changes in the environment in which it operates and, when necessary, adjust its business activities to better reflect the new environment. Most environmental factors can be classified into one of two categories: (1) opportunities, which involve a favorable set of circumstances or (2) threats, which involve an unfavorable set of circumstances.

The two control aspects of managing an offering—performance evaluation and monitoring the environment—are used to evaluate an offering's performance vis-à-vis its marketing plan and, when necessary, modify this plan to better reflect the current situation.

Additional Readings

Aaker, David A. (2007), *Strategic Market Management* (8th ed.). New York, NY: John Wiley & Sons.

Kotler, Philip and Kevin Lane Keller (2008), *Marketing Management* (13th ed.). Upper Saddle River, NJ: Prentice Hall.

Koller, Tim, Marc Goedhart, David Wessels, and Thomas E. Copeland (2005), *Valuation: Measuring and Managing the Value of Companies* (4th ed.). Hoboken, NJ: John Wiley & Sons.

Lehmann, Donald R. and Russell S. Winer (2007), *Analysis for Marketing Planning* (7th ed.). Boston, MA: McGraw-Hill/Irvin.

Walker, Orville C., Harper W. Boyd, and Jean-Claude Larrâechâe (2007), *Marketing Strategy: A Decision-Focused Approach* (6th ed.). London: McGraw-Hill.

Note

[1] The opportunity and threat analyses in this case are very similar to the analyses involved in the SWOT framework. The key difference is that whereas the SWOT framework used in situation analysis involves a comprehensive evaluation of the environment for the purpose of developing a *new* action plan, control analysis focuses primarily on the changes in the environment relative to the initial analysis reflected in the company's *existing* action plan.

Part Two

Strategy

Chapter Five

Managing Company Value

A company is a business entity established for the purpose of creating value for its shareholders. Managing company value involves two key aspects: setting a goal and developing a strategy to achieve that goal. These two aspects of managing company value are the focus of this chapter.

Setting Strategic Goals

Managing company value begins with setting a strategic goal. In Lewis Carroll's *Alice in Wonderland*, when Alice asks the Cheshire Cat which path to take, he responds, "If you don't care where you're going, it doesn't make a difference which path you take." The same logic applies to setting marketing goals. Without a well-defined goal, an organization cannot design an effective marketing strategy or evaluate the success of its current activities. Every action that a company undertakes should be consistent with its strategic goals.

Setting a goal typically involves two decisions: (1) identifying the *focus* of the company's actions and (2) identifying the specific quantitative and temporal *benchmarks* to be reached. These two key aspects of setting strategic goals are discussed in more detail below.

Goal Focus

The focus of a company's goal defines the ultimate criterion for success. Goals vary in their level of generality: Some goals reflect outcomes that are more fundamental than others. In this context, a company's goals can be represented as a hierarchy headed by a company's ultimate goal, which is implemented through a series of more specific, actionable goals.

Setting the Ultimate Goal

The ultimate goal reflects the desired end result associated with a given offering, product line, or the entire company. Based on the nature of the ultimate criterion for success, a company's ultimate goal can be defined through either monetary or nonmonetary outcomes.

- *Monetary goals* are directly related to monetary outcomes and are prevalent in for-profit organizations. The most common monetary goals involve maximizing a company's net income, earnings per share, and return on investment.

- *Nonmonetary goals*, also referred to as functional goals, are not directly linked to monetary outcomes. To illustrate, a company's strategic actions may be guided by the desire to increase customer and/or social welfare—a common goal for nonprofit organizations. Even for-profit organizations often have offerings that do not aim to directly influence the company's bottom line. For example, an offering's ultimate goal may be to facilitate other, more profitable, and/or more strategically important offerings. Thus, Microsoft's Internet Explorer, although not profitable, is strategically important as a technological platform for developing revenue-generating offerings. Similarly, a retailer may set a below-cost price on a popular item (also referred to as loss-leader) in an attempt to build store traffic, thus increasing the sales of more profitable items. A car manufacturer may introduce an unprofitable, entry-level car to gain share among younger customers so that they are more likely to upgrade to the company's more profitable models.

Because its ultimate goal tends to be very general, a company often needs to identify more specific goals that, when acted upon, will enable it to reach its ultimate goal.

Identifying Actionable Sub-Goals

Unlike the company's ultimate goal, which is typically defined in terms of company-focused outcome (e.g., net income), actionable goals often include actions focused on other entities, most often the company's target customers and collaborators. In this context, three common types of actionable goals can be identified: internal company goals, customer-directed goals, and collaborator-directed goals.

- *Internal goals* involve company-specific actions that the company can take to achieve its ultimate goal. Internal goals often focus on factors such as reducing the costs of goods sold, improving the effectiveness and cost-efficiency of the company's marketing actions, and optimizing research and development costs.

- *Customer goals* deal with the customer-related aspect of the company's overall performance and typically involve factors related to sales volume, such as sales revenues, market share, market size, and customer base. Customer goals typically aim to elicit a specific behavioral reaction from target customers (e.g., increasing purchase frequency, switching from a competitive product, or making a first-time purchase of this type of product), which will then enable the company to achieve its ultimate goal. To illustrate, a company might decide to increase net income (ultimate goal) by increasing sales volume from its current customers or by stealing customers from its competitors (customer-focused goals).

- *Collaborator goals* deal with the collaborator-related aspect of the company's overall performance and typically involve factors such as forming strategic alliances and optimizing supply and distribution channels. Collaborator goals typically aim to elicit a specific behavioral reaction from company collaborators, such as lowering product costs (e.g., in cases when the manufacturing is outsourced to a third party), improving the effectiveness of joint marketing activities between the company and its collaborators, and more aggressively promoting the company's offering to target customers.

In addition to setting internal, customer, and collaborator goals, a company might also set goals that focus on the competition. To illustrate, competitive goals involve factors such as creating barriers for entry, increasing market share, and establishing market leadership. It is important to note, however, that competitive goals can rarely have a direct impact on the company's performance; instead, they influence a company's ability to achieve its internal, customer-focused, and/or collaborator-focused goals.

A company can also set context-related goals that deal with factors defining the social, technological, economic, political, legal, and physical environment in which the company operates. For example, compliance with the regulatory environment is an important aspect of the overall corporate goals for companies operating in heavily regulated industries such as pharmaceuticals, automotive, and tobacco, as well as for companies protected by tariffs from foreign competition.

Performance Benchmarks

In addition to determining the focus, setting a goal also involves identifying the particular performance benchmark(s) that the company needs to achieve. Two types of such benchmarks can be distinguished: quantitative and temporal.

- *Quantitative benchmarks* define the specific milestones to be achieved by the company with respect to its focal goals. For example, benchmarks such as "increase market share by 2%," "increase retention rates by 12%," and "improve the effectiveness of marketing expenditures by 15%" quantify the selected goal. Quantitative benchmarks can be expressed in either relative terms (e.g., increase market share by 20%) or absolute terms (e.g., achieve annual sales of one million units).

- *Temporal benchmarks* identify the timeframe for achieving a particular quantitative benchmark. Setting a timeline for achieving a goal is a key strategic decision because the strategy adopted to implement these goals is often contingent on the time horizon. To illustrate, the goal of maximizing next quarter profitability will likely require a different strategy and tactics than the goal of maximizing longer-term profitability. In fact, the time horizon for achieving an offering's goals is often a source of potential conflict among the company's stakeholders. For example, short-term investors and many analysts tend to focus on the short-term performance reflected in a company's quarterly results, whereas longer-term investors tend to focus on the long-term prospects of the company reflected in a company's strategic plan.

To illustrate, a company's ultimate goal may involve generating net income (focus) of $10B (quantitative benchmark) by the end of the fourth quarter (temporal benchmark). An internal actionable goal might involve lowering cost of good sold (COGS) by 25% by the end of the fourth quarter. A customer-specific goal may involve increasing market share by 10% by the end of the fourth quarter. Finally, a collaborator-related goal might involve securing 45% of the distribution outlets by the end of the fourth quarter.

Because achieving sustainable profit growth is the ultimate goal for most companies, the rest of this chapter focuses on understanding the key factors influencing profitability and identifying strategies for effectively managing profit growth.

Managing Profit Growth

Given that net income is a function of revenues and costs, profitability growth can be achieved by increasing revenues (top-line growth) and/or reducing costs (Figure 1). Costs, in turn, can be reduced by managing one of the following three types of expenses: cost of goods sold (COGS), marketing costs, and other costs such as research and development costs, cost of capital, and general and administrative expenses. Revenue growth, on the other hand, can be achieved by an increase in sales volume and/or a change in per unit price.[1] Sales volume, then, can be increased by either growing the share of the company's offering relative to the competition (e.g., by increasing sales to the company's current customers, by stealing customers from its direct competitors), or by growing the size of the entire market (by attracting customers who are new to the particular product category).

Figure 1. The Profit-Growth Decision Tree

The most effective strategy to achieve profit growth varies depending on the circumstances. In some cases, it might involve lowering marketing expenses and/or the costs of goods sold. In other scenarios, profitability can best be achieved by increasing sales volume, for example, by generating incremental volume from current customers. Different strategies for achieving profit growth are outlined in more detail below.

Managing Profit Growth by Increasing Sales Revenues

Sales revenues can be viewed as a function of two main factors: sales volume and unit price. These two aspects of managing sales revenues are discussed in the following sections.

▸ Increasing Sales Revenues by Managing Sales Volume

The development of a sales-volume strategy begins by identifying market opportunities that the company can capitalize on to increase its net income. A functional approach for identifying viable market opportunities is given by the product-market growth framework introduced by Igor Ansoff (also referred to as the Ansoff matrix).[2] This framework can be represented by a 2×2 matrix in which one of the factors is given by the type of offering (existing vs. new) and the other factor by the type of customers (current vs. new). The resulting four product-market strategies are commonly referred to as market penetration, market development, product development, and diversification (Figure 2).

Figure 2. Product-Market Growth Matrix[3]

	Current Customers	New Customers
Current Products	Market penetration	Market development
New Products	Product development	Diversification

These four sales growth strategies can be summarized as follows:

- *Market-penetration* strategies aim to increase sales of an existing offering to a company's current customers. A common market-penetration strategy involves increasing usage rate. To illustrate, airlines stimulate demand from current customers by adopting frequent-flyer programs; packaged goods manufacturers enclose repurchase coupons as part of their product offerings; orange juice manufacturers promote drinking orange juice throughout the day rather than only for breakfast.

- *Market-development* strategies aim to grow sales by introducing an existing offering to new customers. In this case, the company builds on the success of its offerings to attract new customers. The two most common market-development strategies include targeting a new customer segment in an existing geographic area and introducing the offering to a different geographic area (e.g., exporting products to a new country). Market-development strategies aimed at attracting new customers include price promotions (e.g., price reductions, coupons, and rebates), new distribution channels, and communication strategies focused on different customer segment(s).

- *Product-development* strategies endeavor to grow sales by developing new (to the company) offerings for existing customers. In this case, the company builds on its current customer base by offering new products. The two most common product-development strategies include developing entirely new offerings (product innovation) or extending the current product line by modifying existing offerings (product line extension).

- *Diversification strategies* aim to grow sales by introducing new offerings to new customers. Because both the offering and the customers are new to the company, this strategy tends to be riskier than the other product-market strategies. The primary rationale for diversification is to take advantage of growth opportunities in areas in which the company has no presence.

The four strategies identified above are not mutually exclusive; a company could pursue multiple sales growth strategies. Therefore, a company needs to prioritize these strategies based on their market potential and then select the one(s) that will enable it to achieve its long-term goals.

Strategies for managing a company's current offerings are delineated in more detail in Chapter 16, which identifies two basic strategies to increase sales volume: increasing the *rate of adoption* of its offerings (market development) and increasing the *usage rate* of its offerings (market penetration).

▶ Increasing Sales Revenues by Managing Price

Setting the price is a key component in managing a company's profitability. The impact of price on profitability is two-pronged. On one hand, raising price has a direct impact on profitability, whereby, for a given level of sales volume, higher prices lead to higher profits. On the other hand, by influencing sales volume, prices have an indirect impact on profits, whereby higher prices typically lead to a decline in sales volume and, hence, erode overall profits. The impact of price on sales volume is a function of customers' price elasticity, which represents the percentage change in quantity sold relative to the percentage change in an offering's price. Thus, when customers' price elasticity is low, raising prices is unlikely to have a significant impact on sales volume; in contrast, when price elasticity is high, raising prices typically leads to a significant decline in sales volume.

Given the nature of the relationship between an offering's price, sales volume, and profitability, setting a price requires optimizing the impact of its various aspects on profitability. Thus, in cases where the decrease in sales volume caused by a price increase can be offset by the increase in revenues attributed to the higher price, raising the price of an offering can lead to an increase in sales revenues. Lowering the price can also lead to an increase in sales revenues in cases where the lost revenues from a price cut can be offset by an increase in sales volume.

Two issues in managing price merit attention. First, because in most cases the company's offerings are delivered to its customers by a third party (e.g., retailers), the price paid by customers is typically higher than the price the company charges its channel partners. In this context, the (manufacturer) price the company charges its channel partners is the key driver of a company's profitability at a given level of an offering's sales volume rather than the retail price that customers pay. Following the same logic, the impact of price on sales volume is a function of the retail price paid by customers rather than the manufacturer price invoiced by the company.

Second, it is also important to note that the term "price" in the above discussion reflects not only the "list" price of an offering, but also all other monetary aspects of the transaction between the company and its customers and collaborators. These include price reductions, coupons, rebates (in the case of customer transactions), and trade discounts such as volume discounts and allowances (in the case of collaborator transactions). This is an important consideration given the popular practice of disguising price reductions as marketing costs in order to increase reported sales revenues.

Managing Profit Growth by Lowering Costs

An offering's costs can be divided into three broad categories: (1) cost of goods sold (COGS), (2) marketing costs, and (3) other costs, such as research and development costs, cost of capital, and general and administrative costs. These three types of costs are discussed in more detail below.

▸ Managing Costs of Goods Sold

There are two basic strategies to lower COGS. The first is to lower the costs of *inputs*, which involve factors such as the raw materials, labor, and inbound logistics used in developing the company's offering. Lowering the costs of inputs can be achieved by outsourcing, switching suppliers, and adopting alternative technologies that use more cost-effective inputs. The second approach to managing COGS is to lower the costs associated with the *processes* that transform the inputs into the end product, such as optimizing operations and adopting alternative technologies that use more cost-effective processes.

▸ Managing Marketing Costs

Marketing costs can be grouped into four categories: communication costs, costs of incentives, distribution costs, and other marketing costs. Each of these four types of costs is discussed in more detail below.

- *Communications costs* comprise advertising expenditures (e.g., television, radio, print, outdoor, point-of-purchase, and event advertising), public relations expenditures (e.g., press coverage, product placement), and personal selling (e.g., sales force and detailers). Most mass media communication expenditures (e.g., television, radio, print, and outdoor) are fixed costs; they do not depend on the number of units sold. Note, however, that even though their absolute size remains unchanged regardless of the output volume, these expenditures become progressively smaller per unit of output as volume increases (because the fixed costs are allocated over a larger number of output units).

- The *cost of (consumer) incentives* involves consumer-focused promotions such as price reductions, coupons, rebates, contests, sweepstakes, and premiums. Most incentives (e.g., price reductions, coupons, rebates, premiums) are variable costs and, unlike mass media communications, increasing sales volume will not diminish the per-unit cost of the incentives.

- *Distribution costs* are a function of the margins received by distributors, cost of the sales force, and trade incentives such as trade allowances, volume discounts, and co-op advertising allowances.

- *Other marketing costs* reflect the costs of factors such as marketing research and marketing overhead.

▸ Costs Other than COGS and Marketing Expenses

In addition to COGS and marketing expenses, factors such as research and development, various administrative costs, and cost of capital contribute to a company's overall expenses.

Summary

A company is a business entity established for the purpose of creating value for its shareholders. Managing company value involves two key aspects: setting a goal and developing a strategy to achieve that goal.

Setting a goal typically involves two decisions: (1) identifying the focus of the company's actions and (2) identifying the specific quantitative and temporal benchmarks to be reached. The focus of a company's goal defines the ultimate criterion for success and can be represented as a hierarchy headed by this ultimate goal, which is implemented through a series of more specific, actionable goals. The ultimate goal reflects the desired end-result associated with a given offering, product line, or the entire company. Unlike the company's ultimate goal, which is typically defined in terms of company-focused outcome (e.g., net income), actionable goals often include actions focused on other entities, most often the company's target customers and collaborators. Both the company's ultimate goal and its specific actionable goals involve two types of benchmarks: (1) quantitative benchmarks, which define the specific milestones to be achieved by the company with respect to its focal goals and (2) temporal benchmarks, which identify the timeframe for achieving a particular quantitative benchmark.

Achieving sustainable profit growth is the ultimate goal for most companies. Managing profit growth can be achieved by increasing sales revenues and/or reducing costs. Increasing sales revenues can be achieved by managing price and/or by increasing sales volume, which in turn can be achieved by one of four strategies defining the product-market growth matrix: market penetration, market development, product development, and diversification. Managing costs involves decreasing costs of goods sold, optimizing marketing costs (e.g., communication costs, costs of consumer incentives, and distribution costs), as well as lowering various other costs (e.g., research and development costs, administrative costs, and cost of capital).

Relevant Formulas

Alternative strategies for achieving increasing net income can be formally represented as a function of sales volume, unit price, and costs. Sales volume, in turn, can be represented as a function of two factors: the unit share of the company's offering relative to competitors and the overall market size. The resulting profit equation is shown below.

$$\text{Profit} = \underbrace{\text{Market share}_{\text{Unit}} \cdot \text{Market size}_{\text{Unit}}}_{\text{Sales volume}} \cdot \text{Price}_{\text{Unit}} - \text{Costs}$$

In addition to being represented as a function of sales volume, unit price, and total costs, profitability can be viewed as a function of sales volume, unit margins, and fixed costs. In this context, unit margins reflect the difference between an offering's price and its variable costs. Unit margins can be expressed in monetary terms as the difference between an offering's unit price and its unit variable costs, or as a percentage, as the difference between an offering's unit price and its unit variable costs, which is then divided by the offering's unit price.

Calculating margins requires dividing costs into two basic categories: variable and fixed. *Fixed costs* are expenses that do not fluctuate with output volume within a relevant period. Typical examples of fixed costs include research and development expenses, mass media advertising expenses, rent, interest on debt, insurance, plant and equipment expenses, and salary of permanent, full-time workers. In contrast, *variable costs* are expenses that fluctuate in direct proportion to the output volume of units produced. For example, the cost of raw materials and expenses incurred by consumer incentives (e.g., coupons, price discounts, rebates, and premiums) are commonly viewed as variable costs. Other expenses, such as channel incentives (e.g., promotional allowances) and sales force compensation, can be classified as either fixed or variable costs depending on their structure (e.g., fixed salary vs. performance-based compensation). In this context, profitability can be linked to margins as shown in the following equation. This equation implies three basic strategies for growing profits: increasing sales volume, increasing margins, and lowering fixed costs.

$$\text{Profit} = \text{Sales volume} \cdot \underbrace{(\text{Price}_{Unit} - \text{Variable cost}_{Unit})}_{\text{Margin}_{Unit}} - \text{Fixed costs}$$

Relevant Concepts

Economies of Scale: An inverse relationship between the scale of production and marginal production costs. In cases where marginal production costs do not vary as a function of the output volume, there are no economies of scale. If, however, marginal production costs decrease with an increase in production output, then this increase reflects economies of scale. By the same logic, if an increase in production output results in an increase in marginal production costs, then this decrease reflects diseconomies of scale. Typically, marginal production costs decrease until they reach a certain minimum (economies of scale), then increase as firm size increases further (diseconomies of scale).

Experience Curve: The curve describing how costs of production decline as cumulative output increases over time. The concept was introduced by the Boston Consulting Group in 1966 to describe the finding that costs decline approximately 20% to 30% in real terms each time accumulated experience doubles.[4] At present, this term is used in a more general sense to capture the notion that costs tend to decrease with experience. Often used interchangeably with learning curve.

Learning Curve: The curve describing how labor costs of production decline as cumulative output increases over time. The logic behind this concept is that labor hours per unit decline on repetitive tasks. The term learning curve is often used interchangeably with the more general concept of experience curve, although an argument has been made to differentiate the two concepts.[5]

Additional Readings

Aaker, David A. (2007), *Strategic Market Management* (8th ed.). New York, NY: John Wiley & Sons.

Best, Roger J. (2004), *Market-Based Management: Strategies for Growing Customer Value and Profitability* (3rd ed.). Upper Saddle River, NJ: Prentice Hall.

Kumar, Nirmalya (2004), *Marketing as Strategy: The CEO's Agenda for Driving Growth and Innovation.* Boston, MA: Harvard Business School Press.

Notes

[1] When assessing the impact of price on revenues and profitability, note that raising the price does not always increase profitability. In product categories where demand is elastic, a price increase may lead to a sizable decline in sales, such that the loss of revenues from the decline in sales volume is greater than the revenue gained from the price increase. The impact of price on sales volume is discussed in more detail in Chapter 12.

[2] Ansoff, H. Igor (1979), *Strategic Management*. New York, NY: John Wiley & Sons.

[3] Adapted from Ibid.

[4] Henderson, Bruce, D. (1974), "The Experience Curve Reviewed: Why Does It Work?," in *Perspectives on Strategy: From the Boston Consulting Group* (1998), W.S. Carl and J. George Stalk, Eds. New York, NY: John Wiley & Sons.

[5] Henderson, Bruce, D. (1973), "The Experience Curve Reviewed: History," in *Perspectives on Strategy: From the Boston Consulting Group* (1998), W.S. Carl and J. George Stalk, Eds. New York, NY: John Wiley & Sons.

Chapter Six

Managing Customer Value

Managing customer value is a pivotal goal of a company's strategy. Because customers ultimately create value for the company, managing customer value is essential for a company's success. The two key aspects of managing customer value—developing a value proposition and developing a positioning strategy—are the focus of this chapter.

Developing a Customer Value Proposition

Customer needs play a central role in developing an offering's value proposition. Customer needs can be divided into three basic types: functional, monetary, and psychological.

- *Functional needs* are related to the performance benefits sought from an offering. For example, the need for powerful, safe, and reliable transportation may be considered a functional need.

- *Monetary needs* are related to the monetary benefits sought from an offering. For example, the need for resources to finance the purchase of a car may be considered a monetary need.

- *Psychological needs* refer to the psychological benefits sought from an offering. Typical psychological needs involve emotional benefits (e.g., the need for positive affect), social benefits (e.g., the need for social affirmation), and self-expressive benefits (e.g., the need to express one's identity).

When designing an offering, a company should aim to ensure that the offering will deliver superior value to target customers. In particular, the offering's value can be related to the three types of customer needs, as follows.

- *Functional value* refers to the benefits and costs that are directly related to an offering's performance. To illustrate, operation (e.g., engine power), aesthetic (e.g., visual appearance), and safety (e.g., crash test performance) attributes of a car are typically considered functional factors.

- *Monetary value* is related to the monetary benefits and costs associated with the offering (e.g., price, fees, discounts, and rebates).

- *Psychological value* refers to the intangible benefits and costs associated with the offering's image. From a customer's perspective, psychological value can be further divided into three categories: emotional (e.g., the joy of driving a car), social (e.g., group acceptance resulting from ownership of a particular brand of car), and self-expressive (e.g., using the car as a means to express one's identity).

The success of a company's offering, therefore, is a function of the fit between the offering's value proposition and customer needs on each of these dimensions, as illustrated in Figure 1.

Figure 1. Developing a Successful Value Proposition

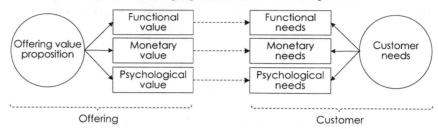

An important aspect of an offering's value proposition is its competitive advantage, i.e., its ability to fulfill customer needs better than the competition's offering. The essence of competitive advantage can be illustrated by examining the concepts of *differentiation* and *parity* and relating them to an offering's ability to deliver value to its target customers. Thus, attributes describing a particular offering can be divided into two broad categories: relevant attributes (or benefits), which create value for a particular customer segment, and irrelevant attributes, which have no significant impact on the value of the offering to this customer segment. Benefits can be further divided into benefits that are shared across all offerings in the market and benefits that are unique to a particular offering. In this context, the term *competitive advantage* refers to benefits that differentiate a particular offering from its competitors, whereas the term *competitive parity* encompasses the benefits that are shared by all offerings targeting a particular customer segment (Figure 2). Thus, only differences on relevant attributes create customer value; differences on irrelevant attributes usually do not add value to the offering.

Figure 2. Competitive Parity and Competitive Advantage.

It is important to note that competitive advantage, competitive disadvantage, and competitive parity reflect customers' perception of the company's and competitors' offerings. It does not matter whether a particular difference is "real"; what matters is whether it is perceived by customers as a differentiating point. To illustrate, customers might not see a difference between a 2 GHz and a 2.1 GHz computer microprocessor, in which case the speed of these two processors are at parity. In contrast, attributes that are objectively at parity may be differentiated in the mind of the customer (e.g., by creating a distinct image of the offering), thereby creating a competitive advantage. To illustrate, Volvo is perceived to be the safest car even though in reality this might not be the case.

The success of a company's offering is measured by the degree to which it can deliver greater value to target customers relative to the competition. In this context, *competitive advantage is a company's ability to deliver greater value to target customers*. The relationship between competitive advantage and customer value can be illustrated as shown in Figure 3.

Figure 3. Competitive Advantage and Customer Value

The relationship between competitive advantage and customer value, depicted in Figure 3, implies that competitive advantage can be quantified as the difference in the value delivered by the company's and competitors' offerings. Thus, competitive advantage is greatest when the benefits delivered by the company's offering perfectly fit the needs of its target customers and competitors' offerings lack any benefits relevant to these customers. This relationship can be summarized as follows:

$$\text{Competitive advantage} = \text{Customer value}_{\text{Company}} - \text{Customer value}_{\text{Competition}}.$$

An offering's ability to provide superior customer value can be further analyzed on three dimensions: functional (e.g., benefits and costs that are directly related to an offering's performance), monetary (e.g., benefits and costs associated with the monetary aspect of the offering), and psychological (e.g., benefits and costs associated with the offering's image). Because competitive advantage captures the difference in the value provided by the company's and competitors' offerings, it can also be represented as a function of the differences in the functional, monetary, and psychological value of the company's and competitors' offerings. In this context, the competitive advantage of a company's offering can also be represented in terms of the differences in the customer value (denoted by Δ) delivered by the company and its competitors on each of the three dimensions (functional, monetary, and psychological).

$$\text{Competitive advantage} = \Delta\text{Functional value} + \Delta\text{Monetary value} + \Delta\text{Psychological value}$$

Developing a Positioning Strategy

An important aspect of developing a customer strategy is designing a positioning strategy for the offering. Positioning reflects the company's view of how the offering should be perceived and remembered by the customer[1]; it is the process of creating a distinct image of the company's offering in a customer's mind.[2,3] For example, Volvo positions its cars as the safest vehicles on the road, Toyota emphasizes reliability, and BMW focuses on the driving experience.

The concept of positioning can be better understood when compared with the concept of value proposition. Unlike value proposition, which captures *all* of the benefits and costs of an offering, positioning focuses customers' attention only on the *most important aspect(s)* of the offering's value proposition. To illustrate, the driving experience is one of the many aspects of BMW's value proposition that the company chose to position its cars in the minds of its customers. In this context, positioning aims to present the advantages of the offering in a way that accentuates its key benefit(s) and provides customers with a compelling reason to choose and/or use the company's offering.

An offering's positioning often can be summarized in a single phrase, commonly used as a tagline in company's communications. To illustrate, consider the following examples: *Fresh, hot pizza delivered in 30 minutes or less, guaranteed* (Domino's); *Better Ingredients. Better Pizza* (Papa John's); *We try harder* (Avis); *If it's got to be clean...it's got to be Tide* (Tide); *It's Everywhere You Want To Be* (Visa); *You never actually own a Patek Philippe. You merely look after it for the next generation* (Patek Philippe men's watches); *You don't just wear a Patek Philippe. You begin an enduring love affair* (Patek Philippe ladies' watches).

Because positioning involves prioritizing the existing benefits and costs of a given offering, the same offering can often be positioned in multiple ways. Consider TiVo, the personal digital video recorder. It offers multiple benefits, such as skipping commercials, pausing live TV, one-step recording, season pass, instant replay and fast-forward features, dual-channel recording, updated program guide, etc. All of these benefits comprise TiVo's value proposition. Successful positioning requires further laddering these benefits and identifying the single most important benefit that delivers value to the customer and differentiates TiVo from the competition. For example, TiVo could be positioned as a device that allows viewers to pause live TV, as a one-step TV recording device, or as a device that allows viewers to record one channel while watching another. In this context, positioning may require ignoring some of the offering's potential benefits to bring its distinct value advantage into focus.

The term positioning can be used in two distinct contexts: desired positioning, which reflects the company's positioning goal with respect to a particular offering; and actual positioning, which reflects customers' perceptions of the offering. Indeed, despite a company's efforts to create a certain image in the minds of its target customers, these customers might have formed a very different perception of the benefits of the company's offering. Thus, the success of a company's positioning strategy can be measured by the overlap of the company's positioning goals and customers' perceptions of the offering.

The process of developing a positioning strategy involves two key decisions: (1) identifying the primary source of the offering's value and (2) defining the reference point used to position the offering. These two aspects of developing a positioning strategy are discussed in more detail below.

Identifying the Primary Source of Value

The process of identifying the primary source of customer value involves evaluating different aspects of the offering's value proposition to select the one(s) to use to position the offering in a customer's mind. This process, often referred to as benefit laddering, aims to prioritize certain aspects of the offering's value proposition to accentuate its key aspect(s) and provide customers with a compelling reason to choose the company's offering.

There are three basic strategies to emphasize the benefits associated with an offering: single-benefit positioning, multi-benefit positioning, and holistic positioning.

The *single-benefit approach* involves identifying a single attribute and emphasizing the value delivered by the offering on this primary attribute (Figure 4). This primary attribute is the one that the company believes will most likely provide customers with a compelling reason to choose and/or use the company's offering. To illustrate, safety is the primary attribute for Volvo and reliability is the primary positioning for Maytag. Note that single-attribute positioning does not imply that the offering is inferior on the other, secondary attributes; it simply identifies an attribute that is likely to be of primary importance to target customers. In this context, the secondary attribute(s) enhances the value delivered by the primary attribute(s), although by themselves, they could rarely serve as a reason for choice.

Figure 4. Single-Benefit Positioning

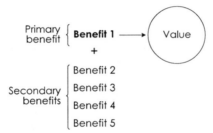

Depending on the nature of the primary benefit used to position the offering, three types of positioning strategies can be identified: functional, monetary, and psychological.

- *Positioning on functional benefits* emphasizes a particular aspect of an offering's performance. For example, Toyota emphasizes reliability and Visa emphasizes its worldwide acceptance.

- *Positioning on monetary benefits* emphasizes the monetary value associated with the offering. To illustrate, Southwest Airlines, Wal-Mart, and Costco emphasize low price as a key aspect of their value proposition. In the same vein, the Discover credit card emphasizes its cash-back feature as "America's number one cash rewards program."

- *Positioning on psychological benefits* emphasizes the intangible benefits associated with the offering's image. For instance, offerings such as Montblanc, Rolls-Royce, Dom Pérignon, and Porsche, are positioned to instill feelings of luxury, exclusivity, and prestige. An offering's positioning may also be influenced by the company's positioning as a leader in innovation (e.g., HP, Apple, Sony, Procter & Gamble) or by its image as a socially responsible organization (e.g., Ben and Jerry's, Newman's Own, and Ecolab). Finally, an offering can be positioned by emphasizing benefits, such as reducing uncertainty and gaining peace of mind.

The *multi-benefit approach* involves emphasizing the benefits delivered by the offering on two or more primary attributes (Figure 5). To illustrate, a classic dual-benefit positioning is the one utilized by Procter and Gamble's Ivory Soap: "*99 $^{44}/_{100}$ % pure: it floats.*" The advantage of multi-benefit positioning over a single-benefit positioning is that it better reflects different aspects of the offering's value proposition. On the downside, however, multi-benefit positioning runs the risk of diluting the offering's image in the mind of the customer and failing to establish a compelling reason for choice. As a result, positioning on more than two primary benefits is not very common.

Figure 5. Multi-Benefit Positioning (Dual-Benefit Scenario)

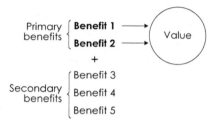

The *holistic* approach emphasizes the overall performance of an offering without identifying individual benefits (Figure 6). Unlike the single-benefit and multi-benefit approaches, the holistic approach entices customers to choose an offering based on its performance as a whole rather than its particular benefits. For example, Gillette's positioning strategy, "*Gillette, the best a man can get,*" is designed to create a perception of superior overall performance. Colgate Total, as implied by its name, claims to offer the best overall package of category benefits. Similarly, Amoco's positioning as "*America's number one premium gasoline,*" Tylenol's positioning as "*the brand most hospitals trust,*" and Hertz' positioning as the "*#1*" car rental company in the world place an emphasis on market leadership as a proxy for the overall performance of these offerings.

Figure 6. Holistic-Benefit Positioning

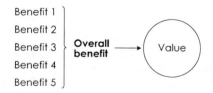

Defining the Reference Point

In defining the reference point, two types of positioning can be distinguished: noncomparative, in which the reference point is a particular customer need, and comparative, in which the reference point involves competitive offerings.

▸ Noncomparative Positioning

Noncomparative positioning directly relates the value of the offering to customer needs without explicitly contrasting it to competitors' offerings. Here, the frame of reference for noncomparative offerings is the needs of the target customers, and the main reason for buying/using the offering is its ability to fulfill these needs.

Noncomparative positioning typically employs one of the two core strategies to relate an offering to customer needs: need-based positioning and category-based positioning.

- *Need-based positioning* directly links the benefits of the offering to an identified customer need. For example, TiVo, the pioneer in personal digital recording, was initially positioned as a device allowing viewers to have their own TV network where they could decide what to watch and when.

- *Category-based positioning* communicates the benefits of the offering by linking it to an already established product category. For example, after TiVo's initial need-based positioning strategy did not work, it was repositioned as a type of digital video recorder with a hard drive.

▸ Comparative Positioning

Comparative positioning relates the value of the offering to customer needs by explicitly contrasting it to other offerings. The frame of reference in comparative positioning is another offering, usually a competitor's. The main reason for buying/using the company's offering is its ability to fulfill customer needs better than the referent offering. The referent offering can be explicitly identified, or it can be broadly described without identifying a particular brand (e.g., "It's not delivery. It's DiGiorno.").

Comparative positioning typically employs one of two core strategies: differentiation-based positioning and similarity-based positioning.

- *Differentiation-based positioning* is by far the prevalent approach, reflecting the belief that differentiation is the key source of the offering's sustainable competitive advantage. The goal here is to establish a single point or multiple points of *differentiation* and steal share from the referent offering by demonstrating the superiority of the company's offering.

- *Similarity-based positioning*, also referred to as "me-too" positioning, aims to show lack of differentiation between the company's offering and other offerings. The goal here is to establish multiple points of *parity* and steal share from the referent company, typically the market leader, because of customer indifference between the two products. For example, Unilever's cosmetic brand Suave claims to "work just as hard as expensive brands."

As a general rule, comparative positioning is usually employed by smaller share offerings aimed at stealing share from the market leader. It is rarely used by the market leader because by comparing its offering to one with a smaller share, the market leader is likely to implicitly promote the referent offering. Note, however, that this principle does not always hold for offerings in different price tiers that do not directly compete for the same customers; in this case, a larger share brand could actually benefit by comparing itself to a smaller share upscale brand (e.g., comparing Honda to Porsche and Mercedes to Bentley).

Developing a Positioning Statement

The positioning statement is an internal document that presents a succinct summary of an offering's targeting and positioning strategy. This statement is used by various divisions within the company (e.g., research and development, sales, and accounting), as well as in a company's communications with its collaborators (e.g., advertising agencies, public relations agencies, and distributors) to ensure that their actions are consistent with the offering's strategy.

The positioning statement identifies three main aspects of an offering's strategy:

- Target customers

- Frame of reference (the reference point used by customers to evaluate the offering, such as product category and competitive offerings)

- The primary reason for buying/using the offering (the key primary source of customer value)

Note that the scope of the positioning statement is broader than just summarizing the offering's positioning. In addition to identifying the two key aspects of the offering's positioning (the frame of reference and the key benefit), it also identifies the customer segment targeted by the offering.

Depending on the frame of reference, two types of positioning statements can be distinguished: noncomparative and comparative. The noncomparative statement defines the key benefit of the offering relative to customer needs without explicitly comparing the offering to the other offerings in the market. The structure of a typical noncomparative positioning statement is illustrated in Figure 7.

Figure 7. Noncomparative Positioning Statement

```
┌─────────────────────────────────────────────────────┐
│  ................................. is the best ................................. │
│              (offering)                    (product category)   │
│                                                       │
│  for ...................................................................  │
│                          (target customers)          │
│                                                       │
│  because ...............................................................  │
│                          (primary reason)            │
└─────────────────────────────────────────────────────┘
```

To illustrate, consider the following noncomparative positioning statements.

Mountain Dew is the soft drink that gives young, active consumers who have little time for sleep the energy they need because it has high level of caffeine.

Gatorade is a smart choice for athletes because it rehydrates, replenishes, and refuels.

Palm Pilot is an electronic organizer that allows busy professionals to back up files on their PC easily and reliably.

For the tradesman who uses power tools to make a living and cannot afford downtime on the job, DeWalt offers dependable professional tools that are engineered to the highest standards and are backed by a guarantee for repair and replacement within 48 hours.

In contrast, the comparative statement defines the offering's key benefit by explicitly relating it to other market offerings. The structure of a typical comparative positioning statement is illustrated in Figure 8.

Figure 8. Comparative Positioning Statement

.... is a better ....
       (offering)   (product category)

than ....
                (competitive offering)

for ....
                (target customers)

because ....
                (primary reason)

To illustrate, consider the following comparative positioning statements.

Mountain Dew is the soft drink that gives young, active consumers who have little time for sleep more energy than any other brand because it has the highest level of caffeine.

Gatorade is a smart choice for athletes because it rehydrates, replenishes, and refuels in ways water can't.

Palm Pilot is an electronic organizer that allows busy professionals to back up files on their PC more easily and reliably than competitive products.

For the tradesman who uses power tools to make a living and cannot afford downtime on the job, DeWalt offers professional tools that are more dependable than other brands because they are engineered to higher standards and are backed by a guarantee for repair and replacement within 48 hours.

Summary

Because customers ultimately create value for the company, managing customer value is essential for a company's success. The two key aspects of managing customer value involve developing a value proposition and developing a positioning strategy.

The value proposition reflects all benefits and costs associated with a particular offering. The success of an offering is determined by the degree to which its value proposition can fulfill customer needs better than the competition. In this context, an offering's competitive advantage is determined by its ability to deliver superior customer value on each of the three value dimensions: functional, monetary, and psychological.

Positioning reflects the company's view of how the offering should be perceived and remembered by the customer; it is the process of creating a distinct image of the company's offering in a customer's mind. Unlike value proposition, which captures *all* of the benefits and costs of an offering, positioning focuses customers' attention only on the most important aspect(s) of the offering's value proposition. Because positioning involves prioritizing the existing benefits and costs of a given offering, the same offering can often be positioned in multiple ways.

The process of developing a positioning strategy involves two key decisions: (1) identifying the primary source of the offering's value and (2) defining the reference point used to position the offering. Identifying the primary source of customer value involves evaluating different aspects of the offering's value proposition to select the one(s) to use to position the offering in a customer's mind. There are three common strategies to position an offering: single-benefit, multi-benefit, and holistic. With respect to defining the reference point, two types of positioning can be distinguished: noncomparative, in which the reference point is a particular customer need, and comparative, in which the reference point involves competitive offerings.

The customer value proposition is summarized in an offering's positioning statement, which identifies three main aspects of the offering's strategy: (1) target customers, (2) frame of reference (the reference point used by customers to evaluate the offering, such as product category and competitive offerings), and (3) the primary reason for buying/using the offering (the key primary source of customer value). Depending on the frame of reference, two types of positioning statements can be distinguished: noncomparative and comparative. The noncomparative statement defines the key benefit of the offering relative to customer needs without explicitly comparing the offering to the other offerings in the market.

Relevant Concepts: Perceptual Mapping

An offering's value proposition can be visually represented using perceptual maps, which reflect a customer's view of how the benefits of the offering relate to their needs vis-à-vis the other offerings in the marketplace. Perceptual mapping offers a unique ability to represent the interrelationships between the various offerings in the marketplace and the factors used by customers to determine the value of these offerings. In general, two types of perceptual maps can be distinguished: attribute-value maps and positioning maps.

Attribute-value maps (also referred to as value curves) capture customer evaluations of an offering's performance on all relevant attributes and relate them to the attribute performance of competitive offerings (Figure 9). Here, higher levels of customer value associated with a particular benefit correspond to higher levels of an offering's performance on that attribute, and the competitive advantage of a company's offering is defined by the differences in its customer value. By capturing an offering's performance on all relevant attributes in a competitive context, attribute-value maps enable the company to better understand the drivers of its unique value proposition to target customers.

One potential shortcoming of attribute-value maps is that they do not take into account the relative importance of each attribute; as a result, they offer little guidance as to which attributes are likely to have greater impact on the overall attractiveness of an offering. To address this limitation, the relative importance of each attribute (typically given as percentages adding to 100) is often incorporated into attribute-value maps.

Figure 9. Attribute-Value Map

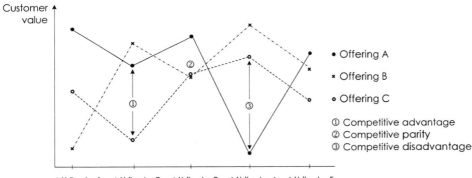

Similar to attribute-value maps, positioning maps are derived from customer evaluations of the various aspects of the offerings available to target customers. Unlike attribute-value maps, which reflect performance on all relevant attributes, positioning maps reflect perceived performance only on the most relevant factors(s). These factors may be individual attributes, such as those used in the attribute-value map or, alternatively, they may reflect holistic evaluations of different aspects of the offerings (e.g., benefits and costs). In addition to plotting the available offerings, perceptual maps can also display consumers' ideal points (or ideal vectors), which reflect customers' ideal combinations of different aspects of the offering.

Perceptual maps can have any number of dimensions, although two-dimensional maps are the most common because they are the easiest to interpret (Figure 10). To illustrate, in the case of headache remedies, a perceptual map can illustrate the relative performance of different drugs on factors such as effectiveness and duration. The most effective and longest lasting drugs will occupy the upper right quadrant of the chart and the least effective and shortest duration drugs will occupy the lower left quadrant.

Figure 10. Positioning Map

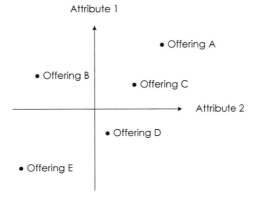

Positioning maps can be derived by asking respondents to rate an option's performance on a set of predefined attributes (as in deriving an attribute-value map) and then aggregating these attribute-based evaluations into a few (usually two) more general factors. Alternatively, positioning maps can be derived based on customers' similarity-based evaluations of the offerings relative to one another to derive the underlying dimensions and plot the offerings onto a two-dimensional space.

Positioning maps offer two main advantages over attribute-value maps. First, by using only a few composite dimensions instead of many individual attributes, positioning maps offer a holistic view of an offering as it is perceived by customers. Second, unlike attribute-value maps, which typically depict an offering's intrinsic value, positioning maps illustrate the offering's value relative to the other offerings in the market. At the same time, a major shortcoming of positioning maps is that they do not capture the impact of individual attributes on an offering's overall attractiveness.

The complementary nature of the benefits and shortcomings of attribute-value and positioning maps indicates that these two tools reflect different aspects of the value-creation process and, therefore, should be used jointly in marketing analysis.

Additional Readings

Barwise, Patrick and Sean Meehan (2004), *Simply Better: Winning and Keeping Customers by Delivering What Matters Most.* Boston, MA: Harvard Business School Press.

Gupta, Sunil and Donald R. Lehmann (2005), *Managing Customers as Investments: The Strategic Value of Customers in the Long Run.* Upper Saddle River, NJ: Wharton School Publishing.

Keller, Kevin Lane (2007), *Strategic Brand Management: Building, Measuring and Managing Brand Equity* (3rd ed.). Upper Saddle River, NJ: Prentice Hall.

Ries, Al and Jack Trout (2001), *Positioning: The Battle for Your Mind* (20th ed.). New York, NY: McGraw-Hill.

Tybout, Alice M. and Tim Calkins (2005), *Kellogg on Branding.* Hoboken, NJ: John Wiley & Sons.

Notes

[1] A broader view of positioning involves creating a distinct image of the offering not only in the minds of customers but also in the minds of the company's employees, stakeholders, and collaborators.

[2] Kotler, Philip (1984), *Marketing Management: Analysis, Planning, and Control* (5th ed.). Englewood Cliffs, NJ: Prentice-Hall.

[3] Ries, Al and Jack Trout (2001), *Positioning: The Battle for Your Mind* (20th ed.). New York, NY: McGraw-Hill.

Chapter Seven

Managing Collaborator Value

Collaboration is an essential component of doing business in today's networked world. To be successful, a company's marketing strategy needs to ensure that collaborators' value is optimized to enhance the value of the company's offering to target customers in a way that benefits the company. The key aspects of identifying collaborator entities, defining their functions, and understanding collaborator dynamics are the focus of this chapter.

The Nature of Collaboration

Collaborators are entities that work with the company to understand, create, communicate, and deliver value to target customers. Collaboration is defined by the collaborating entities and the relationship between these entities.

Collaborator Entities

Virtually any two entities can become collaborators. Yet, some entities are more likely to collaborate with one another than others. Some of the most common collaborator entities are summarized below.

- *Research and development* collaborators work with the company on the development of new products and services. To illustrate, Nike, Samsung, and PepsiCo collaborated with the design company IDEO to develop innovative, customer-centric products.

- *Manufacturing* collaborators assist the company with producing the actual product. For example, NEC provides Dell with removable media storage devices, Intel provides the processors, Nvidia provides graphic cards, and Microsoft provides the operating system.

- *Service providers* collaborate with the company to deliver the service aspect of the company's offering. To illustrate, to gain cost efficiency, companies like AT&T, Sprint, and Dell routinely outsource their customer support service to call centers in regions in which the production processes are more cost efficient.

- *Advertising agencies* assist the company with promoting its offerings to target customers, managing public relations, developing communication and branding strategies, and conducting marketing research. Most of the advertising agencies are either subsidiaries or affiliated with larger communication services groups, such as WPP, Omnicom, Interpublic, Publicis,

Dentsu, and Havas, which enables them to provide a comprehensive set of communication services to large multinational clients.

- *Distributors*, such as wholesalers and retailers, collaborate with the company by facilitating the delivery of its offerings to target customers. For example, consumer packaged good manufacturers, such as Procter & Gamble, Unilever, and Kraft make their offerings available to customers by relying on retail partners such as Wal-Mart, Costco, and Albertsons.

- *Sales force* collaborates with the company to promote and/or deliver its offerings to target customers. To illustrate, Avon employs a multilevel sales force of more than 20,000 independent contractors who are paid a commission on their own sales as well as on the sales of people they recruit and train. Generally, the sales force can be viewed as a form of distribution-based collaboration. It is important to note, however, that the function of the sales force involves promoting and selling, and not necessarily delivering, the actual offering. To illustrate, pharmaceutical companies employ sales representatives to promote their products to physicians without actually selling or delivering the actual drugs (excluding samples).

- *Marketing research* entities enable the company to better understand the company's customers, collaborators, competitors, and the overall context in which the company operates. For example, Procter & Gamble collaborates with marketing research companies such as AC Nielsen and IRI in areas involving the analysis of retail data and test-marketing of new products.

Collaboration Type

From a structural standpoint, two types of collaborators can be distinguished: vertical and horizontal.

- *Vertical collaborators* are located along the value-delivery chain: supplier – manufacturer – distributor – customer (Figure 1). To illustrate, Intel (supplier), HP (manufacturer), and Best Buy (distributor) are vertical collaborators in delivering value to target customers. In fact, most of the distribution channel partnerships between manufacturers such as Procter & Gamble, PepsiCo, and Coca-Cola and retailers such as Wal-Mart, Costco, and Amazon.com can be viewed as a form of vertical collaboration.

- *Horizontal collaborators* usually occupy the same level of the value-delivery chain. For example, the United Mileage credit card, which allows customers to earn frequent flyer miles on each purchase, is a result of the horizontal collaboration between JPMorgan Chase and United Airlines. Similarly, Nike and Apple's collaboration resulted in the unique Nike+iPod product bundle.

The nature of collaboration is typically defined by the extent to which the relationship between the companies is formalized. In this context, two types of collaboration can be identified: explicit and implicit.

- *Explicit collaboration* involves contractual relationships, such as long-term contractual agreements, joint ventures, and franchise agreements. The key advantage of explicit collaboration is that it fosters a long-term relationship between collaborating entities, which ultimately leads to greater effectiveness and cost efficiency of their activities. Explicit collaboration has certain drawbacks, however, such as lower flexibility, greater switching costs, and the strategic risk of creating a potential competitor by sharing know-how and strategic information (e.g., pricing policies, profit margins, and cost structure).

- *Implicit collaboration* typically does not involve contractual relationships and, therefore, tends to be much more flexible than explicit collaboration. This flexibility, however, comes at the cost of inability to predict the behavior of various channel members. Another shortcoming of implicit coordination is a lower level of commitment, resulting in unwillingness to invest resources to customize the channel for a particular manufacturer. Moreover, implicit coordination is likely to lead to lower cost efficiency (vis-à-vis explicit collaboration) resulting from a lower degree of coordination (e.g., resulting from lack of systems integration). An extreme case of implicit collaboration involves complementors—companies with complementary offerings that do not directly collaborate with one another. To illustrate, software developers often create Windows-compatible programs without directly collaborating with Microsoft and numerous companies develop accessories for the iPhone without directly collaborating with Apple.

Key Collaborator Functions

A company's relationship with its collaborators typically involves business-to-business interactions in which they collaborate to deliver superior value to target customers in a way that benefits both the company and its collaborators. Because in most cases customers are the ultimate source of the company's revenues, the primary goal of collaboration is to optimize the value of the offering developed by the company and its collaborators to its target customers.

Collaboration might involve one or more of the following areas: product development, service management, branding, pricing, sales promotions (incentives), communications, and distribution. To illustrate, companies can collaborate to develop a product (research-and-development collaboration), to deliver the offering to the customer (channel collaboration), and/or to create customer incentives (promotional collaboration). These can be categorized into three basic types of collaboration: collaboration to create, communicate, and deliver value. These three types of collaboration are discussed in more detail below.

Collaboration to Create Customer Value

Collaboration to create customer value involves activities aimed at creating an offering that has the potential to deliver superior value to target customers in a way that enables the company and its collaborators to reach their strategic goals. The process of creating customer value involves five key aspects: product, service, brand, price, and incentives. These five aspects are discussed in more detail below.

- *Product development.* Companies often develop products in collaboration with other entities. For example, Palm collaborated with AT&T, Verizon, and Sprint to develop network-specific versions of its Treo smartphone.

- *Service development.* Services are often a result of the joint effort of the company and its collaborators. To illustrate, consider Dell's service delivery process. Phone-based customer support is provided by Dell's collaborators, many of which include call centers both in North America and overseas. Onsite technical support is provided by Dell's collaborators with physical presence in the geographical areas in which Dell offers services. Finally, customer service is also available through multiple user-group sites managed by third-party entities (complementors).

- *Branding.* Similar to products and services, brands often are the result of the combined effort of the company and its collaborators. To illustrate, the Harley-Davidson brand amalgamates the efforts of the Milwaukee-based Harley-Davidson Motor Company, its dealer network, as well as user-based entities such as the Harley Owner Group (H.O.G.).

- *Pricing.* In most cases, pricing is a collaborative effort of the participants in the distribution channel as well as various third-party entities. To illustrate, the suggested retail price (MSRP) set by the manufacturer is typically modified by retailers based on the volume discounts and incentives offered by the manufacturer, as well as on their own profit-maximizing strategy. The retail price is often further adjusted to include a variety of surcharges by third-party entities (e.g., sales taxes).

- *Incentives.* Incentives received by the customer can be offered by the company, its collaborators, and/or third-party entities. To illustrate, incentives for purchasing a hybrid vehicle (e.g., Toyota Prius) can be offered by the manufacturer, by the dealer, as well as by the government offering various tax and usage (e.g., using carpool lanes) advantages.

Collaboration to Communicate Customer Value

The communication of customer value occurs on each of the five dimensions discussed above: product, service, brand, price, and incentives. On each of these dimensions, the company can collaborate with other entities.

- *Product.* Product benefits are often communicated by both the company and its collaborators. For example, the benefits of TiVo, the personal digital recorder, are promoted by its manufacturer, by retailers carrying the product, as well as by many of its current users who actively promote the product.

- *Service.* Service benefits can also be communicated by both the company and its collaborators. To illustrate, awareness of a new movie can be created by the film studio, by its direct collaborators (e.g., distributors, movie theaters), as well as by the word-of-mouth generated by third-party entities such as the media and viewers who have seen the movie.

- *Brand.* Communicating the meaning of the brand can also result from company and collaborator communications. Cult brands such as Harley-Davidson, Apple, and Burton are extensively promoted by loyal users who act as brand ambassadors.

- *Price.* Awareness of an offering's price can also result from company and collaborator communications. To illustrate, customers might learn the price of an offering directly from the company, from retailers, or from other entities such as user groups and online search engines (e.g., froogle.com).

- *Incentives.* The availability of incentives can also be communicated by the company and its collaborators. To illustrate, the news of a temporary price reduction or a frequent-flyer bonus can be disseminated by the airline, its direct collaborators such as travel agencies, and by third-party entities such as user-based forms (e.g., flyertalk.com) and the media.

Collaboration to Deliver Customer Value

As in the case of communications, value-delivery occurs on each of the five dimensions discussed above: product, service, brand, price, and incentives. On each of these dimensions, the company can collaborate with other entities.

- *Product.* Products can be distributed directly by the company and/or through intermediaries such as wholesalers and retailers. To illustrate, Levi Strauss distributes its products directly through its online and brick-and-mortar stores, as well as through retailers such as Macy's, Target, and JCPenney.

- *Service.* Services can be delivered by the company directly or through collaborators. To illustrate, DirecTV outsources satellite dish installation and setup to local independent contractors, FedEx outsources the delivery of its ground packages to local contractors, Sprint outsources its customer service to call centers in the Philippines.

- *Brand.* Brands can be delivered to customers in the form of experiencing the brand's identity and/or essence. This delivery may be carried out directly by the company, as in the case of Disney World, and Nike and Apple retail stores; by direct collaborators, as in the case of Polo Ralph Loren stores located within larger department stores; or by third-party entities such as members of the Harley Owner Group delivering the Harley-Davidson's brand essence.

- *Price.* Customer payments for the company's offerings can be collected directly by the company and/or through collaborators, such as channel members, credit card processors, and banks.

- *Incentives.* Incentives can be distributed to customers directly by the company, by its direct collaborators such as retail stores, by companies specializing in distributing customer promotions, as well as by third-party entities re-distributing the company's incentives.

Collaborator Dynamics

Collaborator dynamics involve issues such as balancing the power between collaborators, collaborator integration, and managing collaborator conflicts. These issues are discussed in more detail below.

Collaborator Power

Collaborator power refers to the ability of a given company to exert influence over another entity. For example, Wal-Mart, Costco, and Home Depot often receive various monetary and nonmonetary benefits such as proprietary volume discounts, promotional allowances, and product-delivery schedules. In general, the balance of power between a manufacturer and a retailer is characterized as follows.

- *Manufacturer power* is high when (1) a manufacturer's offerings are highly differentiated and/or are in high demand, (2) distributors are fragmented and manufacturers are consolidated, (3) there is credible threat of forward integration, (4) the manufacturer's offering generates a significant portion of the distributor's profits, (5) the distributor's contribution to a manufacturer's net income is relatively low, and (6) the cost of switching distributors is low.

- *Retailer power* is high when (1) a manufacturer's offerings are not differentiated and/or are in low demand, (2) manufacturers are fragmented and distributors are consolidated, (3) there is credible threat of backward integration, (4) the manufacturer's offering contribution to distributor's profits is low, (5) the distributor generates a significant part of the manufacturer's net income, and (6) the cost of switching distributors is high (e.g., because of system integration, contracts, and specialization).

Collaborator Integration

Collaborator integration reflects the extent to which different collaborators have common ownership. Collaborator integration most often occurs in the context of distribution channels, where it reflects the extent to which different channel members have common ownership. Depending on the position of the entities in the distribution channel, two types of channel integration are commonly distinguished: vertical and horizontal.

- *Vertical integration* reflects the extent to which a firm owns its upstream suppliers and its downstream buyers. Extending ownership upstream (toward suppliers) is referred to as backward integration, while extending ownership of activities downstream (toward buyers) is referred to as forward integration (Figure 1). For example, a manufacturer establishing its own distribution system (e.g., Apple's decision to establish its own retail locations) is a form of a forward integration, whereas a retailer acquiring a wholesaler and/or a manufacturer is a form of a backward integration. The key advantages of vertical integration include (1) better effectiveness and cost efficiency because of improved coordination between channel members, (2) better control and performance monitoring, (3) increased entry barriers for potential entrants by acquiring proprietary access to scarce resources, and (4) investment in specialized resources that the channel member would not invest in otherwise. Common alternatives to vertical integration include long-term contracts, joint ventures, and franchise agreements.

Figure 1. Vertical Integration Strategies

- In contrast to vertical integration, in which the firm expands along the value-delivery chain into upstream or downstream entities, in the case of *horizontal integration*, the company acquires additional business activities at the same level of the value-delivery chain (e.g., a retailer acquiring another retailer). The key advantages of horizontal integration include (1) greater economies of scale, (2) greater economies of scope (synergies), and (3) increased market power over other channel members.

Collaborator Conflicts

Collaborator conflict describes tension between collaborators, often caused by the differences in their profit-optimization strategies. Although conflicts can occur among collaborators in any domain, they are perhaps most common in distribution channels. The two most common types of channel conflicts involve vertical and horizontal conflicts.

- *Vertical channel conflict* involves different levels of the same channel (e.g., a manufacturer and a retailer) and is often caused by differences in their profit optimization strategies. To illustrate, nondifferentiated product line extensions often lead to vertical channel conflicts, which are driven by the difference in the profit-optimization strategies of the parties in the distribution chain. The nature of the conflict here is the gap between a manufacturer's desire that a retailer carry its entire product line and a retailer's desire to carry only the most profitable, noncompeting offerings from individual manufacturers.

- *Horizontal channel conflict* involves members within the same channel level (e.g., two retailers). Horizontal conflicts occur when different channels target the same customer segment with identical or substitutable offerings (e.g., different retailers selling the same product to the same customers). A common type of horizontal channel conflict occurs when distributors with different cost structures and profit margins sell identical offerings to the same customers.

Summary

Collaborators are entities that work with the company to understand, create, communicate, and deliver value to target customers. Collaboration is defined by the collaborating entities and the type of collaboration, determined by the relationship between these entities.

The most common areas of collaboration include research and development, manufacturing, service delivery, communication, distribution, sales, and marketing research. From a structural standpoint, two types of collaborators can be distinguished: vertical collaborators, located along the value-delivery chain (supplier – manufacturer – distributor – customer), and horizontal collaborators, which usually occupy the same level of the value-delivery chain. The nature of collaboration is typically defined by the extent to which the relationship between the companies is formalized. In this context, two types of collaboration can be identified: explicit collaboration, which involves contractual relationships such as long-term contractual agreements, joint ventures, and franchise agreements, and implicit collaboration, which typically does not involve contractual relationships.

Collaboration might involve one or more of the following three areas: collaboration to create, communicate, and deliver customer value. Collaboration to create customer value involves activities aimed at creating an offering that has the potential to deliver superior value to target customers in a way that enables the company and its collaborators to reach their strategic goals. The process of creating customer value involves five key aspects: product, service, brand, price, and incentives. Communicating and delivering customer value occurs on each of these five dimensions. In addition, the company can collaborate with other entities on each of these five dimensions to communicate the benefits and deliver its offering to target customers.

Collaborator dynamics involve issues such as balancing the power between collaborators, collaborator integration, and managing collaborator conflicts. Collaborator power refers to the ability of a given company (e.g., a manufacturer) to exert influence over another entity (e.g., a retailer). Collaborator integration reflects the extent to which different collaborators have common ownership. In the context of distribution channels, two types of integration are commonly distinguished: vertical integration, in which a company acquires its upstream suppliers or its downstream buyers, and horizontal integration, in which the company acquires additional business entities at the same level of the value-delivery chain. Collaborator conflict describes tension between collaborators, often caused by the differences in their profit-optimization strategies. In distribution channels, there are two common types of conflicts: vertical conflicts, which involve different levels of the same channel (e.g., a manufacturer and a retailer), and horizontal conflicts, which involve members within the same channel level (e.g., two retailers).

Relevant Concepts

Backward Integration: A form of vertical integration that involves upstream expansion of the supply chain.

Forward Integration: A form of vertical integration that involves downstream expansion of the supply chain (e.g., a manufacturer establishing its own distribution system).

Horizontal Channel Conflict: A conflict between members within the same channel level (e.g., between two retailers). Horizontal conflicts occur when different channels target the same customer segment with identical or substitutable offerings (e.g., different retailers selling the same product to the same customer).

Vertical Channel Conflict: A conflict that occurs between different levels of the same channel (e.g., manufacturer–retailer) and is often caused by differences in their profit optimization strategies.

Additional Readings

Anderson, James C. and James A. Narus (2003), *Business Market Management: Understanding, Creating and Delivering Value* (2nd ed.). Upper Saddle River, NJ: Prentice Hall.

Anderson, Erin, Anne T. Coughlan, Louis W. Stern, and Adel I. El-Ansary (2006), *Marketing Channels* (7th ed.). Upper Saddle River, NJ: Prentice Hall.

Prahalad, C. K. and Venkatram Ramaswamy (2004), *The Future of Competition: Co-Creating Unique Value with Customers*. Boston, MA: Harvard Business School Press.

Young, S. David and Stephen F. O'Byrne (2000), *EVA and Value Based Management: A Practical Guide to Implementation*. New York, NY: McGraw-Hill.

Chapter Eight

Managing the Competition

Managing the competition is a key factor for a company's success in the market-place. The process of evaluating market competitiveness, strategies for creating a sustainable competitive advantage, and the key aspects of managing competitive dynamics are the focus of this chapter.

Evaluating Market Competitiveness

Evaluating the competitive nature of a given market involves two key components: identifying a company's key competitors and evaluating the competitive intensity of the marketplace. These two aspects of market competitiveness are outlined in more detail below.

Identifying the Key Competitors

Competitive analysis begins with identifying the key competitors; that is, business entities with offerings positioned to satisfy the same need of the same target customers. Competitors are typically defined relative to the specific needs of a given customer segment rather than simply defined based on the industry in which the company operates. To illustrate, Kodak's film division competes not only in the 35mm film market with companies like Fuji and Agfa, but also with manufacturers of digital cameras, such as Sony and Canon, and even with manufacturers of camera-equipped mobile phones, such as Nokia and Ericsson. Starbucks competes not only with other coffee shops, such as Peet's Coffee & Tea and The Coffee Bean & Tea Leaf, but also with manufacturers of caffeinated energy drinks, such as Red Bull and Monster Energy, and even with producers of caffeinated and vitamin-enhanced water, such as Water Joe and Glacéau. Coca-Cola competes not only with other cola producers, such as Pepsi, but also with the manufacturers of other products, such as juice, bottled water, and milk, that could potentially fulfill the same customer need. In this context, juice, bottled water, and milk are cross-category competitors of Coke because they aim to satisfy the same need of the same target customers.

An important aspect of evaluating market competitiveness is identifying not only current competitors but potential competitors as well. A company's *current competitors* are business entities that currently target the same customers and strive to fulfill the same customer need(s). In contrast, *potential competitors* are business entities that currently do not target the same customers and/or aim to fulfill the same need(s), but nevertheless have the aspirations and/or the capability to satisfy the focal need(s) of the company's target customers. In this context, three groups of potential competitors can be identified.

The first type of potential competitors involves companies with offerings that aim to satisfy the same need as the company's offering but, at present, target a different customer segment. Even though not currently competing with the focal company, their entry into a particular customer segment would be facilitated by their understanding of customer needs and their ability to deliver offerings that could fulfill those needs.

Another set of potential competitors involves companies that currently target the same customer segment but aim to satisfy a different need. Even though these potential competitors are not directly competing with the focal company, their entry into the company's business would be facilitated by their customer expertise, defined by their understanding, access, and relationship with the target customers.

Finally, potential competitors include companies that currently satisfy a different set of needs of different customers. Even though these potential competitors are not competing directly with the focal company and have neither need-based nor customer-based expertise, they may aspire to serve the focal company's customers. They may also have some of the key resources such as strategic assets and core competencies that could facilitate the development of successful competitive offerings. These four types of competitors are shown in Figure 1.

Figure 1. Expertise-Based Approach for Identifying Key Competitors

	Same customers	Different customers
Same need	Current competitors (customer-based and need-based expertise)	Potential competitors (need-based expertise)
Different need	Potential competitors (customer-based expertise)	Potential competitors (no relevant expertise)

Competitors that target the same customers and follow similar strategies to serve the needs of these customers are often referred to as a strategic group. Competitors in the same strategic group often have similar products and services, similar branding strategies, similar pricing and incentive strategies, similar communications campaigns, and/or similar distribution channels. As a result, the competition among companies within the same strategic group tends to be more intense than the competition among companies from different strategic groups.

Evaluating the Competitive Intensity of the Market

The competitive intensity of the market is defined by the extent to which companies' offerings are positioned to satisfy the same need of the same target customers. Market competitiveness can be analyzed by examining the market structure as it relates to a particular offering. In this context, the competitiveness of a given marketplace can be viewed as a function of the relationships among the company, its customers, collaborators, and competitors, as well as the relevant context in which the company operates. These five factors and their relationships are illustrated in Figure 2 and discussed in more detail below.

Customer Factors

The two key customer factors that are likely to influence the competitive nature of a marketplace are the customers' revenue potential and the sustainability of a company's value proposition to these customers.

Figure 2. The Framework for Evaluating Market Competitiveness

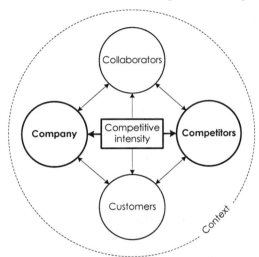

The *revenue potential* of a given customer segment is a function of two key factors: sales volume and margins. Thus, high revenues could result from two distinct strategies: a high-volume (and typically low-margin) strategy or a high-margin (and typically low-volume) strategy. A key factor determining the success of the high-volume strategy is the size of the market. Because large markets have the potential to generate greater revenue streams, they are often associated with greater competitiveness among companies pursuing a high-volume strategy. A key factor determining the success of the high-margin strategy is customers' buying power. Thus, competition is likely to be more intense for customer segments with greater buying power because of the potential for a greater revenue stream generated from these customers.

From the customers' perspective, the *sustainability* of a company's market position is a function of market competitiveness and inherent customer loyalty. Thus, market competitiveness is typically greater when market growth is low, demand is stagnant, and companies have to grow sales by stealing share from each other rather than by attracting new customers. The sustainability of a company's value proposition is also a function of inherent customer loyalty: the degree to which a particular customer segment is prone to switching brands. In general, competition tends to be greater in markets with low inherent loyalty, where customers can easily be induced to switch.

Competitor Factors

The key factors that are likely to influence the degree of competition can be divided into two categories: monetary factors and nonmonetary factors.

The *monetary factors* reflect the relative *profitability* of a given market. In particular, a market is likely to be more competitive when it is highly profitable. Here, the profitability, although a function of the market's revenue potential, also depends on each competitor's unique ability to convert these revenues into profits based on core competencies and strategic assets.

The *nonmonetary factors* are not directly linked to monetary outcomes and are typically functional in nature. The key nonmonetary factor influencing market competitiveness is the strategic importance of this market to competitors. Thus, a given market may be strategically important to a company because of its synergies with other, more profitable offerings. Alternatively, maintaining a strong position in a given market may be important to prevent other competitors from entering the market. The degree of competition could also be a function of behavioral factors such as the rationality of competitors' behavior. To illustrate, factors such as prior competitive history (e.g., price wars, comparative advertising campaigns) and the nature of the personal interactions between managers of competing organizations could have a significant impact on market competitiveness.

Collaborator Factors

Collaborators can influence market competitiveness both directly and indirectly. The *direct* impact of collaborators on market competitiveness reflects the likelihood that a collaborator will become a direct competitor by taking over some or all of the functions currently performed by its partners. To illustrate, a retailer may in-source the manufacturing of the company's offerings, thus becoming a manufacturer's direct competitor. Similarly, a manufacturer may in-source the distribution, thus becoming a retailer's direct competitor.

In addition, collaborators' actions may have an *indirect* impact on market competitiveness by influencing factors such as competitors' profit margins, which, in turn, will affect the intensity of the competition. For example, as retailers become more powerful, they are likely to squeeze manufacturers' margins, forcing them to compete more fiercely for market share to compensate for the loss of margins.

Company Factors

When evaluating the degree of competition in a given market, a company should also evaluate its own impact on the competitive environment. This implies a dynamic view of the environment in which a company evaluates the competition, taking into account how its own actions affect the nature of the marketplace. For example, a company aggressively entering a particular marketplace with a low-price strategy is likely to change the competitive dynamics by influencing the overall market demand and customers' price sensitivity, and potentially provoking a price war among the companies currently serving this market.

Context Factors

Market competitiveness may also be influenced by various social, political, economic, technological, and regulatory factors. Thus, context could have a direct impact on competitiveness by favoring a particular competitor or group of competitors through factors such as proprietary technology and government regulation (e.g., import quotas, licenses, and tax exemptions). In addition, context may influence competition indirectly by affecting factors such as market demand and profit margins. To illustrate, developments in the area of technology often lead to increased productivity, which in turn results in higher profit margins. Changes in technology may also lead to a shift in the strategic assets and core competencies comprising a competitive advantage in a given market. For example, technological developments in digital photography and photocopying have weakened the dominant position of Kodak and Xerox in favor of companies with expertise in digital information processing, such as Sony and Canon.

The above analysis of market competitiveness is conceptually similar to the Five Forces approach for evaluating the competition in a particular industry, outlined by Michael Porter. The key difference is that the approach outlined here describes competitive analysis from the viewpoint of a particular company rather than from an industry perspective. From a company's perspective, this approach is more relevant because it offers a company-specific analysis of the competition. A direct implication of this approach is that the competitive analysis is likely to vary across companies. To illustrate, the competitive analysis for Wal-Mart will differ from the competitive analysis for Target, in part because they face a different set of competitors (e.g., Target has to compete with Wal-Mart, whereas Wal-Mart does not have to compete with itself).

Creating a Sustainable Competitive Advantage

Competitive advantage is the advantage that one firm has relative to competing firms with respect to fulfilling a particular need of a given target market. Thus, a competitive advantage implies not only that a company's offerings are differentiated from competitors' offerings, but that this differentiation creates value for target customers. Differentiation does not necessarily imply a competitive advantage; it is a necessary but not sufficient condition for competitive advantage. Competitive advantage is a company's ability to deliver greater value to target customers.

The key to long-term profitability is the sustainability of the company's competitive advantage. An important aspect of an offering's competitive advantage is the degree to which it can be sustained over time, a factor that is often overlooked by companies. The key to creating a sustainable competitive advantage is ensuring that the company has a long-term strategy for providing superior customer value to its target customers. Because most competitors constantly strive to enhance the value provided by their offerings, a company that does not manage to stay ahead of the competition is bound eventually to lose its competitive edge. To ensure its long-term success in the marketplace, a company must anticipate competitors' actions aimed at enhancing the customer value of their offerings and must develop offerings that exceed the value delivered by the competitive offerings.

To create a sustainable competitive advantage, a company first needs to acquire strategic assets and core competencies that are the source of its ability to deliver superior customer value. The role of strategic assets and core competencies as sources of a sustainable competitive advantage is discussed in more detail below.

Strategic Assets as a Source of Sustainable Competitive Advantage

Strategic assets are the company's resources that (1) are essential for the success of the business in which the company operates and (2) differentiate the company from its competitors. From a marketing standpoint, a company's strategic assets could include some or all of the following factors: business infrastructure, collaborator networks, human capital, intellectual property, brands, customer base, synergistic offerings, access to scarce resources, and access to capital.

- *Business infrastructure* involves four types of assets: (1) manufacturing infrastructure, comprising the company's production facilities and equipment; (2) service infrastructure, which includes assets such as call-center facilities and customer relationship management solutions; (3) supply-chain infrastructure, integrating the manufacturing and service assets into an effective and efficient value-delivery process; and (4) management infrastructure, which involves the company's business management culture.

- *Collaborator network* comprises two types of factors: (1) vertical networks, in which collaborators are located along the supply chain (e.g., suppliers and distributors), and (2) horizontal networks, in which collaborators are not an integral part of the company's supply chain (e.g., research and development, manufacturing, and promotion collaborators). The key to creating sustainable collaborator networks is designing offerings that deliver superior value to the company's collaborators while building relationships that result in switching costs for collaborators (e.g., integrating collaborators' systems into the company's operations).

- *Human capital* involves factors such as the technological, operational, business, and customer expertise of the company's employees. The key to creating sustainable human capital is delivering superior value to the company's key employees and building relationships that enhance the loyalty of these employees.

- *Intellectual property* covers the legal entitlement attached to an intangible asset. Two types of intellectual property can be the source of a competitive advantage: (1) industrial property, which includes inventions, industrial designs, and identity marks such as trademarks, service marks, commercial names and designations—including indications of source and appellations of origin; and (2) copyright, which includes literary and artistic works, such as novels, plays, films, musical works, drawings, paintings, photographs, sculptures, and architectural designs.

- *Brands* create competitive advantage in two ways: (1) by identifying the company and/or its offering and (2) by differentiating it from the competition. The most common brand elements include the brand name, logo, symbol, character, jingle, and slogan. Using these elements, brands provide unique value to customers, the company, and its collaborators.

- *Existing customer base* serves as a competitive advantage by facilitating the acceptance of a company's current and new offerings and by impeding the acceptance of competitive products.

- *Synergistic offerings* are a strategic asset to the degree that they facilitate customer acceptance of related company offerings. To illustrate, the Windows operating system can be viewed as a strategic asset for Microsoft because it facilitates customer adoption of related software offerings.

- *Access to scarce resources,* such as geographic locations and natural resources, is a strategic asset because it provides the company with a distinct competitive advantage.

- *Access to capital* may be considered a strategic asset in cases where it provides the company with a unique competitive advantage. For example, access to capital can influence the resources at a firm's disposal to carry out its strategy: to sustain a price war, to develop new products, and to implement a communication campaign.

To evaluate a company's competitive advantage, managers first need to identify the strategic assets that are essential for success in the marketplace and then evaluate the strength of the company's assets relative to the competition. This comparative analysis is typically used to identify the company's strengths and weaknesses and provide guidance for strengthening its market position.

Core Competencies as a Source of a Sustainable Competitive Advantage

A practical approach to evaluating the sustainability of a company's competitive advantage involves evaluating its strategic assets in relation to its core competencies. Competencies reflect a company's ability to perform various business tasks in an efficient and effective manner. A competency is considered core if it strategically differentiates the company from its competitors. A competency that is central to a company's business operations but is not unique would generally not be considered as a core competency, since it will not meaningfully differentiate the company from its competitors. Thus, a core competency is expertise in an area essential to the company's success, allowing the company to satisfy customer needs better than the competition in a way that enables the company and its collaborators to achieve their strategic goals.

The relationship between strategic assets and core competencies is dynamic. Core competencies reflect the company's expertise in specific functional areas and are a result of focused utilization of strategic assets. At the same time, a company's assets are often derived from its competencies. For example, a competency in database software development is likely to result in competency-specific assets such as business infrastructure, collaborator network, human capital, and intellectual property.

In general, there are four key functional areas in which a company can establish a core competency: business management, operations management, technology development, and customer management. These four areas are discussed in more detail below.

- *Business management.* Competency in business management refers to proficiency in effectively managing business processes, such as identifying business goals, designing strategies and tactics to achieve these goals, and implementing the company's business plan. Business management competency also involves the company's ability to build the collaborator network required for the efficient functioning of the business (e.g., relationships with suppliers and distributors). This competency typically leads to strategic benefits such as business model leadership. To illustrate, Dell's core competency in business management resulted in a direct distribution business model that was one of the key reasons for its success. Other examples of companies with demonstrated competency in business management include McDonalds, Blockbuster, Starbucks, Wal-Mart, and Amazon.com.

- *Operations management.* A competency in operations management refers to an expertise in supply-chain management. Companies with this competency are proficient in optimizing the effectiveness and cost-efficiency of the business processes. This typically leads to the strategic benefit of cost leadership in the marketplace. For example, Wal-Mart's competency in operations management is reflected in its dominant position as the low-cost player in the market. Other examples of companies with demonstrated competency in operations management include Southwest Airlines, Costco, and Home Depot.

- *Technology development.* Competency in technology development refers to a company's ability to design new technological solutions. This competency typically leads to the strategic benefit of technological leadership. Examples of companies that have demonstrated this competency include Motorola, BASF, Google, and Intel. Note that a competency in developing new technologies does not necessarily imply a competency in developing commercially successful products. To illustrate, Xerox and its Palo Alto Research Center (PARC) have invented numerous new technologies such as photocopying, laser printing, graphical user interface, client/server architecture, and the Ethernet, but have been slow in converting these technologies into commercial products.

- *Customer value management.* Competency in customer value management refers to expertise in understanding, creating, and managing customer value. There are three common aspects of competency in customer value management: product management, service management, and brand management. These three aspects are discussed in more detail below.

  - *Product management.* Competency in product management refers to a company's ability to develop products that deliver superior customer value. This competency typically leads to the strategic benefit of product leadership. Examples of companies with demonstrated competency in this area include Microsoft, Merck, Apple, and Palm. Note that competency in product management is not contingent on the company's having competency in technology management. In fact, technologically inferior products delivering need-based functionality are often more successful than technologically superior products that fail to meet customer needs. To illustrate, TiVo, the pioneer in digital video recording, exemplifies a company with competency in developing a successful product based on an existing MPEG-2 digital-encoding technology.

- *Service management.* Competency in service management refers to a company's ability to develop services that deliver superior customer value. This competency typically leads to the strategic benefit of service leadership. Examples of companies with demonstrated competency in this area include Ritz-Carlton, American Express, and Nordstrom.

- *Brand management.* Competency in brand management refers to a company's ability to build strong brands that deliver superior customer value. This competency typically leads to the strategic benefit of brand leadership. Examples of companies with demonstrated competency in this area include Harley-Davidson, Lacoste, Nike, Procter & Gamble, and PepsiCo.

Competitive Dynamics

The constantly evolving nature of the competitive landscape calls for developing strategies to drive and respond to the competitive dynamics in the marketplace. In this context, there are three basic types of competitive strategies: (1) strategies for pioneering new markets, (2) strategies for gaining market position in existing markets, and (3) strategies for defending market position in existing markets. These strategies are discussed in more detail in this chapter.

Pioneering New Markets

The term *pioneer* or *first-mover* is used in different contexts. A company that is first to introduce a new technology is referred to as the *technology pioneer.* A company that is first to commercially introduce a conceptually new ("new-to-the-world") product aimed at satisfying a particular customer need is referred to as a *product pioneer.* A company that is first to introduce a particular business process (e.g., supply-chain management) is referred to as a *process pioneer.* Finally, a company that is first to introduce a given offering to a particular target market is referred to as a *market pioneer.*

For the purposes of marketing analysis, the terms *pioneer* and *pioneering advantage* are used in reference to the first company to introduce its offering to a given market defined by a particular customer need. Thus, a pioneer in a market is the company that first reached a given segment with its offering. Even though, from a chronological standpoint, another company may have pioneered a product by introducing it to a different customer segment, the company that first introduced it to target customers is considered the pioneer for these customers. For example, Apple's iPod, which was introduced in United States in 2001, is typically thought of as the pioneer of portable hard drive MP3 players, even though MPMan, which used the same technology, was introduced in Asia in 1998 by the Korean company Saehan.

When pioneering new markets, a company's goal is not only to gain share but also to create a business model that cannot be copied by its current and future competitors. Thus, creating a sustainable competitive advantage is the underlying mechanism of any successful pioneering strategy. Being the pioneer in a given market offers a company several potential benefits that could be the source of a sustainable competitive advantage. The key benefits of being a market pioneer are as follows:

- By being a pioneer, a company has the unique opportunity to *shape customer preferences* and at the same time create a close association between its brand and the underlying customer need. For example, products like Coke, Xerox, Jeep, Walkman, and TiVo not only helped shape customer preferences (e.g., in terms of flavor, functionality, and design) but also became synonymous with the entire category.

- By being a pioneer, a company has the opportunity to build loyalty by creating *switching costs* for its customers. These switching costs could be functional (e.g., loss of the unique benefits of the pioneer's offering), monetary (e.g., the cost of replacing proprietary equipment or a penalty for breaking a contract), or psychological (e.g., the cost of learning the functionality of a competitor's offering).

- The pioneer can benefit from *preempting scarce resources* such as raw materials, human resources, geographical locations, and collaborator networks. Thus, the pioneer may be able to lock out the competition by securing exclusive access to strategically important mineral resources. Similarly, the pioneer could preempt competitors' access to a particular human resource in short supply, such as engineers, designers, and managers. The pioneer could also preempt strategically important geographic locations in both real space (e.g., Starbucks, Wal-Mart) and cyberspace (e.g., flowers.com, drugstore.com, buy.com). Finally, the pioneer can preempt the competition by forging collaborator alliances with strategically important partners, such as distributors or advertisers. For example, sporting goods manufacturers offer exclusive long-term contracts to promising athletes early in their career when they believe that these athletes are likely to become a strategic asset, differentiating these companies from the competition.

- The pioneer can create *technological barriers to entry* to prevent competitors from entering the market. For example, the pioneer may secure the exclusive rights to use a particular invention or design that is essential for developing offerings that will successfully address a specific customer need. Being the pioneer also enables a company to establish a proprietary technological standard (e.g., operating system, communication protocol, video compression) that ensures the sustainability of the incumbent's technological advantage in the marketplace.

- The pioneer often benefits from *learning curve advantages,* whereby its production effectiveness and efficiency increase as its cumulative output increases over time. Simply put, being in business longer than its competitors often gives the pioneer a competitive edge in technological know-how, level of workforce experience, and production efficiency.

Being a pioneer, however, does not always lead to a sustainable competitive advantage. In fact, pioneers face a distinct set of disadvantages that could actually impede rather than facilitate their strategy.

- *Free riding* is one of the key problems facing the pioneer. A later entrant may be able to free ride on the pioneer's resources, including its investments in technology, product design, customer education, regulatory approval, infrastructure development, and human resource development. To illustrate, after spending millions of dollars to develop the technology and educate the American audience about the advantages of a personal digital recorder, TiVo found itself in competition with cable and satellite operators selling similar services to its already educated target customers. Alternatively, a follower could reverse-engineer the pioneer's product and improve upon it, while investing only a fraction of the resources required to develop the original product. Federal Express built on the idea from DHL to start overnight deliveries in the United States. IBM launched its PC, building on the earlier product introductions from Apple and Atari. Best Buy launched a rapid expansion of superstores based on the success of the Circuit City model.

- *Incumbent inertia* is another very important, yet often overlooked, source of competitive disadvantage. Being a market leader often leads to a feeling of complacency, thus leaving technological and market opportunities open to competitors. To illustrate, IBM's reliance on mainframes, even when mainframes were being replaced by networked computers, enabled competitors such as Dell and Hewlett Packard to get a foothold in its markets and steal some of IBM's most valuable clients. Incumbent inertia may also be driven by a reluctance to cannibalize existing product lines by adapting a new technology or a new business model. For example, brick-and-mortar booksellers, such as Barnes & Noble and Borders, failed to recognize the importance of e-commerce, allowing Amazon.com to establish a dominant presence in online book retailing. Incumbent inertia may also be a result of a "sunk-cost mentality," whereby managers feel compelled to utilize their large investments in extant technology or markets, even when technological advancements and/or market forces make these investments unfeasible. For example, one of the reasons Ford lost its leading market position to General Motors in the 1930s was its reluctance to make the necessary investments to modify existing manufacturing facilities in order to diversify its product line.

- Another potential disadvantage in being a pioneer is the *uncertainty* associated with the offering. Indeed, whereas the pioneer has to deal with the uncertainty surrounding the technology and market demand, a follower can learn from the pioneer's successes and failures and design a superior offering. Because of the uncertainty associated with the introduction of a new offering, companies with strong brands and distribution capabilities often choose to be late market entrants, which enables them to learn from the pioneer's experience and develop an effective and cost-efficient market entry strategy. These companies use their brand and channel power to manage the risk associated with new product development and new market entry, allowing them to be successful late entrants into a given market. To illustrate, the first sugar-free soft drink was introduced in the United States by Cott in 1947, and the first sugar-free cola was introduced by Royal Crown in 1962, only to be overtaken by Coke and Pepsi, which used their branding and distribution power to dominate the consumer soft drink market.

Gaining Market Position

There are two basic strategies for a company to gain market position in an existing market: (1) by stealing share from competitors already serving this market and (2) by growing the market by attracting new customers to the category.

The *steal-share strategy* refers to a company's activities aimed at attracting its competitors' customers (Figure 3). A company's steal-share strategy could vary in terms of its breadth: It can either be narrowly focused on a specific subsegment of competitors' customers with well-defined needs (e.g., Pepsi targeting the younger Coke drinkers with its "new generation" campaign), or it can be broadly focused on the competitor's market as a whole.

Figure 3. Steal-Share Strategy

Current users

To be successful in attracting competitors' customers, a company needs to present these customers with a compelling value proposition. In this context, there are two basic value proposition strategies: a differentiation-based strategy and a similarity-based strategy.

In the case of a *differentiation strategy*, the company's goal is to establish a single or multiple point(s) of differentiation and steal share from the competition by demonstrating the superiority of the company's offering. The differentiation may involve superior benefits (e.g., better performance) and/or lower costs (e.g., lower price).

In contrast, the *similarity strategy*, also referred to as a "me-too" strategy, aims to establish multiple points of parity and steal share from a competitor, typically the market leader, by showing that a company's and a competitor's offerings are, in fact, identical. One particular form of the "me-too" strategy is cloning, which involves emulating the incumbent's offering, usually with slight variations to avoid patent and trademark infringement issues.

The *market growth strategy* refers to a scenario in which, instead of competing for customers who are currently using competitors' products to satisfy a particular need, a company gains market position by attracting customers who have not used any products and services within the same category (Figure 4).

Figure 4. Market-Growth Strategy

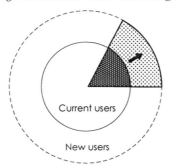

Because it targets customers that are new to the particular product category, the market growth strategy is very similar to pioneering new markets. Thus, pioneering new markets to bring new customers into the category could be viewed as a strategy to gain market position. Note that even with the market growth strategy, the company may as well be stealing share from other companies; the key difference here is that these other companies are not typically viewed as direct competitors because they operate in a different industry and/or target different customer needs.

Defending Market Position

Because business success inevitably attracts competition, a company needs to develop strategies to defend its market position. In general, there are three basic ways in which a company can react to a competitor's actions: (1) by doing nothing, (2) by repositioning its existing offering (e.g., by increasing benefits, decreasing costs, and moving upscale or downscale), and (3) by adding a new offering(s). These strategies are illustrated in Figure 5 and discussed in more detail below.

Figure 5. Defensive Marketing Strategies[1]

▸ Doing Nothing

The decision to ignore a competitor's action(s) reflects a company's belief that either these actions would have no material impact on the company's market position or that the competitive threat is not sustainable and will dissipate by itself. For example, a company may decide that its upscale offering will not be affected by the entry of a low-price, low-quality competitor and, therefore, not consider this action as a direct threat. In the same vein, a company may not react to a competitor's price reduction if it believes that this low-price position is not sustainable in the longer term.

▸ Repositioning the Existing Offering

A company may choose to reposition its offering in one of two ways. It may change the offering's value proposition to become more attractive to the company's current customers or, alternatively, it may reposition the offering to make it appealing to a different customer segment.

- *Enhancing the offering's value to current customers*. Because value is a function of benefits and costs, enhancing the value of an offering may be achieved by two basic strategies: increasing benefits and decreasing costs. These two strategies are outlined in more detail below.

  - *Increasing an offering's benefits*. To enhance the customer benefits of its offering, a company may choose to adopt one of the following three strategies: (1) enhance the functional benefits of its offering (e.g., by improving the offering's performance), (2) increase its monetary benefits (e.g., by adding monetary rewards), and/or (3) increase its psychological benefits (e.g., by enhancing the offering's image). It is important to note that for each of these strategies to be successful, the increase in benefits must actually be perceived as such by customers. Improving the offering's performance on attributes that do not create readily observable customer value will most likely not enhance its customer value.

  - *Decreasing an offering's costs*. As in the case of increasing benefits, decreasing an offering's costs can be achieved by decreasing its functional, monetary, and psychological costs. Because the price of an offering is typically the most important component of customers' costs, price reduction is the most common form of cost decrease. Based on the endurance of price reductions (i.e., whether they are permanent or temporary) and their reach (i.e., whether they are available to all customers or target a particular subset of customers), four types of price reductions can be identified: (1) widespread price cuts in which the price of an offering is permanently reduced; (2) targeted price cuts in which the price of an offering is permanently reduced only to a select group of customers (e.g., senior citizens, students, repeat buyers, high-volume customers); (3) widespread price incentives (e.g., temporary price reductions); and (4) targeted price incentives (e.g., selective discounts, coupons, rebates). These four price-reduction strategies can be summarized in a 2×2 matrix, as shown in Figure 6.

Figure 6. Strategies for Lowering an Offering's Monetary Costs

	Permanent	Temporary
Non-targeted	Widespread price cut	Widespread price incentives
Targeted	Targeted price cut	Targeted price incentives

- *Repositioning the offering to attract new customers.* In addition to increasing an offering's value to existing customers, a company may decide to reposition its offering to better address the needs of target customers. Repositioning implies a change in the value proposition of a given offering and typically involves one of two distinct strategies: vertical or horizontal.

  - *Vertical repositioning* refers to a scenario in which a company modifies the value proposition of an offering by moving it into a different price tier (and typically modifying its benefits). There are two general vertical repositioning strategies: upscale and downscale. In the case of an upscale repositioning, the company increases the price of an offering while at the same time enhancing its benefits. In contrast, in the case of a downscale repositioning, the company decreases an offering's price while at the same time decreasing its benefits.

  - *Horizontal repositioning* refers to a scenario in which a company modifies the value proposition of an offering by altering its benefits without necessarily moving it to a different price tier. To illustrate, in an attempt to break away from the traditional association of prunes as a means to regularity for the elderly and make them appealing to younger customers, in 2002, California prune manufacturers began marketing prunes as "dried plums," highlighting their high level of antioxidants.

▸ Extending the Product Line

In addition to repositioning its existing offering(s), a company can respond to competitive actions by extending its product line. Conceptually, product line extension is similar to repositioning, with the key distinction that instead of modifying the value proposition of an existing offering, the company launches a new offering with a different value proposition. In this context, there are two common product line extension strategies: vertical and horizontal.

- *Vertical extensions* refer to new offerings differentiated by both benefits and price. In this context, two types of vertical extensions can be distinguished: upscale extensions, which are higher performance, higher price offerings; and downscale extensions, which are lower performance, lower price offerings. These can be branded as an extension of the existing brand, as a new (value or premium) brand, or branded by the retailer as a private label. In this context, a downscale offering introduced to shield a major brand from low-priced competitors is commonly referred to as a "fighting brand."

- In contrast, *horizontal extensions* refer to new offerings that are differentiated from the original offering primarily in terms of performance rather than price. The purpose of launching horizontal extensions is to better fulfill the needs of existing customers and/or target a new customer segment.

A more detailed discussion on product line extensions is offered in Chapter 18.

Summary

Managing the competition involves three key aspects: evaluating market competitiveness, creating a sustainable competitive advantage, and managing competitive dynamics.

Evaluating market competitiveness involves identifying the key competitors and evaluating the competitive intensity of the market. A company's competitors are business entities with offerings positioned to satisfy the same need of the same target customers (current competitors), as well as business entities that currently do not target the same customers and/or aim to fulfill the same need(s) but nevertheless have the aspiration and/or the capability to satisfy the focal need(s) of the company's target customers (potential competitors). The competitive intensity of the market is defined by the extent to which companies' offerings are positioned to satisfy the same need of the same target customers. Market competitiveness can be analyzed by examining the market structure as it relates to a particular offering. In this context, the competitiveness of a given market is a function of the relationships among the company, its customers, collaborators, and competitors, as well as the relevant context in which the company operates.

Competitive advantage is the advantage that one firm has relative to competing firms with respect to fulfilling a particular need of a given target market. Differentiation by itself does not necessarily imply a competitive advantage; it is a necessary but not sufficient condition. Competitive advantage is a company's ability to deliver greater value to target customers. The two key antecedents of a company's competitive advantage are its strategic assets and its core competencies. Strategic assets are the company's resources that are essential for the success of the business in which the company operates and that differentiate the company from its competitors. Common strategic assets involve business infrastructure, collaborator networks, human capital, intellectual property, brands, customer base, synergistic offerings, access to scarce resources, and access to capital. A core competency is expertise in an area essential to the company's success, allowing the company to satisfy customer needs better than the competition in a way that enables the company and its collaborators to achieve their strategic goals. There are four key functional areas in which a company can establish a core competency: business management, operations management, technology development, and customer management (product management, service management, and brand management).

Managing competitive dynamics involves three basic types of strategies: (1) strategies for pioneering new markets, (2) strategies for gaining market position in existing markets, and (3) strategies for defending market position in existing markets. The key benefits of pioneering a market involve the opportunity to shape customer preferences, creating switching costs, preempting scarce resources, creating technological barriers to entry, and reaping learning curve benefits. The key drawbacks of being a pioneer involve free riding, incumbent inertia, and the uncertainty associated with the offering's technology and with customer demand. Companies already operating in a given market can gain market position by stealing share from competitors already serving this market (steal-share strategy) and/or by growing the market by attracting new customers to the category (market-growth strategy). To defend its market position against competitive actions, a company can employ one of three basic strategies: do nothing, reposition its existing offering (e.g., by increasing benefits, decreasing costs, and moving upscale or downscale), or add a new offering(s).

Relevant Frameworks: The Five Forces of Competition

The Five Forces framework was advanced by Michael Porter[2] as a conceptual approach for industry-based analysis of the nature of the competition and is often used for strategic industry-level decisions, such as evaluating the viability of entering (or exiting from) a particular industry. According to this framework, the competitiveness within an industry is determined by evaluating the following five factors: bargaining power of suppliers, bargaining power of buyers, threat of new entrants, threat of substitutes, and rivalry among extant competitors (Figure 7). The joint impact of these five factors determines the competitive environment in which a firm operates and allows the firm to anticipate competitors' actions.

Figure 7. The Five Forces of Competition[3]

The five forces influencing the competition in an industry can be summarized as follows.

- *Bargaining power of suppliers.* A supplier is powerful when it is dominated by few companies; the product is differentiated, has switching costs, and has diverse applications (e.g., across industries); there is a credible threat of forward integration.

- *Bargaining power of buyers.* A buyer is powerful when it has concentrated, large-volume purchases; the supplied product is undifferentiated and has no switching costs; the product represents a substantial part of buyers' costs (hence, encouraging more price shopping); the buyer's profit margins are low; the product is not crucial for the buyer; and there is a credible threat of backward integration.

- *Threat of new entrants.* The greater the threat, the greater the overall industry competitiveness. Six main barriers to entry can be identified.

  - *Economies of scale* refer to the benefits from operating the business on a large scale (e.g., in terms of research, production, and distribution). As a general rule, large economies of scale tend to deter new entrants.

  - *Product differentiation* reflects the degree to which competitive products are perceived by consumers to be different. In general, the presence of highly differentiated products is viewed as a deterrent for new entrants.

- *Capital requirements* refer to the magnitude of financial resources required to enter the industry. High capital requirements are likely to deter new entrants.

- *Cost disadvantages* (independent of size) capture factors such as experience curve effects, government subsidies, or favorable locations.

- *Access to distribution channels* refers to new entrants' ability to ensure the availability of its products in distribution channels. In this context, limited access to distribution channels tends to serve as a deterrent for new entrants.

- *Government policy* involves factors such as government regulations, license requirements, and access to technologies (e.g., airlines, power generation, liquor).

• *Threat of substitute products or services.* The introduction of new products tends to increase the competition in an industry and limit the profitability of an industry. In general, the threat of substitutes tends to be greater in cases where the substitutes have clear advantages over the existing products and/or where the profit margins in the industry producing the substitute product are relatively high.

• *Rivalry among existing competitors.* Rivalry tends to be stronger in cases where existing competitors are numerous and comparable in size and power (and hence are likely to have similar goals); industry growth is slow (leading to fights for redistribution of the existing market share); the product is nondifferentiated (leading to price-based competition); fixed costs are high and/or the product is perishable; there is excess capacity; exit barriers are high; and rivals are diverse in terms of goals, strategies, and/or organizational culture.

Additional Readings

Day, George S., David J. Reibstein, and Robert Gunther (2004), *Wharton on Dynamic Competitive Strategy.* New York, NY: John Wiley & Sons.

Kotler, Philip, D. Jain, and Maesincee Suvit (2002), *Marketing Moves: A New Approach to Profits, Growth, and Renewal.* Boston, MA: Harvard Business School Press.

Kim, W. Chan and Renée Mauborgne (2005), *Blue Ocean Strategy: How to Create Uncontested Market Space and Make the Competition Irrelevant.* Boston, MA: Harvard Business School Press.

Prahalad, C. K. and Venkatram Ramaswamy (2004), *The Future of Competition: Co-Creating Unique Value with Customers.* Boston, MA: Harvard Business School Press.

Prahalad, C. K. and Gary Hamel (1990), "The Core Competence of the Corporation," *Harvard Business Review,* (May–June), 79–91.

Treacy, Michael and Fred Wiersema (2006), *The Discipline of Market Leaders: Choose Your Customers, Narrow Your Focus, Dominate Your Market* (2nd ed.). London: Profile.

Notes

[1] Adapted from Hoch, Stephen J. (1996), "How Should National Brands Think about Private Labels?," *Sloan Management Review*, 37 (2), 89–102.

[2] Porter, Michael E. (1979), "How Competitive Forces Shape Strategy," *Harvard Business Review*, 57, 137–145.

[3] Adapted from Ibid.

Chapter Nine

Identifying Target Customers

The discussion so far has focused on managing the strategic aspects of a company's offering aimed at a particular customer segment. An important decision that often precedes optimizing the offering for a given customer segment involves identifying these customers. The process of identifying target customers aims to select customers for whom the company's offering can deliver superior value in a way that enables the company and its collaborators to achieve their strategic goals. Identifying target customers involves two key decisions: segmentation and targeting. The key aspects of these two decisions are the focus of this chapter.

Segmentation

Segmentation is the process of dividing customers into groups with similar characteristics. The process of segmentation is based on the idea that the effectiveness and efficiency of a company's marketing activities can be improved by ignoring the nonessential differences among customers within each segment and treating these customers as if they were a single entity. Thus, through segmentation, the company can reduce the heterogeneity (i.e., diversity) in the marketplace and deal with a relatively small number of customer segments.

Grouping customers into segments serves two main functions. First, it optimizes the *effectiveness* of the offering by identifying the key differences among customers in order to develop a customized offering for each segment. Second, it optimizes the *cost efficiency* of the offering by identifying the irrelevant differences among customers in order to deliver the same offering to customers within each segment. Thus, the key benefit of segmentation is in allowing the company to optimize marketing expenditures by grouping customers who are likely to respond in a similar fashion to the company's offerings. The key disadvantage of segmentation is that grouping customers into segments does not take into account potentially important differences that may exist among customers within each segment.

Segmentation, Mass Marketing, and One-to-One Marketing

The concept of segmentation can be better understood when considered in the context of two alternative marketing approaches: mass marketing and one-to-one marketing. Mass marketing refers to a scenario in which the same offering is given to all customers. A classic example is the strategy adopted by Ford's Model T, in which a single type of car was offered to all customers. In contrast, in one-to-one marketing, the company's offering is customized for each individual customer. In this context, segmentation can be viewed as a compromise between the mass-marketing approach and the one-to-one approach (Figure 1). By recognizing the diversity of customer needs, segmentation allows the company to design offerings that meet the needs of its customers better than the mass-marketing approach. The downside of segmentation vis-à-vis mass marketing is that developing different offerings for each segment could potentially lead to higher product development, communication, and distribution costs.

Figure 1. Segmentation, Mass Marketing, and One-to-One Marketing.

Because in most cases it is not cost efficient to develop an individual offering for each customer (as advocated by the one-to-one approach), segmentation allows companies to effectively reduce the number of offerings by developing offerings for groups of customers with similar needs. However, because grouping customers inevitably ignores some of the differences within each group, segmentation may decrease the effectiveness of the company's offering by not fully customizing the offering to fit the needs of individual customers.

An important issue in segmenting markets is determining the extent to which a market should be segmented and how large each segment should be. Segment size could potentially vary between a single segment encompassing the entire market (mass marketing) and multiple segments of one customer each (one-to-one marketing). As a general rule, segmentation is beneficial when the incremental value from effectively meeting the needs of resulting segments and from optimizing the communications and distribution strategies outweighs the costs of developing separate offerings for each segment. To illustrate, when the cost of customization is relatively high (e.g., durable goods manufacturing), companies tend to develop offerings that serve relatively large segments, whereas in industries where the cost of customization is low (e.g., online information delivery), segmentation can yield relatively small segments.

The process of segmentation is illustrated in Figure 2, in which customers vary on two factors represented by color and shape. Because each of these two factors has three levels, the maximum number of potential segments is nine. In this context, there are three possible segmentation strategies: by color, by shape, and by color and shape. The choice of a particular segmentation criterion is a function of the degree to which this criterion captures strategically important aspects of customer reaction to the company's offering. The depth of segmentation, on the other hand, is determined by the degree of differences among potential buyers, such that more heterogeneous markets are typically associated with a greater number of customer segments. To illustrate, the three scenarios shown in Figure 2 vary in the depth of the underlying segmentation: Compared with Segmentations I and II, the depth of

Segmentation III is greater, as evidenced by the larger number of segments and the lower within-segment heterogeneity.

Figure 2. Market Segmentation Strategies

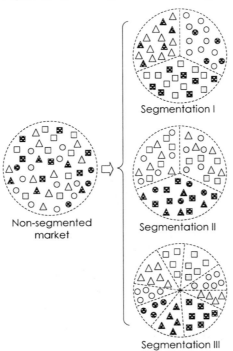

Criteria for Segmentation

When segmenting the market, the company's goal is to produce segments that differ in ways that are meaningful for marketing purposes. Thus, segmentation should yield groups of customers that vary in their response to the company's offering: Customers in the same segment should react in a similar fashion to the offering, while customers in different segments should vary in their response.

As a general rule, a good segmentation should yield segments that are mutually exclusive and collectively exhaustive: They should be sufficiently different from one another so that they do not overlap, and, at the same time, identified segments should include all customers in a given market. This can be achieved by using well-defined criteria to segment the market.

▸ Value-Based vs. Profile-Based Segmentation

Two main factors are used to divide customers into distinct segments: value factors and profile factors.

- *Value-based segmentation* groups customers based on their needs and the benefits they seek from the company's offerings. Value-based segmentation criteria can include three different types of factors: (1) functional factors, such as quality, performance, aesthetics, reliability, durability, safety; (2) monetary factors, such as willingness to pay, financing preferences, promotion preferences; and (3) psychological factors, such as image and social status.

- *Profile-based segmentation* captures some of the observable customer characteristics. In consumer marketing, four types of such characteristics are commonly used: demographic, geographic, psychographic, and behavioral. Each of these characteristics comprises one dimension of the customer profile:

  - *Demographic profile* includes factors such as age, gender, income, education, social status, and stage in the life cycle.

  - *Geographic profile* includes location identifiers such as country, region, city, postal code, and area code.

  - *Psychographic profile* includes relatively stable individual traits, such as personality, moral values, and lifestyle.

  - *Behavioral profile* captures customers' actions related to the company's offering, such as user status, distribution channel used, volume purchased, frequency of repurchase, price sensitivity, promotion sensitivity, and loyalty.

In business marketing, profile-based segmentation, referred to as *firmographics*, is based on factors such as location, size of company, industry, purchasing process, growth, and profitability.

▸ User-Based vs. Occasion-Based Segmentation

Depending on the nature of the segmentation criterion, most segmentations fall into one of two categories: user-based and occasion-based. User-based segmentation groups customers based on their relatively stable individual characteristics, which are likely to determine their needs and/or behavior across different purchase and consumption occasions. To illustrate, a customer may have a strong preference for fast food (e.g., burgers and fries) across different consumption occasions.

In contrast, occasion-based segmentation groups customers based on purchase and consumption occasions. By focusing on usage occasions rather than on the individual characteristics of the customer, occasion-based segmentation implicitly assumes that the same customer is likely to display different needs depending on the occasion. For example, when buying wine, a customer's preference may vary as a function of the occasion (for cooking, for daily consumption, for a special occasion, or for a gift).

In general, user-based segmentation is more appropriate in settings in which customers' needs are relatively stable across purchase occasions and, hence, can be used as a reliable predictor of their behavior on any particular purchase occasion. In contrast, occasion-based segmentation is more useful in cases in which customer needs vary across purchase occasions, and the same customer is likely to fall into different usage-based segments. To illustrate, the preference for regular versus light (diet) soft drinks is fairly stable across individuals and is relatively well captured by a user-based segmentation. In contrast, because the preference for a particular soft drink flavor is likely to vary over time for each individual depending on the usage occasion, in this case, occasion-based segmentation is more appropriate.

Targeting

The concept of targeting is used in two different contexts: (1) as a process of selecting which customers to serve and which to ignore and (2) as a process of identifying the actionable characteristics describing the customers that the company wishes to serve. These two aspects of targeting are discussed in more detail below.

Strategic Targeting

The strategic aspect of a company's targeting decision involves identifying which customers (segments) to serve and which to ignore (Figure 3). Strategic targeting reflects a company's decision to develop an offering that matches the needs of a particular set of customers, as well as customized communication and/or distribution activities to reach these customers. The basic principle underlying the selection of target customers is an offering's ability to deliver superior value to these customers in a way that enables the company and its collaborators to achieve their strategic goals. Because it is guided by the company's ability to fulfill customer needs better than the competition, strategic targeting is typically derived from value-based segmentation rather than from profile-based segmentation.

Figure 3. Strategic Targeting

- Target segment A
- Target segment B
- Target segment C

One of the key issues in strategic targeting analysis is identifying which criteria to use in selecting target customers. In general, three types of targeting criteria can be distinguished: (1) the inherent attractiveness of customers in a given segment, (2) the segment's compatibility with the company's strategic goals, competencies, and assets, and (3) a company's ability to serve the segment better than the competition. These three criteria are discussed in more detail below.

- *Segment attractiveness* reflects the ability of a particular segment to deliver value to the company and its collaborators. Segment attractiveness is a function of two key factors: (1) the long-term revenue potential of the customers in this segment and (2) the cost of reaching these customers. The revenue potential of the segment is typically determined by factors such as segment size, growth, buying power, and inherent loyalty. The cost of reaching customers in the segment, on the other hand, is a function of the company's ability to effectively and cost-efficiently communicate and deliver the offering to these customers.

- *Segment compatibility* reflects the ability of the company to deliver value to the target customers in a way that enables the company and its collaborators to achieve their strategic goals. Segment compatibility is a function of two key factors: (1) the degree to which serving this segment is consistent with the company's strategic goals and (2) the degree to which the company has the resources (i.e., competencies and assets) necessary to serve this segment.

- *Competitive advantage* reflects the company's ability to fulfill the needs of target customers better than the competition. A company's competitive advantage is, to a large degree, a function of the extent to which the competencies and assets necessary to deliver value to the target segment are unique and difficult to imitate by competitors.

Successful targeting requires that a segment meet all of these criteria; failure to meet even one criterion will impede the company's ability to be successful in delivering superior value to target customers in a way that benefits the company and its collaborators. To illustrate, the fact that a particular segment is inherently attractive is not a sufficient reason to target this segment; it is also imperative that serving this segment is consistent with the company's goals and that the company has the resources to deliver value to this segment in a way that cannot be matched by competitors.

Tactical Targeting

Unlike strategic targeting, which involves deciding which customers to target and which to ignore, tactical targeting involves developing an effective and cost-efficient plan to communicate and deliver the offering's value to the already selected target customers. Because of its focus on identifying customers whose needs the company can satisfy better than the competition, strategic targeting is typically derived from a value-based segmentation that groups customers based on their needs. The problem with this approach, however, is that customer needs are not readily observable to the company—a fact that complicates the company's ability to communicate and deliver its offering to target customers in an effective and cost-efficient manner.

In the absence of direct contact with its target customers, a company would need to communicate the value proposition of its offering and make it available to everyone, so that its target customers are aware of the offering and are able to obtain it. This approach, however, often is not cost effective, especially when the targeted customer segment is relatively small. In cases of multiple offerings by the same company, there is also a risk of customer confusion and/or sales cannibalization if all of the offerings are made available to all potential customers. To address this issue, companies often use the readily observable profile characteristics to identify the value-based target segments. For example, airlines tend to identify customers' price sensitivity based on their observable purchase behavior, such as advance purchase, flexibility of travel plans, and length of travel. This process of identifying the value-based segments by linking them to certain observable and actionable characteristics is the essence of tactical targeting (Figure 4).

The efficiency of tactical targeting is a function of the fit between the value-based target segment (customers that share a particular need) and the readily identifiable target segment (customers that share certain identifiable profile characteristics). Thus, on a tactical level, the efficiency of a company's targeting strategy can be expressed as the ratio of the size of the value-based target segment (identified in the process of strategic targeting) and the size of the identifiable profile-based segment. The closer the efficiency ratio is to 1, the more efficient the company's targeting approach.

Figure 4. Tactical Targeting

▲ Value-based segment (unobservable)
⊡ Profile-based segment (observable)

In the ideal scenario, the identifiable segment perfectly matches the value-based segment. In reality, however, achieving such an ideal fit is a challenging task. In this context, three types of errors can be made in tactical targeting: The value-based target segment may be identified too broadly, the target segment may be identified too narrowly, or the target segment may be misidentified (Figure 5). The first type of error, often referred to as a "shotgun approach," leads to inefficient targeting because the company will likely spend significant resources reaching customers who are not interested in its offering. In contrast, the second type of error, often referred to as "oversegmentation," leads to inefficient targeting because the company will likely overlook customers interested in the offering. The decision as to which of the two types of errors the company should accept is a function of the relative benefits and costs and should be consistent with the company's overall goals and strategy. Finally, the third type of error involves misidentifying target customers—a scenario in which the company's communication and distribution efforts are directed to a segment that does not include its target customers.

Figure 5. Common Targeting Errors

Broad target identification   Narrow target identification   Target misidentification

▲ Value-based segment (unobservable)
⊡ Profile-based segment (observable)

Targeting Multiple Segments

A company might target either a single segment or multiple segments. When targeting multiple segments, a company's goals often vary across segments. Furthermore, because different target segments vary in their needs, they often have a different set of competitors and collaborators, rely on different core competencies and strategic assets of the company, and are influenced by different aspects of the overall context in which the company operates. In the same vein, different segments typically require different marketing mix variables, different implementation plans, and different controls. This implies that each individual segment requires its own strategic analysis, as illustrated in Figure 6.

Figure 6. Targeting Multiple Segments

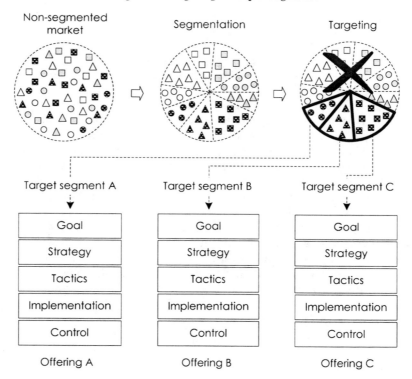

The process of managing multiple offerings comprising a company's product line is discussed in more detail in Chapter 18.

Summary

Identifying target customers involves identifying potential buyers for whom the company will tailor its offering. Identifying target customers typically involves three key decisions: (1) dividing customers into groups with similar characteristics (also referred to as segmentation), (2) selecting which customers to serve and which to ignore (also referred to as strategic targeting), and (3) identifying an effective plan to reach these customers (also referred to as tactical targeting).

Segmentation is the process of dividing customers into groups with similar characteristics. The process of segmentation is based on the idea that the effectiveness and efficiency of a company's marketing activities can be improved by ignoring the nonessential differences among customers within each segment and treating these customers as if they were a single entity. As a general rule, a good segmentation should yield segments that are both mutually exclusive and collectively exhaustive. In other words, identified segments should be sufficiently different from one another so that they do not overlap; at the same time, these segments should include all customers in a given market.

Two main factors are used to divide customers into distinct segments: value factors and profile factors. Value-based segmentation groups customers based on their needs and the benefits they seek from the company's offerings. Profile-based segmentation captures some of the observable customer characteristics. In consumer marketing, four types of characteristics are commonly used: demographic (e.g., age, gender, income, and education), geographic (e.g., country, region, and city), psychographic (e.g., personality, moral values, and lifestyle), and behavioral (e.g., user status, volume purchased, and price sensitivity). In business marketing, profile-based segmentation is usually based on firm-specific factors (e.g., location, company size, and industry).

The strategic aspect of a company's targeting decision involves identifying which customers (segments) to serve and which to ignore. Because it aims to optimize the value to customers, the company, and its collaborators, strategic targeting is typically derived from value-based segmentation rather than from profile-based segmentation. The targeting decision is guided by three key criteria: (1) the inherent attractiveness of the customers in a given segment, (2) the segment's compatibility with the company's strategic goals, competencies, and assets, and (3) a company's ability to serve the segment better than the competition.

The tactical aspect of a company's targeting decision involves developing an effective and cost-efficient plan to communicate and deliver the offering's value to the already selected target customers. In particular, tactical targeting links the (typically unobservable) value-based segments to specific observable and actionable characteristics. Common tactical targeting errors result in three types of biases: segments defined too broadly (i.e., shotgun targeting), segments defined too narrowly (i.e., oversegmentation), and segments that are misidentified.

Relevant Frameworks: S-T-P Framework

The Segmentation-Targeting-Positioning (S-T-P) framework is a relatively simple and very popular approach that offers an insight into the process by which a company selects its "ideal" customers and develops the offering's unique value proposition. The S-T-P framework implies that the process of delivering customer value involves three key decisions: segmentation, targeting, and positioning. Segmenting the market, identifying target customers, and positioning the offering is an iterative process in which the company attempts to identify the customers most likely to benefit from its offering and develops a distinct image of the offering in the minds of these customers.

The S-T-P framework outlines the three key steps in the process of selecting the "ideal" customers and developing the offering's value proposition to these customers. The S-T-P approach does not imply a specific algorithm for dividing the market into segments, identifying which segments to target, and developing a value proposition and a positioning strategy for these customers. Instead, it simply identifies segmentation, targeting, and positioning as key processes in developing an offering's strategy and suggests a particular order in which these processes are to be implemented.

Despite its popularity and intuitive appeal, the S-T-P framework has a number of limitations. One potential limitation is that it focuses only on the customer side of the marketing process and excludes the company and its collaborators from the value equation. As a result, the S-T-P framework does not readily address the process of optimizing the value of the offering to the company and its collaborators. Another potential limitation is that the S-T-P framework implicitly assumes a single positioning strategy without making explicit the fact that a positioning strategy needs to be developed for each target segment. It is also important to note that positioning reflects only one aspect of an offering's value proposition. Whereas the value proposition captures *all* of the benefits and costs associated with a given offering, positioning captures only the *most distinct aspects* of a company's value proposition. By focusing solely on the most distinct aspects of a given offering rather than on its entire value proposition, the S-T-P approach fails to offer a comprehensive view of customer value.

Relevant Concepts

Heterogeneous Market: Market comprised of customers that vary in their response to a company's offering.

Homogeneous Market: Market comprised of customers likely to react in a similar manner to the company's offering (e.g., they seek the same benefits, have similar financial resources, can be reached through the same communication means, and have access to the offering through the same distribution channels).

Niche Strategy: Marketing strategy aimed at a distinct and relatively small customer segment.

Additional Readings

McDonald, Malcolm and Ian Dunbar (2004), *Market Segmentation: How to Do It, How to Profit from It*. Amsterdam: Elsevier.

Weinstein, Art (2004), *Handbook of Market Segmentation: Strategic Targeting for Business and Technology Firms* (3rd ed.). New York, NY: Haworth Press.

Gordon, Ian (2002), *Competitor Targeting: Winning the Battle for Market and Customer Share*. New York, NY: John Wiley & Sons.

Part Three

Tactical Analysis

Chapter Ten

Managing Products and Services

Product and service management aim to optimize the value of the product and service aspects of the company's offering to deliver superior value to target customers, the company, and its collaborators. The key factors for creating and managing the product and service aspects of a company's offering are the focus of this chapter.

Overview

The product and service aspects of an offering capture the offering's key functional characteristics. Products typically change ownership during purchase; once created, they can be physically separated from the manufacturer and distributed to end-users via multiple channels. Products are typically classified into one of two categories: durable or nondurable. Durable goods are consumed over multiple occasions and over an extended period (e.g., cars, household appliances, and machinery). In contrast, nondurable goods are typically consumed on a single occasion and/or over a short period (e.g., food, disposable items, and cosmetics).

The service aspect of the offering is in many respects similar to the product one, with two main exceptions: change of ownership and inseparability. Unlike products, which typically change ownership during purchase, services do not necessarily imply a change in ownership; instead, the customer acquires the right to use the service within a given timeframe. Furthermore, unlike products, which can be physically separated from the manufacturer, services are usually delivered and consumed at the same time.

Because services are created and delivered at the same time, they are difficult to standardize, and their quality varies as a function of the interaction between the service provider and the customer. To illustrate, a customer may experience different levels of service from the same service provider at different times and/or in different locations (service inconsistency), and the same service provider may have different interactions with different customers depending on customers' behavior (service interactivity). The inseparability of creating and delivering value also makes services perishable in the sense that they cannot be inventoried—an important consideration in industries where companies with a fixed service capacity face fluctuating customer demand (e.g., airlines, hotels, and call centers).

Based on the level of uncertainty, product and service characteristics can be classified into one of three categories: search, experience, and credence.[1] *Search characteristics* are associated with the least amount of uncertainty and are typically identifiable through inspection before purchase. *Experience characteristics* carry greater uncertainty and are revealed only through consumption. *Credence characteristics* have the greatest amount of uncertainty and are not identifiable even from ex post observations; as a result, consumers can never be certain of the quality and value of credence attributes even after experiencing the product/service. For example, in the case of toothpaste, size is a search attribute, taste is an experience attribute, and cavity prevention is a credence attribute. It is pertinent to note that the boundaries between these categories are fuzzy, and search–experience–credence categories represent regions in a continuum. In general, search attributes are more common for tangible offerings, whereas credence attributes are more typical for intangible offerings. Because services have more intangible properties relative to products, they are heavy on experience and credence attributes; in contrast, search attributes are more typical for products than services.

A Framework for Managing Products and Services

Managing products and services involves two types of decisions: (1) strategic decisions, aiming to optimize products and services as a function of the offering's market structure and (2) tactical decisions, aiming to optimize products and services as a function of the other marketing mix variables. These two types of decisions are outlined in more detail below.

Product and Service Management: Strategy

From a strategic standpoint, product and service decisions involve five key factors: customers, company, collaborators, competition, and context. These five factors are illustrated in Figure 1 and outlined in more detail below.

Figure 1. Product and Service Management as a Function of Market Structure

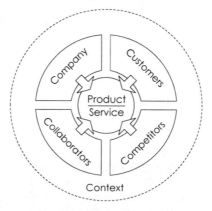

- *Customers.* An offering's product and service strategy is influenced by the characteristics of its target customers. To illustrate, when launching a product/service based on a new technology, a company targeting tech-savvy early adopters is likely to introduce a more advanced, feature-rich, and more expensive version, whereas a company targeting the mainstream market will be more successful introducing a less expensive option that offers only basic features and functionality.

- *Company.* A company's goals, strategic assets, and core competencies are important factors in determining an offering's product and service strategy. For example, a company can manage supply by outsourcing part of its product/service operations, optimize its logistics to use just-in-time manufacturing, and/or offer flexible workforce scheduling (e.g., to address the seasonality of demand, as in the travel, hospitality, and shipping industries). Similarly, to ensure the consistency of the product/service benefits across units and over time, a company can optimize the effectiveness of its operations by employing quality management programs (e.g., Total Quality Management and Six Sigma).

- *Collaborators.* An offering's product and service strategy is also a function of the company's relationship with collaborators. For instance, to increase the benefits to its channel partners, a company can design the product to facilitate inventory management (e.g., by optimizing product nomenclature and labeling), extend the shelf life of perishable products, and optimize the channel's inventory costs (e.g., by creating space-efficient packaging).

- *Competitors.* An offering's product and service strategy is influenced by its competitors' products and services. Thus, when designing its products and services, most companies strive to deliver superior value relative to that of competitive offerings. In this context, competitors' offerings, especially those that have achieved market success, often serve as benchmarks for designing new products and services.

- *Context.* Product and service design is also influenced by various social, economic, political, technological, and regulatory aspects of the environment in which the company operates. To illustrate, most offerings need to comply with product/service specifications and standards imposed by various government and nongovernment agencies (e.g., FDA, FCC, and IEEE[2]).

Product and Service Management: Tactics

From a tactical standpoint, product and service decisions involve analyzing the other marketing mix variables (i.e., brand, price, incentives, communication, and distribution) and their impact on the product and service aspect of the offering. The key elements of this analysis are illustrated in Figure 2 and outlined in more detail below.

Figure 2. Product Management as a Function of the Marketing Mix[3]

- *Product and service.* An offering's product and service strategy is often a function of the interplay between the offering's product and service characteristics. To optimize their customer value proposition, companies often strive to balance the product and service aspects of their offerings. For example, commoditized products are often differentiated by adding services, whereas the intangibility of services often benefits from being enhanced with a tangible product component.

- *Brand.* An offering's product and service strategy is a function of its brand. Thus, the product and service design should be consistent with the essence of the brand. To illustrate, Gillette constantly strives to ensure that all products in its product line are aligned with its image of delivering "the best a man can get."

- *Price.* An offering's product and service strategy is often contingent on its price. For example, the viability of introducing a new product/service feature is a function of the price premium that target customers are willing to pay.

- *Incentives.* Because incentives are, in most cases, added to the offering after the product/service has already been created, their impact is typically not a key factor in product/service design. Nevertheless, by incurring additional expenses, incentives influence the resources available for developing the product/service aspects of the offering.

- *Communication.* The product and service aspects of an offering are also a function of its communication strategy. To illustrate, product design, packaging, and labeling can familiarize target customers with the key aspects of the offering. These aspects can identify the product, brand, and country of origin, describe the product, its contents, recommended usage, as well as provide customers with reasons to buy the product.

- *Distribution.* An offering's product and service strategy is influenced by its distribution. Thus, product design can facilitate its transportation and storage (by both channel members and customers), as well as extend the shelf life of perishable products. For example, Coca-Cola introduced refrigerator-size packaging to facilitate the storage of their products (and in the process ensure that consumers always have a cold drink when they want one). Similarly, containers of products such as ketchup and mustard facilitate the use of the product (e.g., plastic upside-down containers designed to improve the ease of dispensing the product).

Product and Service Decisions

Creating and managing products and services involve decisions concerning a set of key characteristics that include form (e.g., size, shape, and physical structure); features (the discrete characteristics of product/service functionality); performance (the level at which the product/service performs on relevant attributes); consistency (the degree to which all individual products and services are identical and consistent with specifications); durability (the expected length of a product's life cycle); reliability (the probability that the product/service will operate according to its specifications and will not malfunction for the duration of its projected life cycle); compatibility (the degree to which the product/service is consistent with certain readily existing standards); style (the product's look and feel); technological design (the technology used to create the product, as well as the technology used by the product); packaging (the product container); and ease-of-use (the ease of setting up, using, and disposing of the product).

In addition to deciding on the characteristics of the individual products and services, companies have to decide on the mix of products and services they offer. Most product/service mix decisions involve four key aspects: (1) assortment breadth (the number of product lines), (2) product assortment depth (the number of products within each product line), (3) product differentiation (the nature of differences across products in a given product line), and (4) product novelty (the magnitude of differences across products in a given product line). These four aspects are discussed in more detail below.

Product-mix breadth decisions concern the diversity of a company's offering as reflected in the number of product lines it carries. In general, two types of product mixes can be identified: specialized and diversified.

- *Specialized product mix* involves fairly narrow assortments comprised of one or a few product lines. To illustrate, Ferrari (high-performance sports cars), Glacéau (bottled water), and TiVo (digital video recorders) have strategically limited their product mix to a single product line.

- *Diversified product mix* involves fairly broad assortments comprising multiple product lines. For example, companies like General Electric, Procter and Gamble, Johnson and Johnson, and Unilever offer a wide variety of product lines. The primary rationale for a diversified product mix is to take advantage of growth opportunities in areas in which the company has no presence. A company's success in managing diverse product lines is often a function of existing synergies among these lines. Such synergies can be related to company processes (e.g., research and development, manufacturing, and distribution) or personnel (e.g., experienced management, qualified engineers, and knowledgeable sales force).

Product-mix depth decisions concern the number of product items (assortment) offered within each line. These decisions involve evaluating the benefits and costs of offering larger versus smaller assortments.

- *Larger assortments* offer buyers an opportunity for a better match between their preferences and the benefits afforded by the company's product/service. Thus, the greater the variety of available products and services, the greater the likelihood that a buyer will find an attractive product/service. From a company's perspective, however, large assortments tend to increase research and development, manufacturing, and distribution costs associated with the offering.

- *Smaller assortments* are favored by companies because of the cost efficiency of their research and development, manufacturing, and distribution processes. Smaller assortments also tend to be preferred by novice customers, who are often confused by larger assortments. Because products/services comprising smaller assortments are likely to be associated with a higher turnover rate than larger assortments (provided that customer demand does not either increase or increases at a proportionally slower rate than does the assortment size), smaller assortments tend to be preferred by distributors because they offer better shelf-space utilization. The key drawback of smaller assortments, however, is that these offerings are not optimized to match the preferences of all of the company's target customers.

Product-differentiation decisions concern the nature of differences across products in a company's product line. Thus, based on the offerings' overall performance, products and services can be differentiated in one of two ways: vertically or horizontally.

- *Vertically differentiated products* can be easily ordered in terms of the relative attractiveness of their benefits. Because better performance typically comes at a higher price, vertically differentiated products and services typically belong to different price tiers (hence, the name vertical differentiation). The upscale products/services typically deliver a higher level of benefits at a higher price (e.g., Mercedes S-series), whereas the downscale products/services deliver a lower level of benefits, typically at a lower price (e.g., Mercedes A-series). From a company perspective, vertically differentiated products and services typically vary in costs, such that upscale offerings are associated with higher costs than downscale offerings (although the difference in price is typically greater than the difference in costs, which accounts for the typically higher margins associated with upscale products and services).

- *Horizontally differentiated products* and services vary on benefits that do not imply a universal preference ordering; hence, their price is not a key differentiating factor. For example, different types of soft drinks (regular, cherry, vanilla, diet, caffeine-free), different yogurt flavors, and different product colors comprise horizontally differentiated product lines. From a company perspective, horizontally differentiated products and services are typically very similar in terms of their cost structure (unlike in the case of vertically differentiated offerings).

Product novelty decisions concern the magnitude of differences across products in a given product line. Thus, depending on the nature of the functional differences between the products in a company's portfolio, two strategies can be identified: product-variation strategy and product-innovation strategy.

- *Product-variation strategy* leads to product lines in which individual offerings are characterized by relatively minor variations in their functionality. The product-variation strategy is very common in the case of horizontally differentiated offerings. A typical example of this strategy is extending the product line by adding different colors, flavors, tastes, sizes, designs, or packaging variations of the same core products. By adding different product variants, the company can improve the fit between the benefits of its offerings and the needs of its target customers (e.g., different flavors of ice cream, yogurt, or soda). In the case of frequently purchased items, the product variation strategy is often used to address customers' variety-seeking behavior. By adding different product variants, the company can offer its customers more variety while keeping them loyal to company brands. Product variation strategy is also used to customize the offering to the needs of distributors. Thus, product variants are used by companies to avoid channel conflicts that are likely to occur when distributors with different cost structures and profit margins sell identical offerings (also referred to as horizontal channel conflicts). By creating distributor-specific product variants, a company is able to minimize the likelihood of such conflicts.

- Unlike the product-variation strategy, in which offerings are functionally similar, the *product-innovation strategy* leads to product lines in which individual offerings have substantive differences in their functionality. These differences may stem from technology-based innovations, as well as from innovative use of existing technology to design new ways of fulfilling customer needs. The product innovation strategy is often used to develop offerings targeted at customer segments with different underlying needs, which require different benefits from the company's offerings.

Summary

Product and service management aims to optimize the value of the product and service aspects of the company's offering to deliver superior value to target customers, the company, and its collaborators. These aspects capture the offering's key functional characteristics. Products typically change ownership during purchase; once created, they can be physically separated from the manufacturer and distributed to end users via multiple channels. Unlike products, services imply a right of use (rather than a change in ownership) and are delivered and consumed at the same time.

Managing products and services involves two types of analysis: (1) strategic analysis, which examines products and services as a function of the offering's market structure (customers, company, collaborators, competition, and context) and (2) tactical analysis, which examines products and services as a function of the other marketing mix variables (brand, price, incentives, communication, and distribution).

Creating and managing products and services involves decisions concerning a set of key characteristics, such as form, features, performance, (the level at which the product/service performs on relevant attributes), consistency, durability, reliability, compatibility, style, technological design, packaging, and ease of use. In addition to deciding on the characteristics of the individual products and services, managers have to decide on the mix of products and services they offer. Most product/service mix decisions involve four key aspects: (1) product assortment breadth (the number of product lines), (2) product assortment depth (the number of products within each product line), (3) product differentiation (the nature of differences across products in a given product line), and (4) product novelty (the magnitude of differences across products in a given product line).

Additional Readings

Barlow, Janelle and Paul Stewart (2006), *Branded Customer Service: The New Competitive Edge* (1st ed.). San Francisco, CA: Berrett-Koehler.

Berry, Leonard L. (2004), *Marketing Services Competing through Quality*. New York, NY: Free Press.

Lehmann, Donald R. and Russell S. Winer (2005), *Product Management* (4th ed.). Boston, MA: McGraw-Hill/Irwin.

Lovelock, Christopher H. and Jochen Wirtz (2007), *Services Marketing: People, Technology, Strategy* (6th ed.). Upper Saddle River, NJ: Prentice Hall.

McGrath, Michael E. (2001), *Product Strategy for High Technology Companies: Accelerating Your Business to Web Speed* (2nd ed.). New York, NY: McGraw-Hill.

Zeithaml, Valarie A., Mary Jo Bitner, and Dwayne D. Gremler (2006), *Services Marketing: Integrating Customer Focus across the Firm* (4th ed.). Boston, MA: McGraw-Hill/Irwin.

Notes

[1] Nelson, Phillip (1970), "Information and Consumer Behavior," *Journal of Political Economy*, 78 (March–April), 311–29.

[2] The Institute of Electrical and Electronics Engineers is a developer of voluntary, consensus-based industry standards in a broad range of industries, including energy, healthcare, and information technology.

[3] Figure 2 illustrates the impact of marketing mix analysis on product design; the analysis of the impact of the marketing mix on services is conceptually identical, with the exception that the concepts of product and service are switched.

Managing Brands

Brands are essential marketing tools used to create value for customers, the company, and its collaborators. The key aspects of creating and managing brands are the focus of this chapter.

Overview

A brand is a marketing tool created with the purpose of differentiating a company's offering from the competition and creating value for customers, the company, and its collaborators. A brand has two key aspects: (1) brand identity, which includes identifying characteristics, such as name, sign, symbol, character, and/or design; and (2) brand meaning, which reflects a set of offering-related associations in the mind of the buyer. To illustrate, the identity of BMW is captured by elements such as its distinct name and logo, whereas its meaning—"the ultimate driving machine"—reflects the mental associations that target customers make with the brand. The key aspects of the identity and the meaning of a brand are delineated in more detail below.

Brand identity is typically achieved through attributes such as brand name, logo, symbol, character, slogan, jingle, product design, and packaging. The key criteria for deciding on brand identity elements are that they should be (1) unique, (2) memorable, (3) likeable, and (4) consistent with the other brand elements and with the meaning of the brand. Brand elements should also be flexible and adaptable to changes in the market environment (e.g., to accommodate shifts in consumer preferences) and the company's product line (e.g., to be extendable to other product categories). Furthermore, the company should be able to protect the uniqueness of its brand elements against infringement by competitors.

Brand meaning reflects the brand-related perceptions and beliefs held by the brand's current and potential customers; it reflects customers' understanding of this brand's value proposition, often referred to as a brand's promise. The meaning of the brand has dual impact on customers' perceptions of value: (1) it signals the quality of the products and services associated with the brand and (2) it adds value above and beyond the one provided by the underlying product or service. This added value can involve factors such as emotional benefits (e.g., the satisfaction from using and owning the brand), social benefits (e.g., group acceptance resulting from ownership of a particular brand), and self-expressive benefits (e.g., using the brand as a means to express one's identity).

In general, brand identity aims to *identify* the company's offering and *differentiate* it from the competition. In contrast, brand meaning aims to *create value* (for customers, the company, and its collaborators) that goes beyond the product and service characteristics of the offering. A brand's identity can exist independently from its target customers; in contrast, a brand's meaning is subjective in nature and exists primarily in the minds of the buyers.

A Framework for Managing Brands

Managing brands involves two types of decisions: (1) strategic decisions, aiming to optimize brands as a function of the offering's market structure and (2) tactical analysis, aiming to optimize brands as a function of the other marketing mix variables. These two types of decisions are outlined in more detail below.

Managing Brands: Strategy

From a strategic standpoint, branding decisions involve analyzing five key factors: customers, company, collaborators, competition, and context. These factors are illustrated in Figure 1 and outlined in more detail below.

Figure 1. Brand Management as a Function of Market Structure

- *Customers.* Because one of the primary functions of any brand is to create value for its target customers, understanding these customers' needs is essential for building and managing successful brands. In this context, changes in customer preferences often lead to repositioning the brand in a way that maximizes its value to customers.

- *Company.* An offering's branding strategy is influenced by the existing brands in the company's brand portfolio. To illustrate, a company with a portfolio of strong brands can build on these brands for its new offerings.

- *Collaborators.* An offering's branding can be influenced by the branding strategies of its collaborators. For example, collaboration in the area of branding often leads to the development of long-term co-branding strategies (e.g., co-branding between Microsoft and Intel, between Coca-Cola and Splenda, and between Citibank, American Airlines, and MasterCard). In this context, understanding a collaborator's branding strategy is essential for developing and managing a company's own brands.

- *Competitors.* Competitors' branding strategy can have a significant impact on designing and managing an offering's brand. Indeed, because one of the primary goals of brands is to differentiate a company's offering from the competition, competitive differentiation is essential for successful brand management. Of particular relevance here are the concepts of points of parity (associations that are shared by competing brands) and points of difference (associations that are unique to a particular brand), which are used by companies to position their brands vis-à-vis those of their competitors.

- *Context.* An offering's branding strategy is also influenced by the social, economic, political, technological, and regulatory aspects of the environment in which it operates. For instance, the protectability of a brand name is a function of the degree to which it has been adopted by the population and has become synonymous with the associated category. Thus, because of their common use as a generic term, brands such as Aspirin, Thermos, and Escalator have lost their legal trademark-protected status.

Managing Brands: Tactics

From a tactical standpoint, branding decisions involve analyzing the other marketing mix variables (product, service, price, incentives, communication, and distribution) and their impact on the offering's brand. The key aspects of this analysis are illustrated in Figure 2 and outlined in more detail below.

Figure 2. Brand Management as a Function of the Marketing Mix

- *Product and service.* An offering's brand is directly linked to the product and service characteristics of the offering. To illustrate, the more commoditized a company's product or service is, the less observable its benefits are and the greater the importance of branding in differentiating the offering. For instance, brand characters are typically used to differentiate commoditized products with benefits that are not readily observable, such as the Michelin Man (tires), Green Giant (processed vegetables), Tony the Tiger (cereal), and Mr. Clean (cleaning products). An offering's brand can also be enhanced by its packaging. For example, the swirl design of Coca-Cola's bottle, the frosty design of the Gray Goose vodka bottle, and the signature blue Tiffany's box are important brand elements that create value in the minds of customers above and beyond that of the actual product.

- *Price.* An offering's pricing is an important factor in branding. For example, low prices can hurt the image of an upscale brand and high prices are inconsistent with the image of a value brand.

- *Incentives.* An offering's brand is a function of the nature of incentives. Because monetary incentives emphasize the importance of price, they typically tend to erode the strength of the brand. In contrast, nonmonetary incentives and promotions that are consistent with the brand image (e.g., toys and games involving the brand's character) can ultimately strengthen the brand.

- *Communication.* An offering's communication strategy is a key factor in building and managing brands. Thus, the impact of an offering's communications on branding is a function of the nature of the communicated message. For example, brand-related communications tend to strengthen the brand, whereas communications focused on price and monetary incentives typically have the opposite effect and erode the brand image.[1]

- *Distribution.* An offering's brand is a function of its distribution strategy. For example, the increasing role of online and warehouse retail formats decreases the role of personal selling in branding in favor of point-of-sales branding through packaging and in-store communications. An offering's distribution channels can also become a vehicle for brand delivery. For instance, Disney World theme parks and Nike Town retail stores function as channels delivering Disney and Nike brands.

Brand Hierarchy

Brand hierarchy (also referred to as brand architecture) reflects the relationship between different brands in a company's portfolio. There are several popular approaches to managing multiple brands:

- *Individual branding* involves creating a separate brand for each product or product line. To illustrate, Tide, Cheer, Bold, and Era are individual brands of laundry detergents created by Procter & Gamble. Chevrolet, Pontiac, Buick, Cadillac, Saturn, GMC, and Hummer are individual brands of General Motors. Campbell Soup Company uses Campbell's for soups, Pepperidge Farm for baked goods, and V8 for juices. Sears uses Kenmore for appliances, Kraftsman for tools, and DieHard for batteries. In some cases, the brand names for different products may even have the same origin: Nescafé, Nesquik, Nestea, and Nespresso are used by Nestlé to brand different beverages.

- *Umbrella branding* involves using a single brand for all of a company's products. For example, General Electric, Heinz, Virgin, and Costco (Kirkland Signature) use a single brand for nearly all of their products. The main advantage of using umbrella branding is that it leverages the equity of an existing brand, benefiting from the instant recognition of the core brand while avoiding the costs associated with building a new brand. A drawback of using umbrella branding is that a poor performance of any particular product carrying the brand name can easily hurt the reputation of the entire brand. Using a single brand may also limit the company's ability to attach a specific meaning to the brand across different product categories.

- *Sub-branding* involves combining two or more brand names, one of which typically is the umbrella brand. For instance, Courtyard by Marriott, Residence Inn by Marriott, Fairfield Inn by Marriott, and SpringHill Suites by Marriott exemplify using sub-brands in the context of umbrella branding. Similarly, Porsche uses sub-branding for the different offerings in its product line: Carrera, Boxster, Cayenne, and Cayman. Using this strategy enables the company to leverage an existing brand name while minimizing the spillover risk of potential negative associations to the parent brand.

- *Co-branding* involves combining two or more independent brand names, typically from different product categories, such as United Airlines–Chase–Visa credit cards, Lexus "Coach edition" sport-utility vehicles, and HP–iPod MP3 players. A form of co-branding involves ingredient branding in which an ingredient or component of a product has its own brand identity, such as Teflon surface protector, Gore-Tex fabrics, NutraSweet and Splenda sweeteners, and Intel microprocessors.

Companies with multiple product lines may also employ hybrid brand structures that involve a variety of individual, umbrella-branding, and sub-branding strategies. To illustrate, Chevrolet, Pontiac, Buick, Cadillac, Saturn, and Hummer are individual brands of General Motors; at the same time, each one serves as an umbrella brand for its sub-brands (Camaro, Impala, Corvette, Malibu, Monte Carlo, and Blazer are Chevrolet sub-brands; CTS, STS, XLR, and Escalade are Cadillac sub-brands, and G6, Solstice, GTO, Grand Prix are Pontiac sub-brands).

Brand Dynamics

Once created, brands evolve over time. There are two common types of changes in an offering's branding strategy: (1) brand repositioning, which involves changes to an existing brand, most often to make the brand more relevant to its target customers, and (2) brand extensions, which involve broadening the set of underlying product categories to which the brand is applied. These two types of brand dynamics are discussed in the following sections.

Brand Repositioning

Brand repositioning involves changing a key aspect of a brand's identity and/or image. There are several common reasons to reposition an existing brand, including: (1) in response to a change in target customers, (2) when reaching a new target market, and (3) in reaction to a change in the positioning of a competitor's brand. These reasons are illustrated in more detail below.

- *Reacting to a change in the target customers.* One of the most common reasons for repositioning a brand is to ensure that it remains relevant in the context of the changing needs of its target customers. For example, to reflect the changing values and lifestyles of women, General Mills has consistently refined the image of Betty Crocker—a fictitious character designed to offer cooking advice to consumers. Over the years, she has had eight different "looks," from the first stern, gray-haired, older woman in 1936 to today's olive-skinned, dark-haired Betty. Similarly, to increase its appeal to younger customers, Procter and Gamble repositioned its half-century-old beauty brand, Oil of Olay. The key changes introduced in 2000 included changing the name to Olay (to avoid associations equating oil to "greasy"), streamlining its logo, replacing the woman's image (which resembled a nun) on the label with a younger one, and cleaning up the packaging design. In response to customers' concerns over fried food, Kentucky Fried Chicken abbreviated its name to KFC to project a healthier image.

- *Reaching a new target market.* Companies often reposition their brands when entering new markets so that the brand image reflects the specifics of that market and better resonates with the needs and values of target customers. For example, Philip Morris' Marlboro brand was originally introduced in 1924 as a woman's cigarette, tagged "Mild as May"; it was repositioned in 1954 using the rugged cowboy image of the Marlboro Man, which was more likely to appeal to male smokers. Procter and Gamble's cleaning product Mr. Clean was introduced as Mr. Proper in Germany, Flash in the United Kingdom, Monsieur Propre in France, Mastro Lindo in Italy, Don Limpio in Spain (from *limpiar*—"to clean"), and Maestro Limpio in Mexico.

- *Reacting to a change in a competitor's positioning.* Because companies strive to create superior customer value relative to that of other offerings in the marketplace, a change in the positioning of a competitor's offering often induces the company to reposition its brand to preserve and/or enhance its competitive advantage. To illustrate, the popularity of the Energizer Bunny in the United States forced Duracell to discontinue the use of its brand mascot—the Duracell Bunny—that is now used to brand Duracell batteries only outside of North America.

Brand Extensions

Brand extension refers to the strategy of using the same brand name in a different context, such as a different product category or a different price tier. For example, Montblanc—which, over a century, built a reputation for producing the finest quality pens—extended its brand to include items such as luxury watches, sunglasses, cufflinks, wallets, briefcases, and even fragrances. In a similar manner, Oakley extended its brand from eyewear to other domains such as apparel, footwear, bags, and watches.

Brand extensions can be better understood when considered in the context of product line extensions. Product line extensions involve adding a new offering to a company's existing product line. In contrast to product line extensions, brand extensions involve the development of a branding strategy for an existing product line extension. To illustrate, consider the decisions of Toyota and Volkswagen to enter the luxury car market. Both companies have made the decision to extend their product

Chapter 11   Managing Brands   **107**

line upscale but have chosen different branding strategies. Believing that its existing brand name cannot convey the luxury image required to successfully compete with Mercedes S-class and BMW 7-series, Toyota launched a new brand—Lexus—rather than trying to extend its existing brand. In contrast, Volkswagen launched its upscale extension branded as Volkswagen Phaeton, prominently featuring the VW logo on the front and the back of the car. Thus, in Volkswagen's case, the product line extension went hand in hand with a brand extension, whereas in Toyota's case the product line extension involved launching a new, freestanding brand.

In general, the primary reason for extending an existing offering is to develop a new value proposition to better address the needs of a specific customer segment. The primary reason to extend the brand is to leverage the equity of an existing brand by applying it to a new offering. The popularity of brand extensions stems from the fact that building new brands is a costly and time-consuming task. As a result, when entering a new product category, companies often choose to leverage the equity of their existing brands rather than invest in creating new ones.

Based on their breadth, there are two main types of brand extensions: within-category extensions and cross-category extensions. In within-category brand extensions, the same brand name is applied to several products within the same product category. In contrast, in cross-category brand extensions, the same brand name is applied to products in different categories. To illustrate, extending the Starbucks name to different coffee flavors is typically referred to as a within-category brand extension, whereas extending it to ice cream is considered a cross-category brand extension.

Based on their relation to the offering's pricing, two types of brand extensions are commonly distinguished: vertical and horizontal.

- *Vertical brand extensions* stretch the brand to a product or service in a different price tier. Depending on the direction in which the original offering is being extended, two types of vertical brand extensions can be distinguished: upscale and downscale. Examples of *upscale brand extensions* include Gallo's entry into the premium wine segment with Gallo Family Vineyards Estate Series, Volkswagen's (unsuccessful) extension into the luxury car segment with VW Phaeton, and Levi's (unsuccessful) entry into the designer suit category in the 1980s. Because the image of the core brand generally hurts rather than helps the upscale extension, launching a successful upscale brand extension is a challenging task.

- Examples of *downscale brand extensions* include the BMW 1-series, Porsche's Boxster, and Armani Exchange. Because they leverage the image of the core brand, downscale extensions tend to be more successful than upscale ones. The potential shortcomings for downscale brand extensions include dilution of the image of the core brand and cannibalization of its sales by the downscale brand. A downscale brand extension launched with the primary purpose of fending off low-priced competitors is often referred to as a fighting brand.

- *Horizontal brand extensions* involve applying the brand to a different product category in the same price tier. For example, Ralph Lauren's Polo brand was successfully extended from clothing to home furnishings like bedding and towels, Timberland extended its brand from boots to outerwear and travel gear, and Porsche extended its brand from sport cars to include sport-utility vehicles.

Brand Equity

The term brand equity is used in reference to the financial value of the brand; it is the net present value of the financial benefits derived from the brand. Thus, brand equity reflects the financial outcome from brand ownership and determines the premium that should be placed on a company's valuation because of brand ownership.

The key component of a brand's equity is the brand's strength. Brand strength (also referred to as brand power or customer-based brand equity[2]) reflects the brand's ability to differentiate the offering from the competition and create customer value through meaningful associations. Unlike brand equity, which reflects the value of the brand to the company, brand strength reflects the value of the brand among current and potential customers.[3]

Brand equity is a function of brand strength, as well as a number of additional factors reflecting the company's utilization of the strength of its brand (e.g., sales revenues). Thus, a stronger brand does not necessarily imply greater brand equity. For example, although Armani, Möet & Chandon, Audi, and Lexus brands would be considered stronger than GAP, McDonalds, Volkswagen, and Toyota brands, respectively (as measured by the greater price premium they command over identical unbranded products), the equity of the latter set of brands is estimated to be higher than that of the former (e.g., the brand equity of Toyota is higher than the brand equity of Lexus).[4]

Brand strength can be defined as the differential impact of brand knowledge on consumer response to an offering's marketing efforts.[5] Thus, a brand has greater strength when customers react more favorably to the various aspects of an offering (product, service, price, incentives, communications, and distribution) when the brand is identified relative to when it is not identified. To illustrate, one of the benefits of brand strength is the price premium customers are willing to pay for the branded (as opposed to the identical unbranded) product. In addition to the price premium, other dimensions of brand strength include greater loyalty; enhanced perceptions of product performance; greater licensing, merchandising, and brand extension opportunities; less vulnerability to service inconsistencies and marketing crises; more elastic response to price decreases and more inelastic response to price increases; greater communications effectiveness, and increased channel power.

Measuring Brand Equity

Knowing the monetary value of a company's brand(s) is essential for company valuation (e.g., for mergers and acquisitions, sale of assets, licensing, financing, and estimating benefits or damages to the brand). Despite the importance of brand equity, there is no commonly agreed upon methodology for its calculation; instead, there are several alternative methods, each placing emphasis on different aspects of brand equity. The three most common approaches to brand equity measurement are outlined below.

- *Cost-based approach* involves calculating brand equity based on the costs involved (e.g., marketing research, advertising, and legal costs) if the brand needs to be created from scratch at the time of valuation.

- *Market-based approach* involves calculating brand equity based on the difference in the cash flows generated from the branded product and a functionally equivalent but nonbranded product, adjusted for the costs of creating the brand. The market-based approach can be summarized in the following equation:

$$\text{Brand equity} = \text{Sales revenues}_{\text{Brand}} - \text{Sales revenues}_{\text{Generic}} - \text{Branding costs}.$$

- *Financial approach* involves calculating brand equity based on the net present value of the cash flows derived from the brand's future earnings. This approach typically involves three key steps: (1) estimating the company's future cash flows, (2) estimating the contribution of the brand to these cash flows, and (3) adjusting these cash flows using a risk factor that reflects the volatility of the earnings attributed to the brand. The financial approach can be summarized in the following equation:

$$\text{Brand equity} = \text{NPV of future cash flows} \cdot \text{Brand contribution factor} \cdot \text{Risk factor}.$$

The financial approach to estimating brand equity can be illustrated using Interbrand's methodology, which is the basis for *Business Week's* annual ranking of the top 100 brands. Interbrand's method involves three steps. The first step consists of estimating the percentage of the overall revenues that can be attributed to the brand. Based on reports from analysts at JPMorgan Chase, Citigroup, and Morgan Stanley, Interbrand projects five years of earnings and sales for the products and services associated with the brand. Interbrand then deducts the estimated earnings that can be attributed to tangible assets, on the assumption that the income generated beyond that point is due to intangible assets. The next step involves stripping out the nonbrand intangibles such as patents, trademarks, technological know-how, and management strength to determine the portion of the company's income generated by intangible assets that can be attributed to the brand. The final step involves assessing the risk profile of these projected earnings based on a variety of factors such as market leadership, stability, market growth, global reach, trend, support (e.g., investment in the brand), and protection. The discount rate resulting from this risk analysis is applied to brand-related earnings to produce the net present value of the brand.

Summary

A brand is a marketing tool created for the purpose of differentiating a company's offering from the competition and creating value for customers, the company, and its collaborators. A brand has two key aspects: (1) brand identity, which includes identifying characteristics such as name, sign, symbol, character, and/or design; and (2) brand meaning, which reflects a set of offering-related associations in the mind of the buyer. Brand identity aims to *identify* the company's offering and *differentiate* it from the competition. In contrast, brand meaning aims to *create value* (for customers, the company, and its collaborators) that goes beyond the product and service characteristics of the offering.

Managing brands involves two types of analysis: (1) strategic analysis, which examines brands as a function of the offering's market structure (customers, company, collaborators, competition, and context) and (2) tactical analysis, which examines brands as a function of the other marketing mix variables (product, service, price, incentives, communication, and distribution).

Two important branding decisions involve managing the brand hierarchy and managing the brand dynamics. Brand hierarchy reflects the relationship between different brands in a company's portfolio. Popular approaches to managing multiple brands include: individual branding, umbrella branding, sub-branding, and co-branding. Brand dynamics reflect the brand evolution over time. The two common types of brand dynamics are brand repositioning, which involves changes to an existing brand, most often to make the brand more relevant to its target customers, and brand extension, which involves broadening the set of underlying product categories to which the brand is applied.

Brand equity is the net present value of the financial benefits derived from the brand. Brand equity is a function of brand power, as well as a number of additional factors reflecting the company's utilization of the strength of its brand. Brand power reflects the brand's ability to differentiate the offering from the competition and create customer value through meaningful associations. Unlike brand equity, which reflects the value of the brand to the company, brand power reflects the value of the brand among current and potential customers. The three most popular approaches to measuring brand equity are cost-based (the cost of recreating the brand), market-based (the difference in the cost-adjusted cash flows of a branded and nonbranded product), and financial (the net present value of the cash flows of the offering's future earnings that are attributed to the brand).

Relevant Concepts

Brand Audit: A comprehensive analysis of a brand, most often to determine the sources of brand equity.

Brand Essence: The fundamental nature of the brand, also referred to as "brand promise." Brand essence distills the meaning of the brand into one key aspect—the positioning of the brand. One way to think about brand essence is to think of the "ness" of the brand, such as "BMW-ness," "Apple-ness," and "Microsoft-ness."

Copyright: A legal term describing rights given to creators for their literary and artistic works. The types of works covered by copyright include: literary works such as novels, poems, plays, reference works, newspapers and computer programs; databases; films, musical compositions, and choreography; artistic works such as paintings, drawings, photographs, and sculpture; architecture; and advertisements, maps, and technical drawings.

Fighting Brand: A downscale (lower priced) brand introduced to shield a major brand from low-priced competitors.

Generification: Colloquialized use of brand names (e.g., in reference to the products they are associated with). The use of a brand name as a generic term can lead to the loss of a company's right to the exclusive use of that brand name. To illustrate, Trampoline, Brazier, Escalator, Thermos, Yo-Yo, and Aspirin lost their trademark-protected status because of popular use; Xerox, Rollerblade, Velcro, and Google are considered to be at risk of following them.

Global Brand: A brand with a comprehensive international distribution system, such as Coca-Cola, Pepsi, and Sony.

Industrial Property: A type of intellectual property that involves (1) inventions (patents), (2) industrial designs, and (3) identity marks such as trademarks, service marks, commercial names, and designations, including indications of source and appellations of origin. An invention is a product or process that provides a new way of doing something or offers new solutions to technical problems; a patent is an exclusive right granted for an invention. An industrial design is the aesthetic aspect of a product and may consist of three-dimensional features, such as shape or surface, or two-dimensional features, such as patterns, lines, or color. Industrial design is primarily of an aesthetic nature and does not protect any technical aspects of the product to which it is applied. Identity marks such as trademarks, service marks, commercial names, and designations are designed to identify an offering or a company and protect it from the competition. Thus, a trademark (or service mark in the case of services) is a distinctive sign that identifies certain goods or services as those produced or provided by a specific entity. A geographical indication is a sign used on goods that have a specific geographical origin and possess qualities or a reputation that stem from the place of origin. Geographical indications may be used for a wide variety of agricultural products, such as "Tuscany" for olive oil produced in a Tuscany, Italy, or "Roquefort" for cheese produced in the Roquefort area in France.

Intellectual Property: The legal entitlement attached to the expressed form of an idea, or to some other intangible subject matter. Intellectual property is divided into two categories: (1) *industrial property*, which encompasses inventions, industrial designs, and identity marks such as trademarks, service marks, commercial names and designations, including indications of source and appellations of origin; and (2) *copyright*, which includes literary and artistic works such as novels, poems and plays, films, musical works; artistic works such as drawings, paintings, photographs and sculptures; and architectural designs.

National Brand: A brand available nationwide.

Private Label: Branding strategy in which an offering is branded by the retailer (e.g., Kirkland Signature, Costco's private brand; Kenmore, Sears' brand for home appliances; White Cloud, Wal-Mart's private label for laundry detergents). Private labels (also referred to as store brands) are often contrasted with national brands, which are branded by the manufacturer or a third party rather than by the retailer (e.g., Coca-Cola, IBM, and Nike). Typically, private labels tend to be less expensive than national brands, although there are many exceptions, such as private labels offered by upscale retailers (e.g., Nordstrom, Marks & Spenser).

Regional Brand: A brand available only in a particular geographic region.

Store Brand: See *private label*.

Additional Readings

Aaker, David A. (1991), *Managing Brand Equity: Capitalizing on the Value of a Brand Name.* New York, NY: Free Press.

Aaker, David A. (1996), *Building Strong Brands.* New York, NY: Free Press.

Aaker, David A. (2004), *Brand Portfolio Strategy: Creating Relevance, Differentiation, Energy, Leverage, and Clarity.* New York, NY: Free Press.

Hart, Susannah and John M. Murphy (1998), *Brands: The New Wealth Creators.* New York, NY: New York University Press.

Keller, Kevin Lane (2007), *Strategic Brand Management: Building, Measuring and Managing Brand Equity* (3rd ed.). Upper Saddle River, NJ: Prentice Hall.

Kapferer, Jean-Noël (2008), *The New Strategic Brand Management: Creating and Sustaining Brand Equity Long Term* (4th ed.). Sterling, VA: Kogan Page.

Kumar, Nirmalya and Jan-Benedict E. M. Steenkamp (2007), *Private Label Strategy: How to Meet the Store Brand Challenge.* Boston, MA: Harvard Business School Press.

Lamons, Bob (2005), *The Case for B2B Branding: Pulling Away from the Business to Business Pack* (1st ed.). Mason, OH: Thomson/South-Western.

Tybout, Alice M. and Tim Calkins (2005), *Kellogg on Branding.* Hoboken, NJ: John Wiley & Sons.

Notes

[1] With the exception of companies such as Wal-Mart, Costco, and Home Depot, where low prices are directly related to the essence of the brand.

[2] Keller, Kevin Lane (2007), *Strategic Brand Management: Building, Measuring and Managing Brand Equity* (3rd ed.). Upper Saddle River, NJ: Prentice Hall.

[3] Note that the use of the terms "brand equity" and "brand strength" varies across companies. A popular approach involves using the term "brand value" in reference to the monetary valuation of the brand (i.e., the net present value of the future cash flows attributable to the brand), while the term "brand equity" is used in reference to the brand's value to current and potential customers (i.e., the equivalent of brand strength).

[4] *Business Week* (2007), "The 100 Top Brands 2006". August 6, p. 59–64.

[5] Keller, Kevin Lane (2007), *Strategic Brand Management: Building, Measuring and Managing Brand Equity* (3rd ed.). Upper Saddle River, NJ: Prentice Hall.

Chapter Twelve

Managing Price

Setting and managing an offering's price is one of the key factors in determining the value of the offering to customers, the company, and its collaborators. Of all marketing mix variables, price is the only one that produces revenue for the company; all the others are costs. The key aspects of price management are the focus of this chapter.

Overview

There are three popular approaches to determine an offering's price. The first approach involves setting the price based on the company's costs. In the most extreme case, referred to as *cost-plus pricing* (or *markup pricing*), the offering's final price is determined by adding a fixed markup to the cost of the offering. Another approach, often referred to as *competitive-parity pricing*, involves setting the offering's price in a way that puts the offering's value at parity with that of competitors. The third approach, often referred to as *customer-value pricing*, focuses on customer demand, determined by customers' willingness to pay for the benefits afforded by the company's offering. While each of these approaches has its advantages, they miss the point that the pricing decision is not an isolated decision but a key component of the offering's strategy and tactics.

The key to determining the optimal price is to consider its implications on an offering's value to customers, collaborators, and the company in a broad context that involves all other aspects of the company's strategy and tactics. Setting the price is really a decision about value, not just price. Thus, the "optimal" price is a price that, in combination with the other marketing mix variables (product, service, brand, incentives, communications, and distribution), delivers superior value to target customers, the company, and collaborators. This approach is outlined in more detail in the following sections.

A Framework for Managing Price

Managing price involves two types of decisions: (1) strategic decisions, which aim to optimize price as a function of the offering's market structure and (2) tactical decisions, which aim to optimize price as a function of the other marketing mix variables. These two types of decisions are outlined in more detail below.

113

Managing Price: Strategy

From a strategic standpoint, pricing decisions involve analyzing five key factors: customers, company, collaborators, competition, and context. These five factors are illustrated in Figure 1 and outlined in more detail below.

Figure 1. Price Management as a Function of Market Structure

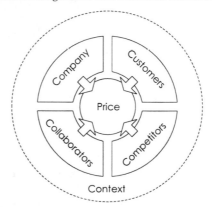

- *Customers.* An offering's pricing is a function of customers' willingness to pay for the benefits it offers, such that greater willingness to pay is typically associated with higher price. Pricing based entirely on customers' willingness to pay is often referred to as demand pricing.

- *Company.* Pricing is a function of the strategic assets and core competencies of the company, which determine its cost structure. To illustrate, a lower cost structure provides the company with the strategic option to lower its price without incurring a loss. Pricing based entirely on the company's costs is often referred to as cost-based pricing.

- *Collaborators.* Pricing is also influenced by the goals and resources of company collaborators (e.g., channel partners). For example, the price of offerings sold though consolidated distribution channels such as Wal-Mart is likely to be influenced by the profit optimization strategies of these channels.

- *Competitors.* Prices of competitive offerings have a direct impact on an offering's price. For instance, based on its strategic goals, a company may set the price of its offering at par, below, or above that of competitors. Pricing based entirely on competitors' prices is often referred to as competitive pricing.

- *Context.* Pricing is also a function of various social, economic, political, technological, and regulatory factors describing the environment in which the company operates. To illustrate, the price of travel services is influenced by seasons; the price of high-tech products is a function of the availability of superior technologies; the price of gasoline, tobacco, and alcohol products is a function of government regulations and taxation.

Managing Price: Tactics

From a tactical standpoint, pricing decisions involve analyzing the other marketing mix variables (product, service, brand, incentives, communication, and distribution) and their impact on the offering's price. The key aspects of this analysis are illustrated in Figure 2 and outlined in more detail below.

Figure 2. Price Management as a Function of the Marketing Mix

- *Product and service.* Product and service characteristics of an offering are key drivers of the offering's price. Thus, price is a function of the monetary value that target customers are willing to pay for the benefits provided by the company's products and services. Typically, a company can set higher prices for highly differentiated products and services than for commoditized offerings.

- *Brand.* In addition to the product and service characteristics of the offering, its brand has a significant impact on pricing. To illustrate, strong brands command substantial price premiums over weaker brands and nonbranded offerings. In fact, the price premium associated with a given brand is also used to measure the strength of this brand.

- *Incentives.* Incentives are typically used to make further adjustments to the offering's price to better meet the needs of target customers, collaborators, and the company. As a result, incentives have become an integral component of a company's pricing strategy, such that an offering's price is typically augmented by some form of monetary incentive that is offered to channel members (e.g., volume discounts and promotional allowances) and/or customers (e.g., price reductions and coupons).

- *Communications.* Pricing decisions are also influenced by the offering's communication strategy. For example, an offering may be priced 50% less than the market leader to more effectively communicate its benefits ("half-price").

- *Distribution.* An offering's price is also a function of its distribution system, such as channel structure (e.g., direct, indirect, or hybrid), channel ownership (e.g., ownership-based, contractual, or implied), channel type (e.g., specialized vs. broad), and channel coverage (e.g., limited vs. extensive). To illustrate, a company selling through indirect channels typically cannot directly set the retail prices; it can only suggest the price at which the offering should be sold to customers (manufacturer's suggested retail price, or MSRP).

Psychological Pricing

Successful pricing strategies take into account the fact that people do not always perceive pricing information objectively; instead, price perception is often a function of factors such as the availability of other prices and the price format. The psychological aspects of pricing have an important impact on people's perception of an offering's value. Many of these effects are also very robust and tend to hold even when buyers are made aware of their implications. The four most common effects—reference-price effects, price–quantity effects, price-tier effects, and price-ending effects—are outlined below.

- *Reference-price effects.* To assess the price of a given offering, people typically evaluate it relative to another price, which serves as a reference point. This reference price can be either internal (e.g., a remembered price from a prior purchase occasion or advertising) or external (e.g., a competitor's price, the manufacturer suggested retail price). Understanding the reference prices that buyers use when evaluating the offering can provide the company with valuable information that may be relevant for setting the offering's price. Furthermore, by strategically choosing the reference price, a company can frame the price of its offering in a way that makes it more attractive (e.g., by comparing it to a more expensive competitive offering).

- *Price–quantity effects.* People tend to be more sensitive to changes in price than to changes in quantity. To illustrate, the sales volume of a 10-pack of hotdogs priced at $2.49 is likely to decline further following a $.50 price increase (a 10-pack for $2.99) than following a two-item reduction in unit volume (an 8-pack for $2.49), even though on a per-item base, the 8-pack is more expensive than the 10-pack.

- *Price-tier effects.* People tend to encode prices in tiers, such that an item priced at $1.99 is typically encoded into "$1+" price tier, whereas an item priced at $2.00 is typically classified into "$2+" price tier. This tiered price encoding leads to the somewhat paradoxical perception that the difference between items priced at $1.99 and $2.00 is one dollar rather than one cent.

- *Price-ending effects.* In many cases, prices ending in "9" tend to create the perception of a discount, whereas prices ending on "0" tend to create perception of quality.

Pricing Dynamics

Price is one of the more dynamic marketing mix variables. Indeed, changing the price, either directly or by offering price incentives, is often much easier to conceive and implement than changing the product and service characteristics of the offering or repositioning its brand. As a result, competition typically occurs in the domain of pricing. Because companies increasingly rely on monetary incentives as a tool for managing the dynamic aspect of pricing, the following discussion examines the joint impact of price and monetary incentives. In particular, the focus is on two key aspects of price dynamics: the impact of price dynamics on customer demand and the use of pricing as a competitive tool.

Customer Reaction to Changes in Price

Because in most cases sales volume is a function of price, the company has to determine the price level at which it is most likely to achieve its goals. Typically, sales volume is inversely related to price: Lowering the price results in an increase in the sales volume, and vice versa. The impact of changes in price on sales volume is a function of customers' price sensitivity. Lowering the price to increase volume is most effective in cases where demand is elastic, so that a small change in price leads to a large change in sales volume. In contrast, in cases where demand is inelastic, profits may be increased by raising the price since the decrease in sales volume resulting from the change in price is likely to be relatively small.

The price–quantity relationship is quantified through an offering's price elasticity. Price elasticity represents the percentage change in quantity sold relative to the percentage change in price for a given product or service. Because the quantity demanded decreases when the price increases, this ratio is negative; however, for practical purposes, the absolute value of the ratio is used, and price elasticity is often reported as a positive number.

$$E_p = \frac{\Delta Q\%}{\Delta P\%} = \frac{\Delta Q \cdot P}{\Delta P \cdot Q}$$

To illustrate, price elasticity of -2 means that a 5% price increase will result in a 10% decrease in the quantity sold. In cases where price elasticity is greater than one ($|Ep| > 1$), demand is said to be elastic in the sense that a change in price causes an even larger change in quantity demanded. In contrast, when price elasticity is less than one ($|Ep| < 1$), demand is said to be inelastic, meaning that a change in price results in a smaller change in quantity demanded. When price elasticity is equal to one ($|Ep| = 1$), demand is said to be unitary, meaning that a change in price results in an equal change in quantity demanded.

It is important to note that because price elasticity reflects proportional changes, it does not depend on the units in which the price and quantity are expressed. Note also that because price elasticity is a function of the initial values, the same absolute changes in price can lead to different price elasticity values. For example, the impact of lowering the price by 5 cents will vary based on the initial price: it is 5% of an initial price of $1.00 but only 1% of an initial price of $5.00.

Competitive Reaction to Price Dynamics: Managing Price Wars

Price wars do not necessarily involve direct price reductions on the part of manufacturers. They may be a result of a change in different aspects of an offering's value proposition to customers and/or collaborators. To illustrate, an increase in a manufacturer's incentives (e.g., volume discounts, allowances) may prompt retailers to lower the offering's prices, thus provoking a price war. Because price wars often stem from a change in the value proposition of a particular offering, it is also possible that a price war may be caused by increasing the level of benefits while holding price constant. In this case, to preserve their market share, competitors may decide to lower their prices rather than match the increased level of benefits, thus initiating a price war.

In most cases, price wars start when a company is willing to sacrifice margins to gain market share. Not every price cut initiated by a particular company, however, leads to a price war. In general, price wars are more likely to occur in the following cases:

- Offerings are undifferentiated.

- Capacity utilization is low.

- Significant economies of scale can be achieved by increasing volume.

- Markets are mature, and to grow sales, a company has to steal share from its direct competitors.

- Customers' price sensitivity is high and switching costs are low.

Price cuts, the forerunner of price wars, are very popular among managers for several reasons:

- Price cuts are easy to implement and typically produce fast results.

- Price cuts are an effective tool to increase sales volume. Thus, even though most price cuts ultimately result in loss of profits, companies focused on sales volume can achieve their sales-volume goals by lowering price.

- Unlike most of the other marketing mix variables, changes in price can be easily reversed or further modified based on market response.

- Lowering the price to match or beat a competitor's price is consistent with the competitive-focus mentality among many managers who focus on competitors' behavior instead of on developing strategies to better serve the needs of their customers in a way that is profitable to the company.

- The manager has misjudged a competitive reaction based on the assumption that competitors would not react to the company's attempt to steal their customers.

Price wars are easy to initiate but costly to win. Indeed, wining a price war often comes at the expense of significant loss of profits, making it more like a Pyrrhic victory than a true success. Price wars are detrimental to a company's profitability for several reasons:

- Price reductions have an exponential impact on profitability. To illustrate, reducing the price of an offering with a 10% profit margin by 1% will result in a 10% decrease in operating income unless there is a significant increase in sales volume.

- Because price reductions can be easily implemented by all competitors, they rarely lead to a sustainable competitive advantage. Any firm can quickly lower its prices in response to a competitor's action.

- Price wars often result in a shift in customers' future price expectations, such that the lowered prices become the reference points against which all future prices are judged.

- Emphasis on price tends to erode brand strength. This effect is exacerbated by the heavy price-focused communication campaigns that tend to accompany most price wars. Indeed, to justify lowering the price of an offering, a company needs to promote the low price so that the lost profits resulting from the decrease in price can be offset by the incremental profits achieved by generating new sales.

Price wars rarely enable companies to achieve their strategic goals, and in most cases, the only true beneficiaries of a price war are the companies' customers. Quite often, the best strategy for a company to win a potential price war is to avoid it.

Even if a company is not seeking a price war, it may end up being confronted with a scenario in which a competitor initiates a price cut. There are many strategies to handle such situations. A three-step approach for developing a strategic response to a competitor's price cut is outlined below.

The first step is to verify the validity of the threat of a price war. Price wars are often caused by miscommunication of pricing information or misinterpretation of a competitor's strategic goals. Thus, when competitive prices are not readily available (e.g., in contract bidding), a company may perceive that a particular competitor has significantly lowered its price without this actually being the case. It is also possible that a competitor's price decrease is driven by internal factors (e.g., clearing the inventory prior to introducing a new model) rather than by an intention to initiate a price war.

The second step involves identifying customers who are most likely to be affected by competitors' price cut and prioritizing these customers based on their value to the company and their price sensitivity. Thus, based on their value to the company and price sensitivity, customers may be classified into one of four categories: high-value/loyal customers, high-value/price-sensitive customers, low-value/loyal customers, and low-value/price-sensitive customers (Figure 3). Identifying which of these customers are likely to be affected by a competitor's price cut and the impact of this price cut on a company's profitability aids the development of a segment-specific response strategy.

Figure 3. Customer Loyalty Matrix

	Low price-sensitivity	High price-sensitivity
High value	High-value loyals	High-value switchers
Low value	Low-value loyals	Low-value switchers

The third step involves developing segment-specific strategies to address the competitive threat. There are four basic strategies to fight a price war: do nothing, increase benefits, decrease costs, and launch a fighting brand. These strategies are summarized below.

- *Do nothing.* The decision to ignore a competitor's price cut reflects a company's belief that either the price cut will not have a significant impact on the company's market position, that the price cut is not sustainable and will dissipate by itself, or that serving the customer segment targeted by the price cut is no longer viable (e.g., low-value, price-sensitive customers).

- *Increase benefits.* Instead of lowering its price, a company may react to a competitors' price cut by increasing the overall value of its offering.

- *Decrease costs.* The most common practice (although not necessarily the best) of responding to a competitor's price cut is a corresponding price reduction. This decrease in price can be accomplished either on a permanent basis by lowering the actual price or as a temporary solution by offering price incentives (e.g., discounts, coupons, and rebates).

- *Launch a fighting brand.* A fighting brand is a downscale offering introduced to shield a major brand from low-priced competitors. Using a fighting brand enables the company to compete for price-sensitive customers without discounting its core brand, while at the same time mitigating the potential for the low-priced extension to cannibalize the sales of the core brand.

Summary

The key to determining the optimal price is to consider its implications on an offering's value to customers, collaborators, and the company in a broad context that involves all other aspects of the company's strategy and tactics. Setting the price is really a decision about value, not just price. Thus, the optimal price is one that, in combination with the other marketing mix variables (product, service, brand, incentives, communications, and distribution), delivers superior value to target customers, the company, and collaborators.

Managing price involves two types of analysis: (1) strategic analysis, which examines price as a function of the offering's market structure (customers, company, collaborators, competition, and context) and (2) tactical analysis, which examines price as a function of the other marketing mix variables (product, service, brand, incentives, communication, and distribution).

Successful pricing strategies take into account that people do not always perceive pricing information objectively; instead, price perception is often a function of a variety of psychological effects such as reference-price effects, price–quantity effects, price-tier effects, and price-ending effects.

Competing on price often results in price wars, which typically start when companies are willing to sacrifice margins to gain market share. Price wars are likely to occur in the following cases: when offerings are undifferentiated, when capacity utilization is low, when significant economies of scale can be achieved by increasing volume, when markets are mature and a company has to steal share from its direct competitors to grow sales, and when customers' price sensitivity is high and switching costs are low. An effective approach for developing a strategic response to a competitor's price cut involves the following three steps: (1) verifying the validity of the threat of a price war, (2) prioritizing customers that are most likely to be affected by the competitors' price cut based on their value to the company and price sensitivity, and (3) developing segment-specific strategies to address the competitive threat (i.e., do nothing, increase benefits, decrease costs, or launch a fighting brand).

Relevant Concepts

Captive Pricing: See *complementary pricing*.

Complementary Pricing: Pricing strategy applicable to uniquely compatible, multipart offerings, whereby a company charges a low (relative to its cost) introductory price on the first part and higher prices for the other parts. Classic examples include razors and blades, printers and cartridges, and cell phones and cell phone service. Note that the unique compatibility is crucial to the success of complementary pricing: Only the printer manufacturer should be able to sell cartridges that fit its printers.

Cost-Plus Pricing: A pricing method in which the final price is determined by adding a fixed markup to the cost of the product. It is easy to calculate and is commonly used in industries where profit margins are relatively stable. Its key drawback is that it does not take into account customer demand and competitive pricing.

Cross-Price Elasticity: The percentage change in quantity sold of a given offering caused by a percentage change in the price of another offering.

Deceptive Pricing: The practice of presenting an offering's price to the buyer in a way that is deliberately misleading. Deceptive pricing is illegal in the United States.

Everyday Low Pricing (EDLP): Pricing strategy in which a retailer maintains low prices without frequent price promotions.

Experience Curve Pricing: Pricing strategy based on an anticipated future lower cost structure resulting from scale economies and experience curve effects.

High-Low Pricing: Pricing strategy in which a retailer's prices fluctuate over time, typically a result of heavy reliance on sales promotions.

Horizontal Price Fixing: The practice whereby competitors explicitly or implicitly collaborate to set prices. Price fixing is illegal in the United States.

Image Pricing: See *price signaling*.

Loss Leadership: Pricing strategy that involves setting a low price (often at or below cost) in an attempt to increase the sales of other products and services (e.g., a retailer sets a low price for a popular item in an attempt to build store traffic, thus increasing the sales of other, more profitable items).

Manufacturer's Advertised Price Strategy: Pricing strategy in which the manufacturer sets a recommended retail price and offers incentives to encourage retailers not to undercut the recommended price. For example, a common strategy to ensure channel cooperation involves advertising allowances that reimburse the retailer only if the retail price does not drop below a specified level. This strategy is typically used to reduce multichannel conflict by establishing a price floor to control underpricing.

Penetration Pricing: Pricing strategy aimed at rapidly gaining market share. This strategy often leads to higher sales volume, albeit at lower margins.

Predatory Pricing: A strategy that involves selling below cost with the intent of driving competitors out of business. In most cases, predatory pricing is illegal in the United States.

Prestige Pricing: Pricing strategy whereby the price is set at a relatively high level for the purpose of creating an exclusive image of the offering.

Price Discrimination: A strategy that involves charging different buyers different prices for goods of equal grade and quality.

Price Fixing: The practice in which companies conspire to set prices for a given product and/or service. Price fixing is illegal in United States.

Price Segmentation: See *price discrimination*.

Price Signaling: (1) Pricing strategy that aims to capitalize on price-quality inferences (i.e., higher priced products are also likely to be higher quality). Primarily used when the actual product benefits are not readily observable (also known as prestige pricing); (2) Indirect communication (direct price collusion is prohibited by law) between companies, aimed at indicating their intentions with respect to their pricing strategy.

Price Skimming: Pricing strategy in which a firm sets a high initial price to maximize profit margins, usually at the expense of market share.

Product-Line Pricing: Pricing strategy in which the price of each individual offering is determined as a function of the offering's place in the relevant product line (e.g., the price of BMW's 3-series models is a function of the prices of its 5- and 7-series models).

Second Market Discounting: Pricing strategy in which a company charges a lower price for the products/services it offers in more competitive markets (e.g., exports for developing countries).

Two-Part Pricing: See *complementary pricing*.

Vertical Price Fixing: The practice whereby channel partners (e.g., a manufacturer and a retailer) explicitly or implicitly collaborate to set prices. Price fixing is illegal in the United States.

Yield Management Pricing: Pricing strategy whereby the price is set to maximize revenue for a set amount of capacity at a given time (typically used by airlines and hotels).

Additional Readings

Baker, Ronald J. (2006), *Pricing on Purpose: Creating and Capturing Value*. Hoboken, NJ: John Wiley & Sons.

Marn, Michael V., Eric V. Roegner, and Craig C. Zawada (2004), *The Price Advantage*. Hoboken, NJ: John Wiley & Sons.

Nagle, Thomas T. and John E. Hogan (2006), *The Strategy and Tactics of Pricing: A Guide to Growing More Profitably* (4th ed.). Upper Saddle River, NJ: Pearson/Prentice Hall.

Chapter Thirteen

Managing Incentives

Incentives offer solutions, typically short term, aimed at enhancing the value of the offering by providing additional benefits and/or reducing costs. Because they tend to increase the value of the offering to customers and collaborators, and typically lead to an increase in sales volume, incentives are often referred to as sales promotions. The key aspects of managing incentives are the focus of this chapter.

Overview

Most incentives fall into one of three categories: incentives given to customers (e.g., coupons, loyalty programs, sweepstakes, contests, and premiums), incentives given to the company's collaborators, most often channel partners (e.g., price cuts, volume discounts, allowances, and co-op advertising), and incentives given to the company's employees (e.g., bonuses, rewards, and contests). These three types of incentives are illustrated in Figure 1.

Figure 1. The Flow of Incentives

Incentives can be further divided into two categories: monetary, such as volume discounts, price reductions, coupons, and rebates; and nonmonetary, such as premiums, contests, and rewards. In contrast to monetary incentives, which typically aim to reduce an offering's costs, nonmonetary incentives often aim to enhance the offering's benefits. The most popular incentives, organized by their target (customers, collaborators, and company) and type (price and nonprice), are given in Table 1.

Deciding on the optimal mix of these various incentives can be facilitated using a systematic approach, outlined in more detail in the following sections.

Table 1. Incentive Types

	Price incentives	Nonprice incentives
Customer incentives	Coupons, rebates, price reductions, volume discounts	Premiums, rewards, sweepstakes
Collaborator incentives	Advertising allowances, slotting allowances, stocking allowances, display allowances, market-development allowances, spiffs, volume discounts, volume rebates, off-invoice incentives	Contests, bonus merchandise, buyback guarantees, sales support and training
Company incentives	Performance bonuses, monetary prizes, spiffs	Contests, recognition awards, free goods and services, vacation and travel incentives

A Framework for Managing Incentives

Managing incentives involves two types of decisions: (1) strategic decisions, aiming to optimize incentives as a function of the offering's market structure and (2) tactical decisions, aiming to optimize incentives as a function of the other marketing mix variables. These two types of decisions are outlined in more detail below.

Managing Incentives: Strategy

From a strategic standpoint, incentive decisions involve analyzing five key factors: customers, company, collaborators, competition, and context. These five aspects of incentive analysis are illustrated in Figure 2 and outlined in more detail below.

Figure 2. Incentives Management as a Function of Market Structure

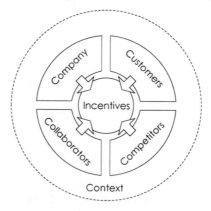

- *Customers.* An offering's incentive strategy is a function of customer factors, such as their needs, price sensitivity, and product knowledge. In general, companies are more likely to rely on incentives in cases where buyers understand the commodity nature of many products; when the relative importance of brands is declining at the expense of the importance of price;

and when customers become more deal oriented and accustomed to buying only in the presence of a sales promotion.

- *Company.* An offering's incentive strategy is also influenced by the company's goal, strategic assets, and core competencies. To illustrate, the use of incentives is often driven by a company's desire to achieve certain performance benchmarks within a specified timeframe (e.g., sales revenues by the end of the fiscal year). Because of their immediate impact on sales, a company can increase sales volume in a very short period, thus allowing managers to time the offering's market performance. Although not optimal from a long-term perspective, this use of incentives often results from pressure by the company's shareholders and business analysts concerned with quarterly accountability of sales-related (rather than profit-based) benchmarks.

- *Collaborators.* A company's collaborators, and in particular its channel partners, have a major impact on its incentive strategy. For example, the increased reliance on trade incentives is due to pressure from channel partners, who are gaining power because of consolidation of many retail chains, concentrated buying, stagnant shelf space, and the growth of private labels.

- *Competitors.* Companies often offer incentives in response to pressure from competitors who are using incentives as a universal offensive and defensive tool. This widespread use of incentives often contributes to the escalation of promotional expenditures of most companies in a given market.

- *Context.* The use of incentives is also a function of context factors, such as overall economic conditions and advances in technology. Thus, adverse economic conditions can lead to greater reliance on incentives to stimulate demand. Technological advancements can facilitate the use of incentives by making the process of identifying target customers and delivering incentives to these customers more effective and cost efficient.

Managing Incentives: Tactics

From a tactical standpoint, incentive decisions involve analyzing the other marketing mix variables (product, service, brand, price, communication, and distribution) and their impact on the offering's incentives. The key aspects of this analysis are illustrated in Figure 3 and outlined in more detail below.

Figure 3. Incentives as a Function of the Marketing Mix

- *Product and service.* A company's use of incentives is a function of the characteristics of the product and service aspects of the offering. To illustrate, the increased standardization and commoditization of products and services resulting from technology developments and outsourcing make it more difficult to differentiate offerings based on functional benefits, which, in turn, leads to increased reliance on incentives.

- *Brand.* The use of incentives is a function of the strength of the offering's brand. Thus, a decline in a brand's strength (e.g., resulting from brand proliferation and/or commoditization of the underlying products and services) often forces companies to rely on incentives as a means of differentiating their offerings. In contrast, incentives are not a key strategic element for strong brands such as Apple, Lacoste, and Porsche. In addition, the nature of the brand and its elements can be used as the basis for developing incentives (e.g., using Tony the Tiger, the cartoon character associated with Kellogg's Frosted Flakes cereal, to launch a contest, game, or sweepstakes).

- *Price.* An offering's pricing strategy plays a key role in its use of incentives. Thus, certain pricing strategies (e.g., everyday low pricing) imply limited use of incentives, whereas others (e.g., high-low pricing) heavily rely on incentives. As an integral part of an offering's pricing strategy, incentives offer greater flexibility in managing increasingly complex pricing structures.

- *Communications.* An offering's incentives are a function of its communication strategy. Thus, companies relying on direct-to-customer communications (pull strategy) are also more likely to utilize customer incentives to promote their offering to customers, whereas companies with limited or no direct-to-customer communications (push strategy) are more likely to rely on trade incentives to induce channel members to promote the offering to customers.

- *Distribution.* An offering's distribution can have an important impact on incentives as well. To illustrate, a distribution strategy that involves using consolidated, powerful channels (e.g., Albertsons, Home Depot, and Macy's) is typically associated with greater reliance on trade incentives.

Customer Incentives

Customer incentives vary based on the entity creating and delivering the incentive. Thus, customer incentives can be created by either the manufacturer (manufacturer incentives) or the channel member (retailer incentives). Manufacturer incentives can then be delivered either directly by the manufacturer or indirectly by the retailer. In the latter case, because the incentives are created by the manufacturer and then given to retailers to distribute to target customers, they are often referred to as pass-through incentives.

Most customer incentives serve one of two goals: (1) temporarily increasing sales volume by enhancing the value of the offering, thus giving target customers additional reasons to buy the offering and (2) serving as a segmentation tool by selectively enhancing the value of the company's offering to target customers. For example, sales-focused incentives designed to stimulate sales volume within a given timeframe are typically driven by company, competitor, and channel-related factors (e.g., meeting quarterly sales goals, responding to a competitor's promotion, or reducing inventory). In contrast, segment-focused incentives serve as a segmentation tool by making the offering attractive to a particular customer segment. An incentive can combine both sales-focused and segment-focused functions by selectively increasing sales from a particular segment.

Based on the type of reward, customer incentives can be divided into two groups: monetary and nonmonetary. Monetary incentives aim to reduce an offering's costs by providing customers with a monetary inducement to purchase the offering. The most common forms of *monetary* incentives are coupons, rebates, price reductions, and volume discounts.

- *Coupons* entitle the buyer to receive a price reduction for a given product or service at the time of purchase.
- *Rebates* involve cash refund offers that are fulfilled after the purchase has been made.
- *Price reductions* involve straightforward price discounts that do not require any action from customers.
- *Volume discounts* involve price reduction offers conditional upon the purchase of multiple items.

The most common forms of *nonmonetary* incentives are premiums, prizes, contests, sweepstakes, games, and loyalty programs.

- *Premiums* involve bonus products or services offered for free or at deeply discounted prices as an incentive for purchasing a particular offering. Premiums can be delivered instantly with the purchase (e.g., packaged with the product) or may require the customer to send in a proof of purchase to receive the premium.
- *Prizes* offer customers the opportunity to win an award as an incentive for purchasing a particular offering. Unlike premiums, where the reward (bonus products or services) is given with every purchase, in the case of prizes, the actual reward is given to a relatively small number of participants. Prizes can be both monetary and nonmonetary.
- *Contests, sweepstakes,* and *games* involve prizes that typically require customers to submit some form of an entry and are usually not contingent on customers purchasing the offering. Winners are selected by a panel of judges (e.g., in the case of contests), by drawing (e.g., in the case of sweepstakes), or by an objective criterion, such as points collected (e.g., in the case of games).
- *Loyalty programs* involve rewards related to the frequency, volume, and type of products and services purchased. Loyalty programs can be both monetary (e.g., cash-back credit cards offering a reward based on purchase volume) and nonmonetary (e.g., frequent-flyer awards).

Based on their reach (whether they are available to all customers or target a particular subset of customers), customer incentives can be organized into three categories: (1) widespread incentives, readily available to all target customers (e.g., temporary price reductions), (2) widespread conditional incentives, which require a certain action on the part of potential buyers (e.g., possession of a coupon, completion of a survey), and (3) targeted incentives available to a particular subset of customers (e.g., senior citizens, students, repeat buyers, high-volume buyers). Most conditional incentives are used as a tool for price segmentation, since price-sensitive buyers who are willing to expend time and effort to receive a discount are more likely to take advantage of the incentive.

Collaborator Incentives

The most common form of collaborator incentives are those offered to members of the distribution channel. These incentives, also referred to as trade incentives, can have multiple objectives, such as (1) to gain distribution through a particular channel, (2) to encourage channel members to stock the offering at certain inventory levels (e.g., to avoid stock-outs or to transfer the inventory from the manufacturer to intermediaries and customers), and (3) to encourage channel members to promote the company's offering.

Similar to customer incentives, trade incentives can be divided into two main types: monetary incentives, such as discounts and allowances, and nonmonetary incentives, such as contests and buyback guarantees.

Monetary incentives involve payments or price discounts given as encouragement to purchase the product or as an inducement to promote the product to customers. The nature of monetary incentives is a function of the nature of the business relationships between channel members. Typical monetary incentives include the following.

- *Slotting allowance*: an incentive paid to a distributor to allocate shelf space for a new product.

- *Stocking allowance*: an incentive paid to a distributor to carry extra inventory in anticipation of an increase in demand.

- *Cooperative advertising allowance*: an incentive paid by the manufacturer to a distributor in return for featuring its offerings in a retailer's advertisements. The magnitude of the allowance can be determined as a percentage of the distributor's advertising costs or as a fixed dollar amount per unit.

- *Market-development allowance*: an incentive for achieving certain sales volume in a specific customer segment.

- *Display allowance*: an incentive paid by the manufacturer to a distributor in return for prominently displaying its products and/or services (e.g., by offering attractive shelf space or store location).

- *Spiffs[1]*: incentives such as cash premiums, prizes, or additional commissions given directly to the salesperson (rather than the distributor) as a reward for selling a particular item. Because they encourage the retailer's sales personnel to "push" the product to customers, spiffs are often referred to as "push money."

- *Volume discount*: price reductions determined based on purchase volume.

- *Volume rebate* (also referred to as volume bonus): an incentive paid by the manufacturer to a distributor as a reward for achieving certain purchase-volume benchmarks (e.g., selling 1,000 units per quarter).

- *Off-invoice incentive*: any temporary price discounts offered by manufacturers to distributors.

- *Cash discount*: price reductions for payments made instantly or within a short timeframe.
- *Inventory financing* (also referred to as floor planning): loans provided to a distributor for acquiring manufacturers' goods.

Nonmonetary incentives involve nonmonetary inducements designed to encourage channel support for the company's offering. Typical nonmonetary incentives include the following:

- *Contests*: performance-based rewards (e.g., vacation trips, cars, and monetary compensation) given to the best achievers.
- *Bonus* merchandise: free goods offered as a reward for purchasing a particular item.
- *Buyback guarantees*: an agreement that the manufacturer will buy back from the distributor product quantities not sold within a certain timeframe.
- *Sales support* and *training*: various forms of aid offered by the manufacturer to distributors that are designed to familiarize the distributor with the offering and facilitate sales.

Company Incentives

In addition to incentives focused on target customers and collaborators, companies often develop incentives designed to motivate and reward their own personnel. Company-focused incentives typically aim to motivate employees to achieve better performance.

Company incentives commonly involve rewards for employees who meet certain performance benchmarks. Typical company incentives include performance-based awards such as contests, monetary bonuses, employee recognition awards, free goods and services, vacation and travel incentives, prizes, sweepstakes, and games. Some sales force incentives, such as spiffs, may be applied at the company level as well.

Summary

Incentives offer solutions, typically short term, aimed at enhancing the value of the offering by providing additional benefits and/or reducing costs. Most incentives fall into one of three categories: incentives given to customers (e.g., coupons, loyalty programs, sweepstakes, contests, and premiums), incentives given to the company's collaborators, most often channel partners (e.g., price cuts, volume discounts, allowances, and co-op advertising), and incentives given to the company's employees (e.g., bonuses, rewards, and contests).

Managing incentives involves two types of analysis: (1) strategic analysis, which examines incentives as a function of the offering's market structure (customers, company, collaborators, competition, and context) and (2) tactical analysis, which examines incentives as a function of the other marketing mix variables (product, service, brand, price, communication, and distribution).

Most customer incentives serve one of two goals: (1) temporarily increasing sales volume by enhancing the value of the offering, thus giving target customers additional reasons to buy the offering, or (2) serving as a segmentation tool by selectively enhancing the value of the company's offering to target customers. Customer incentives can be divided into two categories: monetary incentives that typically aim to reduce an offering's costs (e.g., coupons, rebates, price reductions, and volume discounts) and nonmonetary incentives, which often aim to enhance the offering's benefits (e.g., premiums, prizes, contests, and loyalty programs).

Most collaborator incentives involve incentives offered to members of the distribution channel. Also referred to as trade incentives, they can have multiple objectives, such as (1) to gain distribution through a particular channel, (2) to encourage channel members to stock the offering at certain inventory levels (e.g., to avoid stock-outs or to transfer the inventory from the manufacturer to intermediaries and customers), and (3) to encourage channel members to promote the company's offering. Similar to customer incentives, trade incentives can be divided into two main types: monetary incentives (such as discounts and allowances), and nonmonetary incentives (such as contests, bonus merchandise, and buyback guarantees).

Relevant Concepts

Free-Standing Inserts (FSI): Leaflets or coupons inserted into newspapers.

Incentives Ratio: Percentage of sales that involves an incentive relative to the company's total sales.

$$\text{Incentives ratio} = \frac{\text{Sales revenues with incentives}}{\text{Total sales revenues}}$$

Pass-through Incentives Ratio: Percentage of the incentives provided to customers by a channel member (e.g., a retailer) relative to the incentives provided to that channel member (e.g., by a manufacturer).

$$\text{Pass-through incentives} = \frac{\text{Incentives provided to customers by a channel member}}{\text{Incentives provided to the channel member}}$$

Push and Pull Promotions: Based on the flow of promotions (incentives and communications) from the manufacturer to target customers, two core promotion strategies can be identified: pull and push. Pull strategy refers to the practice of creating demand for a company's offering by promoting the offering directly to end-users, who in turn demand the offering from intermediaries, ultimately "pulling" the offering through the channel (Figure 4). To illustrate, the manufacturer may extensively advertise its products and services to end-users and/or promote its offerings using means such as direct mail, coupons, contests, etc. In contrast, push strategy refers to the practice of creating demand for a company's offering by incentivizing channel members, who in turn push the product downstream to end-users. For example, the manufacturer may offer high margins on their products and services so that retailers have a vested interest in selling the product. The manufacturer may also educate a retailer's sales force about the benefits of its offerings and provide the retailer with promotional materials, thus facilitating the sales process.

Figure 4. Pull and Push Promotion Strategies

Run-Of-Press Coupons: Coupons that appear in the actual pages of a newspaper (rather than being inserted as a separate page). Sometimes run-of-press coupons are part of an advertisement promoting the same offering.

Slippage: The percentage of customers who fail to redeem a promotional offer made with the purchase.

Trade Allowance: A broad range of trade incentives (e.g., slotting allowance, stocking allowance, and advertising allowance) offered as a reward for conducting promotional activities on behalf of the manufacturer. Trade allowances are typically implemented as a discount from the wholesale price rather than as a separate promotional payment. From an accounting standpoint, they are often considered as a discount to the channel rather than as a separate marketing expense.

Additional Readings

Blattberg, Robert C. and Scott A. Neslin (1990), *Sales Promotion: Concepts, Methods, and Strategies*. Englewood Cliffs, NJ: Prentice Hall.

Neslin, Scott A. (2002), *Sales Promotion*. Cambridge, MA: Marketing Science Institute.

Schultz, Don E., William A. Robinson, and Lisa Petrison (1998), *Sales Promotion Essentials* (3rd ed.). Lincolnwood, IL: NTC Business Books.

Note

[1] Contrary to popular belief, "spiff" is not an acronym (e.g., Sales Promotion Incentive Fund) but is connected with the use of the word in the middle of the nineteenth century in reference to somebody smartly dressed (hence *to spiff up*—to improve the appearance of a place, a product, or a person).

Chapter Fourteen

Managing Communications

The communication aspect of the marketing mix involves the process of informing the target audience (customers and collaborators) about the specifics of the company's offering. The key aspects of managing communications are the focus of this chapter.

A Framework for Managing Communications

Managing communications involves two types of decisions: (1) strategic decisions, which aim to optimize communications as a function of the offering's market structure and (2) tactical decisions, which aim to optimize communications as a function of the other marketing mix variables. These two types of decisions are outlined in more detail below.

Managing Communications: Strategy

From a strategic standpoint, communication decisions involve analyzing five key factors: customers, company, collaborators, competition, and context. These five factors are illustrated in Figure 1 and outlined in more detail below.

Figure 1. Communication Management as a Function of Market Structure

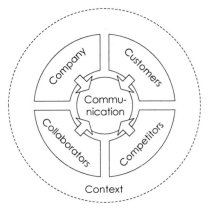

- *Customers.* An offering's communication strategy is a function of the characteristics of its target customers. To illustrate, customers' familiarity and attitudes toward the offering play an essential role in determining the goals of the communication campaign. Thus, for customers unaware of the company's offering, a key communication goal is to create awareness, whereas for customers who are already familiar with the offering, the communication campaign may focus on strengthening their preference for the offering, forming an intent to purchase the offering, and/or acting on their already formed purchase intent.

- *Company.* The nature of the communication campaign is often influenced by company-specific factors, such as available resources and communications expertise, as well as the company's overall strategic goals. For instance, the scale of the communications campaign (i.e., budget) and the media selection (e.g., television, radio, print, and/or online) are often a function of the resources available to the company, as well as of the legacy budgeting and media policies.

- *Collaborators.* An offering's communication strategy is often coordinated and sometimes even developed jointly with the company's collaborators. For example, companies collaborating in the area of product development, services, and branding often choose to develop a joint communication campaign. In addition, particular aspects of a company's communication campaign are often implemented by its collaborators (e.g., point-of-sale promotions and co-op advertising implemented by distribution channels).

- *Competitors.* Competitors' communications often have a major influence on a company's own communication strategy. To illustrate, an increase in competitive spending often leads to a corresponding increase in the company's own communication budget (a strategy referred to as competitive parity budgeting). In the same vein, the nature of a competitor's message can directly influence the company's own message (e.g., comparative advertising often evokes a competitive response).

- *Context.* An offering's communication campaign is also a function of the political, economic, social, technological, and legal environment in which the offering operates. For instance, by enabling companies to reach their target customers in a more effective and cost-efficient manner, recent technological developments are changing the traditional media strategies in favor of targeted one-on-one communication strategies. An offering's communication campaign is also contingent on the existing regulations concerning specific products and services (e.g., tobacco, alcohol, and pharmaceuticals), as well as the use of specific communication strategies (e.g., comparative and benefit-specific claims).

Managing Communications: Tactics

From a tactical standpoint, communication decisions involve analyzing the other marketing mix variables (i.e., product, service, brand, price, incentives, and distribution) and their impact on the offering's communications. The key aspects of this analysis are illustrated in Figure 2 and outlined in more detail below.

Figure 2. Communication Management as a Function of the Marketing Mix

- *Product and service.* An offering's communications are a function of the nature of the attributes describing the offering. To illustrate, communications depend on the balance between the tangible and intangible characteristics of the offering. Thus, in the case of offerings with predominantly intangible characteristics (e.g., service-based offerings), communications often aim to highlight their tangible characteristics (e.g., creating tangible symbols such as the Rock of Gibraltar for Prudential). In the same vein, to better differentiate offerings with predominantly tangible attributes (e.g., product-based offerings), communications often strive to highlight their intangible characteristics (e.g., emphasizing the service, reliability, and durability aspects of the product).

- *Brand.* Communications also depend on the identity and meaning of the offering's brand. For instance, brands with mass appeal (e.g., Coca-Cola) are more likely to rely on communications utilizing mass media, whereas nonmainstream brands appealing to a specific market segment (e.g., Harley-Davidson, Burton, and Red Bull) often rely on nontraditional communication strategies focused on user-based communities.

- *Price.* An offering's communications are also a function of its price. For example, to minimize potential price–quality inferences in the case of low-priced offerings, pricing information is sometimes communicated by distributors rather than manufacturers, so that the cause of the low price is attributed to the cost efficiency of the distributor rather than the quality of the offering.

- *Incentives.* An offering's incentives often have a direct impact on communications. Indeed, because incentives often aim to increase revenues by generating new sales that would not have occurred in their absence (e.g., by attracting new customers or by inducing current customers to make incremental purchases), informing target customers about these incentives is a crucial factor for ensuring their success (i.e., without promoting the incentive, the only buyers who would take advantage of the incentive are those who would have purchased the offering anyway).

- *Distribution.* An offering's communications are also influenced by its distribution strategy. For example, the popularity of the self-serve retail format and the growth of online commerce has diminished the role of personal selling in favor of product-based (e.g., packaging) and in-store communication formats (e.g., flyers, promotional displays, and shelf talkers). In addition, the increasing power of retailers has resulted in a shift of the promotional budget in favor of channel-based communications and incentives in lieu of traditional mass media communications.

The Communication Process

Managing the communication aspect of an offering involves six key decisions: setting the goal, developing the message, selecting the media, developing the creative solution, implementing the communication campaign, and evaluating the campaign results. The key steps are illustrated in Figure 3 and are briefly outlined below.

Figure 3. Planning a Communication Campaign

```
        ┌─────────────────────┐
        │        Goal         │
        └─────────────────────┘
                  ⇩
        ┌─────────────────────┐
        │       Message       │
        └─────────────────────┘
                  ⇩
        ┌─────────────────────┐
        │        Media        │
        └─────────────────────┘
                  ⇩
        ┌─────────────────────┐
        │  Creative solution  │
        └─────────────────────┘
                  ⇩
        ┌─────────────────────┐
        │   Implementation    │
        └─────────────────────┘
                  ⇩
        ┌─────────────────────┐
        │       Control       │
        └─────────────────────┘
```

- The *goal* identifies the criteria to be achieved by the communication campaign within a given timeframe.

- The *message* identifies the information to be communicated to target customers. The message can focus on one or several of the five value-creation marketing mix variables: product, service, brand, price, and incentives. To illustrate, a company can choose to promote the benefits of its product and service, communicate the meaning of its brand, publicize its price, and inform customers about its current incentives.

- The *media* describes the means used by the company to convey its message. The media decision involves three aspects: media budget, media type, and media scheduling.

- The *creative solution* involves the execution of the company's message in a given media. Among the key aspects of the creative solution are appeal type (e.g., information-based or emotion-based) and execution style (e.g., text, format, and layout).

- The *implementation* aspect of marketing communications identifies the timeline and the logistics of executing the message, media, and creative decisions. Implementation has two key aspects: (1) the processes involved in executing the message, media, and creative strategy (e.g., producing the advertisement and placing it in the appropriate media channel), and (2) the people managing these processes.

- The *control* aspect of marketing communications involves evaluating the success (effectiveness and cost efficiency) of the communication campaign with respect to achieving its goals.

A concept that has gained popularity in recent years is that of *integrated marketing communications*. This concept calls for consistency of an offering's communication campaign on at least three levels: (1) consistency between communication strategy and the company's overall marketing goal and strategy, (2) consistency between the communications and the other elements of the offering's tactics, and (3) internal consistency across the six elements of the communication campaign illustrated in Figure 3.

- *Strategic consistency* implies coordination between the different aspects of the communication campaign and the elements of the offering's overall marketing strategy.

- *Tactical consistency* implies coordination among the value-creation, value-communication, and value-delivery aspects of the offering. Thus, an offering's message should be consistent with the perceived product and service benefits, brand image, price, incentives, and distribution channel.

- *Internal consistency* implies that the message, media, creative solution, implementation, and control metrics evaluating the success of the campaign need to be consistent with the communication goal as well as in and of themselves. The concept of internal consistency can also be applied with respect to the different media types (e.g., advertising, public relations, and direct marketing) so that they work in a coordinated fashion rather than independently from one another.

Setting a Communication Goal

Setting a goal typically involves two decisions: (1) identifying the focus of the communication campaign and (2) identifying the specific performance benchmarks to be reached.

Setting the *focus* of the communication campaign involves identifying the ultimate criterion for success. There are three fundamental goals, any of which can be the focus of a given communication campaign:

- Create and/or raise *awareness* of the company's offering.

- Create and/or strengthen buyer *preferences* for the company's offering.

- Incite an *action* (e.g., purchase the offering, contact the company for information). In certain cases (e.g., when the offering is not readily available), communications may aim to create a behavioral intent (e.g., purchasing the offering) rather than incite an immediate action. For example, movie releases are often preceded by preannouncements designed to form a predisposition in target customers to view the movie when it is released.

Note that these goals are interdependent, such that some can be viewed as prerequisites for others. Thus, enhancing an offering's attractiveness implies that target customers are aware of its existence. Similarly, a call for action implies that customers are already aware of the offering and find it attractive (Figure 4).

Figure 4. Communication Goals

As a general rule, communication goals are rarely tied directly to sales and/or profits. The rationale for this is that even though advertising can influence sales and profits, its impact is moderated by a variety of factors such as the other marketing mix variables (e.g., product, service, brand, price, incentives, and distribution), by competitors' and collaborators' actions, as well as by the overall economic, social, political, and regulatory context.

The *benchmark* aspect of the goal provides measurable *criteria* for success (e.g., creating awareness among 40% of a given market), as well as an identifiable *timeframe* for achieving these criteria (e.g., two weeks prior to launching the new product).

Developing the Message

The message can concern any of the five value-creation marketing mix variables (product, service, brand, price, and incentives) as well as the availability of the offering. For each of these marketing mix factors, the message articulates the specifics of the company's offering as follows:

- The *product- and service-related message* informs target customers of the characteristics of the company's products and services.

- *The brand-related message* focuses on the identity and the meaning of the company's or offering's brand.

- The *price-related message* communicates the offering's price.

- The *incentives-related message* depicts the incentives associated with the offering, such as temporary price reductions, volume discounts, rebates, coupons, and premiums.

- The *distribution-related message* highlights the offering's availability in distribution channels.

A particular message can communicate multiple aspects of the offering. To illustrate, the iPhone press conference in January 2007 aimed to inform target customers about the product and service benefits of the iPhone, enhance the iPhone and Apple brands, and inform customers about the price, the relevant incentives, and the availability of the iPhone in June 2007.

An alternative approach to defining the message content is based on the type of value it communicates. In this context, three types of messages can be distinguished: functional, monetary, and psychological.

- The *functional-value message* informs target customers of the performance aspect of the offering (e.g., reliability, durability, and safety).

- The *monetary-value message* focuses on the monetary aspect of the offering (e.g., its price and price incentives).

- The *psychological-value message* communicates the psychological benefits of the offering (e.g., its emotional, social, and self-expressive benefits).

With respect to the strategy used to communicate the offering's value proposition, two types of messages can be distinguished: comparative and noncomparative. *Comparative messages* define the value of the offering by comparing it to a competitive offering. In contrast, *noncomparative messages* define the value of the offering in terms of its inherent ability to meet a particular customer need without necessarily comparing it to competitive offerings. In this context, the focus of comparative messages is on differentiating the company's offering and emphasizing the uniqueness, whereas the focus of noncomparative messages is on emphasizing the offering's fit with customers' needs. Furthermore, the frame of reference (i.e., how the customer should think about the offering) for the comparative message is the other offerings in the product category (e.g., product X is better than product Y), whereas in the case of noncomparative messages, the frame of reference is customer needs (e.g., product X fulfills need Z).

Selecting the Media

The media decision involves three aspects: media budget, media type, and media scheduling. These three aspects are discussed in more detail in the following sections.

Media Budget

Deciding on the magnitude of communications expenditures is one of the key decisions in planning a promotional campaign. There are several approaches to determine the total communication budget:

- *The goal-driven* approach is based on an estimate of the resources required to achieve the company's strategic goal. To illustrate, if the communication goal is to increase awareness of a company's new offering by 10% within three months, then the budget will reflect the estimated costs of achieving this goal, taking into account factors such as media costs, number of customers reached through a single exposure to the company's message per media dollar spent, and the average number of exposures necessary to create awareness.

- The *percentage-of-sales* approach implies setting the budget as a fraction of the company's sales revenues.

- The *competitive-parity* approach implies setting the budget at par with a key competitor (or a set of competitors). The approach in which the budget is set proportionally to the desired share of total media expenditures in a given category is also referred to as share-of-voice budgeting.

- The *legacy* approach implies setting the budget based on prior-year expenditures.

- The *affordability* approach implies setting the budget based on resources available for promotional activities.

While all of the above budgeting strategies have merit (some more than others), the goal-driven approach tends to dominate the others in its ability to estimate most effectively the resources required to achieve the company's communication goals. Competitive-parity and percentage-of-sales approaches can also provide useful insights into the budgeting decision. Because they are detached from market realities, the legacy and affordability approaches are the least likely to provide an accurate budget estimate.

Media Type

Media type involves the means used by the company to convey its message. The most popular types of media include advertising, public relations, direct marketing, personal selling, event sponsorship, product-based communications, and product samples. These media types are discussed in more detail below.

- *Advertising* involves nonpersonal marketing communications, in which the company/sponsor develops the message and absorbs most or all of the media costs (air time, print space). The most popular forms of advertising involve audio–visual (television, video, film), radio, print (promotional brochures, advertisements in newspapers and magazines, newspaper and magazine inserts), online (website advertisement), outdoor (posters, billboards), point-of-sale (front-of-the-store, end-of-aisle, and shelf-talkers—signs displayed in close proximity to the promoted item). In the United States, advertising is the most popular media format, with most of the advertising dollars spent on television commercials.

- *Public relations* involve communications by third parties that are not controlled by the company. Unlike advertising, with public relations the company does not pay for the media and does not control the content of the message; all it can do is encourage a third party (opinion leaders, press) to promote the offering (in newspaper, television, and radio coverage). Because the message comes from a third party that typically has no vested interest in the company's offering, public relations communications are often viewed as more credible than communications directly initiated by the company.

- *Direct marketing* involves individually targeted communications (e.g., catalogs, direct mail, telemarketing, and online), typically designed to elicit a direct response.

- *Personal selling* involves direct (typically face-to-face) interaction with a company representative (e.g., a salesperson).

- *Event sponsorship* involves sponsoring events and activities of interest to the offering's target customers. A form of event sponsorship is product placement, where the sponsor company secures the rights to embed (place) its offering within a particular form of entertainment, such as a sports event, television show, or a movie.

- *Product-based communications* are those embedded in the product itself, such as product labels, signs, and packaging.

- *Product samples* and *free trials* enable customers to experience product benefits directly.[1] Samples and free trials are often used in new product introductions to encourage customers to try the offering and are typically distributed via direct mail (e.g., in the case of consumer packaged goods); online (e.g., in the case of digital content products such as electronic newspapers, music samples, and movie trailers); or at the point of sale (e.g., in the case of items that can be readily consumed, such as food samples).

The allocation of resources across different media types is a function of the effectiveness and cost-efficiency of each media format with respect to its ability to communicate the desired message. For certain types of products (e.g., alcohol and tobacco), legal restrictions exist that also determine the choice of advertising medium.

In addition to deciding on the allocation of resources across different types of media, the media decision involves determining the specific media channels within each of the media types. For example, within the domain of television advertising, the media channel decision involves selecting particular shows and time slots in which the company's message will be best positioned to reach and influence its target customers. Thus, beer companies often choose to advertise during popular sport events with predominantly male audiences, whereas beauty products are typically advertised during shows with predominantly female audiences.

Media Scheduling

Deciding on media scheduling involves identifying factors such as time horizon, pattern, reach, and frequency.

- Based on the *time horizon*, media scheduling typically involves two types of planning: macro-scheduling and micro-scheduling. Macro-scheduling involves deciding on the allocation of media impact within a longer term timeframe, such as on an annual basis (e.g., in the case of seasonal products like flowers, chocolates, and champagne) or as a function of the offering's business cycle (e.g., when launching a new offering, the media impact is typically greater at the time of introduction, slowing down as the offering reaches the desired level of market penetration). In contrast, micro-scheduling involves media allocation decisions within a shorter timeframe, such as a month, a week, or a day.

- Based on the *pattern*, three common scheduling formats can be distinguished: continuous, concentrated, and intermittent. Continuous scheduling (also referred to as flighting) involves allocating exposures evenly throughout the individual periods within a given timeframe. Concentrated scheduling involves allocating the majority of exposures in a single period. Intermittent scheduling (also referred to as pulsing) involves alternating periods with high and low (or zero) levels of advertising (e.g., every other week). The decision on a particular timing format is a function of the characteristics of the company's offering and target customers' pattern of product adoption and usage.

- The communication *frequency* decision reflects the number of times target customers are exposed to a particular message over a given period. The number of exposures necessary is a function of a variety of factors, such as communication goals (e.g., create awareness, strengthen preferences, or incite action), the novelty of the offering's benefits, the relevance of these benefits to customers' goals, the nature of the media carrying the message (e.g., television commercial, print advertisement, or direct mail), the creative solution used to generate awareness, and the level of involvement of the target customers viewing the advertisement. In certain cases, a single exposure could be sufficient, although in most cases, multiple exposures are required to achieve communication goals.

- The communication *reach* decision reflects the number of target customers that are exposed to a particular message at least once in a given period. The communication reach is typically a function of the size of the target market.

Creative Solution

The *creative solution* involves translating the company's message into the language of the selected media format (e.g., television, print, or radio advertising). The creative solution has two key aspects: appeal type and execution style.

- *Appeal type* refers to the approach used to communicate the company's message. Most creative solutions involve at least one of two types of appeals: information-based (also referred to as cognitive) and emotion-based (also referred to as affective). Information-based appeals typically rely on methods such as factual presentations (straightforward presentation of the relevant information), demonstrations (illustrating the key benefits of the offering by showing it in a staged environment), slice-of-life stories (illustrating the key benefits of the offering by showing it in everyday use), testimonials (praise by an individual based on his or her experience with the offering and endorsements by ordinary users or celebrities). In contrast, emotion-based appeals typically play on emotions such as love, romance, humor, and fear. Communication campaigns often combine informational and emotional appeals—an approach consistent with the "Think-Feel-Do" paradigm, according to which consumer actions are preceded by learning and affective evaluation of the offering.

- *Execution style* refers to the method used to translate a particular appeal into the language of the selected media format. Style decisions are media specific. Thus, print advertising involves decisions concerning the copy text (e.g., wording of the headline and the body text), visual elements (e.g., pictures, photos, graphics, logos), format (e.g., size, color scheme), and layout (i.e., the arrangement of different parts of the advertisement). Radio/audio advertising involves decisions concerning the text (e.g., wording of the dialogue and narration), audio (e.g., music, dialogue, and sound effects), and format (e.g., length). Television/video advertising involves decisions concerning the visual/video elements (e.g., imagery), text (e.g., wording of the dialogue, voice-over narration, and printed text), audio (e.g., music, dialogue, and sound effects), and format (e.g., length).

Implementing the Communication Campaign

The implementation of a communication campaign involves two decisions: defining the processes that enable the company to implement the message, media, and creative solutions, and identifying the people managing these processes.

- The *processes* aspect of implementation typically involves four steps: preproduction (e.g., identifying the technical aspects of the message, media, and creative solution), production (e.g., the actual filming, videotaping, recording, or printing of the advertisement), postproduction (e.g., editing, duplicating, legal compliance, and client approval), and distribution (e.g., airing, printing, and shipping).

- The *people* aspect of implementation involves identifying the key personnel, such as campaign managers, creative staff (e.g., writers, directors, and producers) and actors.

Evaluating Communication Effectiveness

John Wanamaker's famous quote, uttered nearly a century ago, "I know that half of my advertising money is wasted. I just don't know which half," adequately reflects the current state of evaluating communication effectiveness. There is no general agreement on the part of marketers, advertising agencies, and research companies as to the best way to measure advertising effectiveness. As a result, companies use diverse criteria to measure the effectiveness of an advertising campaign. The most commonly used criteria involve measuring the following six factors: exposure, comprehension, recall, persuasion, intent, and behavior. These six factors are discussed in more detail below.

- *Exposure* reflects the number of times a given advertisement has been seen by the target audience.

- *Comprehension* reflects the degree to which the target audience understood the message embedded in the advertisement.

- *Recall* reflects the degree to which an advertisement is remembered by the target audience. Two types of recall measures are commonly utilized: aided and unaided. In the case of aided recall, respondents are given a list of brand names following the presentation of a series of advertisements and are asked to recall whether they have seen any of these brands. In contrast, in the case of unaided recall, respondents are simply asked to recall all brands they have seen during the presentation. Overall, retention is a very popular (although not always very useful) benchmark among advertising agencies.

- *Persuasion* reflects the degree to which the advertisement is able to change the attitudes of the target audience and enhance their preference for the advertised product. Because preferences for established brands (which often are among the largest advertisers) are difficult to change with a single advertisement, many advertising agencies measure the attitude toward the advertisement (rather than the attitude toward the brand) on the premise that if the target audience likes the advertisement, then this attitude will translate into liking the brand.

- *Intent* reflects a mental disposition in the consumer to act favorably toward the offering (e.g., buy the product, visit the store, or contact the company). Intent is typically measured by asking respondents to indicate the likelihood of purchasing the product within a given timeframe.

- *Behavior* reflects the impact of an advertisement on respondents' actual behavior, such as purchasing the product, inquiring about product features, and researching the product on the Internet. Behavior is typically measured by the number of sales, sales inquiries, and website visits.

It is important to understand that none of the above measures is a reliable indicator of the effectiveness of a given advertisement. Intuitively, it may seem that sales volume is the best measure of communication effectiveness. Unfortunately, this is not the case. The key problem with relying on customers' behavior as a measure of communication effectiveness is that in most cases, the impact of communications is not immediate (especially in cases of brand-building communications); as a result, the impact of communications is confounded with a variety of nonrelated factors such as changes in price, incentives, competitive actions, and purchase cycle.

The key to deciding which metric to use involves the goal of the campaign, the selected media format, and the message being communicated.

- Measuring the success of a communication campaign is a function of the nature of *communication goals*. Thus, in cases where the communication goal is to create awareness (e.g., in the case of a new product introduction), then exposure,[2] comprehension, and/or recall should be measured. In cases where the communication goal is to strengthen preferences, then the persuasiveness of the advertisement should be measured. Finally, in cases where the communication goal is to incite action, then behavior should be measured.

- Measuring the effectiveness of a communication campaign is also a function of the particular *media format*. Thus, in cases where the media are not directly linked to a particular performance measure, such as public relations and event sponsorship, performance tends to be measured through indirect measures of awareness and preference. In contrast, in cases where the media are directly linked to performance measures (e.g., direct marketing, personal selling, and click-through advertising), the effectiveness of the communication campaign could be directly estimated using behavior-based measures.

- Evaluating the effectiveness of a communication campaign is also a function of the nature of the *communication message*. To illustrate, unlike communicating incentives that tend to have an immediate impact on sales, building a brand has a delayed impact on sales. As a result, using sales as an effectiveness benchmark is likely to lead to an underestimation of the impact of brand-building communications, while at the same time overestimating the role of incentive-focused communications. In the same vein, it is also important to account for the fact that incentive-focused communications merely inform target customers of an existing incentive; in contrast, brand-focused communications typically not only inform customers about the offering's brand, they also create brand equity.

Summary

Managing communications involves two types of analysis: (1) strategic analysis, which examines communications as a function of the offering's market structure (customers, company, collaborators, competition, and context), and (2) tactical analysis, which examines communications as a function of the other marketing mix variables (product, service, brand, price, incentives, and distribution).

Managing the communication aspect of an offering involves six key decisions: setting the goal, developing the message, selecting the media, developing the creative solution, implementing the communication campaign, and evaluating the campaign results.

The goal identifies a set of criteria (e.g., create awareness, strengthen preferences, and incite action) to be achieved by the communication campaign within a given timeframe.

The message identifies the information to be communicated to target customers. The message can focus on one or several of the five value-creation marketing mix variables: product, service, brand, price, and incentives.

The media describes the means used by the company to convey its message. The media decision involves three aspects: media budget (goal-based, percentage of sales, competitive parity, legacy, and affordability), media type (advertising, public relations, personal selling, product samples, event sponsorship, and product placement), and media scheduling (time horizon, pattern, reach, and frequency).

The creative solution involves the execution of the company's message in a given media. Among the key aspects of the creative solution are appeal type (e.g., information-based or emotion-based) and execution style (e.g., text, format, and layout).

The implementation aspect of marketing communications identifies the timeline and the logistics of executing the message, media, and creative decisions.

The control aspect of marketing communications involves evaluating the success (effectiveness and cost efficiency) of the communication campaign with respect to achieving its goals. The most commonly used criteria involve measuring the following five factors: exposure, comprehension, recall, persuasion, intent, and behavior.

Relevant Concepts

Above-the-Line (ATL) Communications: Company communications are often divided into two categories: Above-The-Line (ATL) communications, which encompass mass media advertising, such as television commercials, radio, and print advertisements; and Below-

The-Line (BTL) communications, which include public relations, event sponsorship, personal selling, and direct mail. Historically, the term ATL was used in reference to communications for which an advertising agency charged a commission to place in mass media, whereas the term BTL was used in reference to communications that involved a standard charge rather than a commission. Currently, the terms ATL and BTL are loosely used to indicate an emphasis on mass media (ATL) versus one-to-one communications (BTL). The current use of BTL often includes customer and trade incentives as well.

Advertising Allowance: A form of trade promotion in which retailers are given a discount in exchange for promoting a product in their own advertisements.

Advertising Awareness: The number of potential customers who are aware of the offering. Awareness is a function of the total volume of advertising delivery to the target audience and the number of exposures necessary to create awareness. In cases where a single exposure is sufficient to create awareness, the awareness level equals the advertising reach.

$$\text{Awareness} = \frac{\text{Advertising reach} \cdot \text{Frequency of exposure}}{\text{Number of exposures necessary to create awareness}}$$

Affiliate Marketing: A communications strategy that involves revenue sharing between advertisers and online content providers. An affiliate is rewarded based on specific performance measures, such as sales, click-throughs, and registrations, or a combination of these factors.

Awareness Rate: The number of potential customers aware of the offering relative to the total number of potential customers. Depending on the manner in which it is measured, two types of awareness are commonly distinguished: aided awareness, in which respondents are provided with the name of the target offering (e.g., "Have you seen any advertisements for Coca-Cola in the past month?"), and unaided awareness, in which respondents are not provided with any offering-specific information (e.g., "Which soft drinks have you seen advertised during the past month?").

Below-the-Line (BTL) Communications: See *Above-the-Line Communications.*

Carryover Effect in Advertising: Impact of an advertising campaign that extends beyond the timeframe of the campaign. To illustrate, an advertising effort made in a given period may generate sales in subsequent periods.

Comparative Advertising: Advertising strategy whereby a given offering is directly compared with another offering.

Competitive Parity Budgeting: Budget allocation strategy based on (1) matching the competitors' absolute level of spending or (2) the proportion per point of market share.

Cooperative Advertising: Advertising strategy in which a manufacturer and a retailer jointly advertise their offering to consumers. In this case, the manufacturer pays a portion of a retailer's advertising costs in return for featuring its products, services, and brands.

Cost Per Point (CPP): Measure used to represent the cost of a communications campaign. CPP is the media cost of reaching one percent (one rating point) of a particular demographic.

$$\text{CPP} = \frac{\text{Advertising cost}}{\text{GRP}}$$

Cost Per Thousand (CPM): Measure used to represent the cost of a communications campaign. CPM is the cost of reaching 1,000 individuals or households with an advertising message in a given medium (M is the Roman numeral for 1,000). For example, a TV commercial that costs \$200,000 to air and reaches 10M viewers has a CPM of \$20. The popularity of CPM derives in part from its being a good comparative measure of advertising efficiency across different media (e.g., TV, print, and Internet).

$$CPM = \frac{Advertising\ cost}{Total\ impressions} \cdot 1,000$$

Frequency: The number of times the target audience is exposed to an advertisement in a given period. Also used in reference to the number of times an advertisement is repeated through a specific medium during a specific period.

Gross Rating Point (GRP): A measure of the total volume of advertising delivery to the target audience. It is equal to the percent of the population reached times the frequency of exposure. To illustrate, if a given advertisement reaches 60% of the households with an average frequency of three times, then the GRP of the media is equal to 180. GRP can also be calculated by dividing the gross impressions by the size of the total audience. A single GRP represents 1% of the total audience in a given region.

$$GRP = Reach \cdot Frequency$$

Impression: A single exposure of an advertisement to one person.

Institutional Advertising: Advertising strategy designed to build goodwill or an image for an organization (rather than to promote specific offerings).

Integrated Marketing Communications (IMC): The strategy of designing marketing communications programs to coordinate all communication activities (e.g., advertising, public relations, and personal selling) to provide a consistent message across different communication channels.

Net Promoter Score: A popular metric designed to measure customers' word of mouth about a company and/or its products.[3] The basic idea is fairly simple: A company's current and potential customers are asked to indicate the likelihood that they will recommend the company and/or its products to another person (e.g., "How likely is it that you would recommend this company to a friend or colleague?"). Responses are typically scored on a 0–10 scale, with 0 meaning extremely unlikely and 10 meaning extremely likely. Based on their responses, customers are categorized into one of three categories: promoters (those with ratings of 9 or 10), passives (those with ratings of 7 or 8), and detractors (those with ratings of 6 or lower). The Net Promoter Score is then calculated as the difference between the percentage of a company's promoters and detractors. For example, if 40% of a company's customers are classified as promoters and 25% are classified as detractors, the company's Net Promoter Score is 15%.

Point-of-Purchase Advertising: Promotional materials displayed at the point of purchase (e.g., in a retail store).

Public Service Announcement (PSA): Nonprofit advertising that uses free space or time donated by the media.

Reach: The size of the audience that has been exposed to a particular advertisement at least once in a given period (multiple viewings by the same audience do not increase reach). Reach may be stated either as an absolute number or as a fraction of a population. For example, if 40,000 of 100,000 different households are exposed to a given commercial at least once, the reach is 40%.

Reminder Advertising: Advertising strategy designed to maintain awareness and stimulate repurchase of an already established offering.

Share of Voice: A company's communications expenditures relative to those of the entire product category.

$$\text{Share of voice} = \frac{\text{An offering's communications expenditures}}{\text{Product category's communications expenditures}}$$

Target Rating Point (TRP): A measure of the total volume of advertising delivery to the target audience. TRP is similar to GRP, but its calculation involves using only the target audience (rather than the total audience watching the program) as the base. Thus, a single TRP represents 1% of the targeted viewers in any particular region.

Teaser Advertising: Communication strategy designed to create interest in an offering while providing little or no information about it.

Top-of-Mind Awareness: The first brand identified by respondents when asked to list brands in a given product category.

Total Impressions: The number of times each recipient has been exposed to the message.

$$\text{Total impressions} = \text{Number of recipients} \cdot \text{Number of exposures per recipient}$$

Wearout: A decrease in the effectiveness of a communication campaign from decreased consumer interest in the message, often resulting from repetition.

Additional Readings

Belch, George E. and Michael A. Belch (2007), *Advertising and Promotion: An Integrated Marketing Communications Perspective* (7th ed.). Boston, MA: McGraw-Hill Irwin.

Ogilvy, David (1983), *Ogilvy on Advertising* (1st American ed.). New York, NY: Crown.

Sutherland, Max and Alice K. Sylvester (2000), *Advertising and the Mind of the Consumer: What Works, What Doesn't, and Why* (2nd ed.). St. Leonards, NSW: Allen & Unwin.

Wells, William, John Burnett, and Sandra E. Moriarty (2006), *Advertising: Principles & Practice* (7th ed.). Upper Saddle River, NJ: Pearson/Prentice Hall.

Notes

[1] Product samples are often misclassified as a form of incentive. Because product samples aim to inform customers about the benefits of the offering without influencing its value proposition, they should be viewed as a form of communication rather than as an incentive.

[2] Exposure is also a useful metric to determine whether a particular quantity benchmark has been achieved (e.g., number of exposures per target customer).

[3] Reichheld, Fred (2003), "The One Number You Need to Grow," *Harvard Business Review*, December

Chapter Fifteen

Managing Distribution

The distribution aspect of the marketing mix involves the processes of delivering the company's offering to its target customers and collaborators. The key aspects of managing distribution channels are the focus of this chapter.

A Framework for Managing Distribution

Managing distribution involves two types of decisions: (1) strategic decisions aiming to optimize distribution as a function of the offering's market structure, and (2) tactical decisions aiming to optimize distribution as a function of the other marketing mix variables. These two types of decisions are outlined in more detail below.

Managing Distribution: Strategy

From a strategic standpoint, channel decisions involve analyzing five key factors: customers, company, collaborators, competition, and context. These five factors are illustrated in Figure 1 and outlined in more detail below.

Figure 1. Distribution Management as a Function of Market Structure

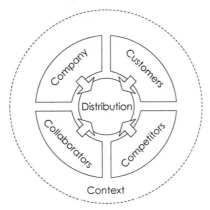

- *Customers.* An offering's distribution strategy is influenced by its target customers. Thus, offerings pursuing a mass-marketing strategy are more likely to involve extensive distribution through different channels and across different geographic markets, whereas offerings with a smaller customer base, such as niche offerings, are more likely to involve a more selective distribution strategy.

- *Company.* A company's goals, strategic assets, and core competencies have a great influence on the distribution of its offerings. To illustrate, a company seeking market share dominance is likely to utilize diverse channels for its offerings in order to achieve extensive distribution coverage. In the same vein, an offering's distribution strategy is influenced by the company's existing strategic assets and core competencies, such as an established distribution network and expertise.

- *Collaborators.* An offering's distribution strategy reflects the company's relations with its collaborators and, in particular, its channel partners. Indeed, because indirect distribution implies collaboration with intermediaries, it is influenced by their goals, strategic assets, and core competencies. An offering's distribution strategy can be also influenced by the dynamics of the relationship between the company and its collaborators and, in particular, by the balance of power between channel partners. For example, a company may choose to shift from a single to multiple distributors to minimize the percentage of sales through an individual intermediary, thus reducing the power of any particular channel. Similarly, a company may adopt a direct distribution strategy (e.g., by opening its own retail stores) to decrease its reliance on its collaborators.

- *Competitors.* An offering's distribution strategy is also influenced by its competitors' distribution strategy. For instance, the increasing competition in the traditional distribution channels has forced many companies to seek alternative distribution formats. Similarly, in the case of new offerings, the likelihood that competitors will also enter the market is a key factor in determining the coverage and speed of the distribution strategy.

- *Context.* Distribution is also a function of various social, economic, political, technological, and regulatory factors describing the environment in which the offering is delivered to its customers. To illustrate, the consolidation of retail outlets and the emergence of superstores and specialized retail chains in many industries have resulted in increased power of retailers with respect to the other channel members (e.g., manufacturers and wholesalers).

Managing Distribution: Tactics

From a tactical standpoint, distribution decisions involve analyzing the other marketing mix variables (product, service, brand, price, incentives, and communication). The key tactical aspects of managing distribution are illustrated in Figure 2 and outlined in more detail below.

Figure 2. Distribution Management as a Function of the Marketing Mix

- *Product and service.* An offering's distribution strategy is a function of the characteristics of its product and service characteristics. For example, offerings defined by predominantly experience and credence attributes (characteristics that are unobservable at the time of purchase, such as reliability, durability, and consumption experience) are more likely to benefit from the endorsement of an established distribution channel than offerings characterized by predominantly search attributes (characteristics that are readily observable, such as color, size, and shape). In the same vein, novel, complex, and/or nondifferentiated products tend to benefit from being distributed through channels offering higher levels of sales support.

- *Brand.* To ensure the success of an offering, its distribution strategy needs to be consistent with its branding strategy. To illustrate, brands associated with a distinct lifestyle (e.g., Ralph Lauren, Lacoste, Apple, and Cartier) tend to benefit from employing a direct distribution model that enables the company to achieve better control over the environment in which its brand is delivered to customers.

- *Price.* An offering's distribution channel is a function of its pricing strategy. For instance, penetration pricing is typically associated with extensive distribution through multiple channels and in different geographic areas, whereas skim pricing is typically associated with limited distribution through selected channels and/or geographic areas. Similarly, the price tier of the distribution channel is typically selected based on the price tier of the offering.

- *Incentives.* The selection of a distribution channel is contingent on the offering's incentive strategy. For example, a promotional strategy that implies frequent use of incentives typically calls for channels that also frequently utilize sales promotions (sometimes referred to as "High–Low" retailers), whereas a promotional strategy that implies limited use of incentives is more consistent with an everyday low pricing (EDLP) retail strategy.

- *Communication.* An offering's distribution channel is also an important vehicle for implementing its communication strategy. In this context, the selection and design of a distribution channel is often a function of its ability to effectively communicate the offering's benefits. To illustrate, offerings relying on a "push" strategy, in which the channel is a key factor in promoting the offering to target customers, are likely to use channels that can facilitate this function (e.g., retailers with extensive and experienced sales force).

Distribution Channel Design

The process of designing and managing distribution channels involves several pivotal decisions: channel structure, channel coordination, channel type, channel coverage, and channel exclusivity. The key aspects of these decisions are discussed in the following sections.

Channel Structure

Based on their structure, three basic types of value-delivery models can be identified: direct, indirect, and hybrid (Figure 3). These three types of distribution channels and their pros and cons are discussed in more detail below.

Figure 3. Distribution Channel Structure

Direct distribution involves a business model in which the manufacturer and the end-customer interact directly with each other without intermediaries.

The direct distribution model affords multiple advantages, such as (1) a more effective distribution system resulting from better coordination of the different aspects of the value-delivery process, (2) greater cost efficiency resulting from eliminating intermediaries, (3) greater control over the environment in which the offering is delivered to customers (level of service, product display, and availability of complementary offerings), and (4) closer contact with the end user, allowing the manufacturer to have first-hand information about their needs and their reaction to its offerings.

Despite its numerous advantages, the direct-distribution model also has a number of disadvantages: (1) establishing a direct-distribution channel, especially a brick-and-mortar one, takes time; (2) in most cases, it is difficult to achieve the same breadth of distribution outlets with direct distribution as with multiple intermediaries; (3) launching and managing a distribution channel requires a different set of strategic assets and core competencies that many manufacturers do not readily have; (4) in most cases, direct-distribution channels require a large upfront fixed-cost investment.

Indirect distribution involves a business model in which the manufacturer and the end customer interact with each other through intermediaries, such as wholesalers and retailers.

The indirect distribution model has a number of advantages, such as: (1) rapid distribution that can be implemented instantly, (2) broad coverage that enables the company to reach all or the majority of its target customers, (3) greater effectiveness of the value-delivery process since manufacturers can benefit from the assets and core competencies of intermediaries, (4) potential economies of scale because intermediaries perform similar activities for a variety of manufacturers, and (5) no large upfront investment necessary because a manufacturer using intermediaries is "renting" rather than buying shelf space for its products.

Despite its advantages, the use of intermediaries in the indirect distribution model is associated with a number of disadvantages, such as: (1) more complex channel structure could have a negative impact on the efficiency of the distribution system; (2) the possibility that intermediaries can add an extra layer of profit margins, thus increasing the total costs of the indirect distribution system; (3) loss of control over the selling environment; (4) greatly diminished ability to communicate with and collect information directly from customers; and (5) potential for vertical channel conflicts resulting from different strategic goals and profit-optimization strategies for the manufacturer and its intermediaries.

Hybrid distribution involves a business model in which the manufacturer and the end customer interact with each other through multiple channels, for example, directly and through intermediaries such as wholesalers and/or retailers.

The hybrid channel has numerous advantages that stem from combining the benefits of direct and indirect distribution. At the same time, hybrid channels are also subject to many of the disadvantages of both direct and indirect channels. An additional problem with using hybrid channels is the potential for a channel conflict in cases where the both the company and its intermediaries target the same customers and aim to perform the same value-delivery function (e.g., selling an offering that will satisfy the same need of the same target customers). For example, Apple's launch of its own retail stores in 2001 ended up cannibalizing sales of existing resellers of Apple products.

Channel Coordination

Conventional marketing channels comprise independent companies (e.g., manufacturers, wholesalers, and retailers), each maximizing their own profitability. Because the profitability of the channel as a whole can be increased by coordinating the activities of each individual member, there is an increasing trend toward channel coordination. The coordination could be (1) ownership-based, in which different channel members are parts of the same company; (2) contractual, in which coordination is achieved through binding contractual agreements between channel members (e.g., between manufacturers and distributors); and (3) implicit, in which channel coordination is achieved without explicit contractual agreements. The pros and cons of these channel coordination strategies are outlined below.

Channel coordination based on *common ownership* of channel members offers numerous potential advantages, such as: (1) better optimization of channel functions, resulting in greater effectiveness and cost-efficiency (e.g., through joint profit optimization and system integration), (2) greater degree of information sharing, and (3) better control and performance monitoring.

Despite its multiple advantages, single-ownership distribution channels have a number of potential disadvantages: (1) high initial investment; (2) potential internal inefficiencies because of lack of competition; (3) lower cost efficiency resulting from a smaller scale; (4) the need to develop distribution channel expertise when moving from one business function (e.g., manufacturing) to another (e.g., distribution). In addition, in the case of hybrid distribution in which some but not all channels are company owned, ownership often results in channel conflicts with independent distributors.

Channel coordination based on *contractual relationships*, such as long-term contractual agreements, joint ventures, and franchise agreements, has several key advantages: (1) lower initial investment, (2) fast implementation, and (3) lower cost efficiency resulting from partners' scale and/or specialization. Despite its advantages, contractual channel coordination has a number of drawbacks: (1) potential inefficiencies stemming from less coordination, (2) strategic risk of creating a potential competitor (e.g., in the case of backward integration) by sharing know-how and strategic information (e.g., pricing policies, profit margins, and cost structure), and (3) monitoring performance.

Implicit channel coordination is similar to contractual coordination with the advantage of being much more flexible. This flexibility, however, comes at the cost of the inability to predict the behavior of various channel members. Another shortcoming of implicit coordination is a lower level of commitment, resulting in unwillingness to invest resources to customize the channel for a particular manufacturer. Implicit coordination is also likely to lead to lower cost efficiency resulting from a lower degree of channel coordination (e.g., resulting from lack of systems integration).

Channel Type

Channels vary in terms of the breadth and depth of their assortments. Based on the breadth of assortment of items carried by a distributor, channels can be classified into one of two categories: specialized or broad. Specialized distributors, e.g., Foot Locker, Office Depot, CarMax, and Toys "R" Us, tend to carry a relatively narrow assortment. In contrast, nonspecialized distributors, e.g., Wal-Mart, Costco, and Carrefour, tend to carry much more extensive assortments.

Based on the depth of the item assortment carried by a distributor, channels can be classified into one of two categories: limited and extensive. Limited-assortment distributors (e.g., 7-Eleven and Circle K), carry relatively small assortments, whereas extensive-assortment distributors, such as Home Depot and Wal-Mart, carry fairly large assortments. Specialized retailers carrying an extensive assortment of items (e.g., Home Depot, Office Depot, and Sport Mart) are also referred to as category killers.

Channel Coverage

Channel strategies vary in the degree to which they can make an offering available to customers in a given market (e.g., the number of outlets at which offerings are made available to target customers). Extensive distribution implies that an offering is readily accessible by a fairly large proportion of customers in a given market, whereas limited distribution implies that the accessibility of the offering is fairly limited (e.g., the offering is available only through specialized retailers). The key trade-off here is between achieving high offering availability, which typically comes at a high cost and often leads to channel conflicts, and limited availability, which aims to achieve more targeted distribution at the risk of missing some potential customers.

Channel Exclusivity

Channel exclusivity refers to the degree to which an offering is made available through different distribution channels. Channel exclusivity is commonly used to reduce the potential for horizontal channel conflicts, which occur when distributors with different cost structures and profit margins sell identical offerings to the same customers. To mitigate the negative impact of a direct price comparison of the same offering across retailers, manufacturers often release channel-specific product variants in which individual offerings vary in functionality and, therefore, cannot be directly compared.

Distribution Channel Functions

Channels facilitate the value exchange between the company and its customers. Their primary function is delivering the company's offering to its target customers. In addition to its value-delivery functions, channels often take part in the process of enhancing the value of the company's offering and communicating the offering benefits to target customers. The value-delivery, value creation, and value communication functions of distribution channels are discussed in more detail in the following sections.

Value-Delivery Functions of a Distribution Channel

Channel functions are not limited to delivering the company's products and services to customers; they can involve all five value creation marketing mix variables: product, service, brand, price, and incentives.

- *Delivering products.* The product-delivery function involves transfer of the physical possession and ownership rights (title) of the product from the manufacturer to intermediaries (e.g., wholesales and retailers) to end users. It can involve value-added functions such as storage, inventory management, assorting, and repackaging.

- *Delivering services.* The service-delivery function involves performing services (customization, repair, technical assistance, and warranty support) that are part of the company's offering.

- *Delivering brands.* The brand-delivery function involves enabling customers to experience the brand. To illustrate, Apple, Sony, and Harley-Davidson retail stores function as channels delivering these brands to their customers.

- *Delivering prices.* The price-delivery function involves collecting and processing payments from customers. Note that, unlike other marketing mix variables, in the case of pricing the flow is reversed: The price is collected from customers and delivered to the company.

- *Delivering incentives.* The incentive-delivery function involves the mechanisms for distributing incentives to customers (e.g., delivering coupons, rebates, and premiums to customers), as well as the processes established to implement these incentives (e.g., implementing price reductions, processing coupons, and rebates).

In addition to delivering the offering to target customers, the functions of distribution channels also involve managing reverse flow, often referred to as reverse logistics (Figure 4). Reverse logistics can involve product-delivery (processing returns), price-delivery (processing refunds and partial credits), and incentives-delivery (collecting and processing coupons and rebates).

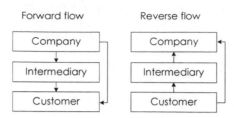

Figure 4. Value-Delivery Flow

Value-Creation and Value-Communication Functions of a Distribution Channel

In addition to their value-delivery function, channels typically participate in the process of creating and communicating the value of the offering. The value-creation function of distribution channels can involve products (e.g., product assembly), services (e.g., financing and extended warranty), brand (e.g., using the retail environment to enhance the meaning of the brand), price (e.g., negotiating the price to the end-user), and incentives (e.g., managing channel-specific incentives). The value-communication function of distribution channels can involve products and services (e.g., explaining product and/or service benefits), brands (e.g., communicating the brand essence), price (e.g., informing customers about the offering's price), and incentives (e.g., making customers aware of the availability of an incentive). The value-communication function of channels also involves managing the reverse flow—customer feedback, suggestions, and complaints.

Summary

Managing distribution involves two types of analysis: (1) strategic analysis, which examines distribution as a function of the offering's market structure (customers, company, collaborators, competition, and context), and (2) tactical analysis, which examines distribution as a function of the other marketing mix variables (product, service, brand, price, incentives, and communications).

The process of designing and managing distribution channels involves several pivotal decisions: channel structure (direct, indirect, and hybrid), channel coordination (ownership-based, contractual, and implicit), channel type (specialized vs. broad, and limited vs. extensive), channel coverage (limited vs. extensive), and channel exclusivity.

Channels facilitate the value exchange between the company and its customers. Their primary function is delivering the company's offering (product, service, brand, price, and incentives) to its target customers. In addition to its value-delivery functions, channels often take part in the process of enhancing the value of the company's offering and communicating the offering benefits to target customers.

Relevant Concepts

All-Commodity Volume (ACV): A measure of an offering's availability, typically calculated as the total annual volume of the company's offering in a given geographic area relative to the total sales volume of the retailers in that geographic area across all product categories (hence, the term "all-commodity volume"). Also refers to the gross sales in a specific geographic area (i.e., total sales of all stores).

$$ACV = \frac{\text{Total sales of stores carrying the company's offering}}{\text{Total sales of all stores}}$$

Category Killers: Specialty retailers that focus on one product category, such as electronics or business supplies at very competitive prices (e.g., Home Depot, Office Depot, and PetSmart).

Contractual Vertical Marketing System: Channel structure in which the relationships between the manufacturer and the distributor are set on a contractual basis (rather than common ownership).

Corporate Vertical Marketing System: Channel structure in which the manufacturer and the distributor have common ownership rather than a contractual relationship.

Detailers: Indirect sales force promoting pharmaceuticals to doctors and pharmacists so that they, in turn, recommend the brand to the consumer.

Direct Channel: Distribution strategy in which the manufacturer and the end customer interact directly with each other without intermediaries.

Forward Buying: Increasing the channel inventory (also referred to as "channel stuffing"), usually to take advantage of a manufacturer's promotion and/or in anticipation of price increases.

Gray Market: A market in which products are sold through unauthorized channels.

Hybrid Channel: Distribution strategy in which the manufacturer and the end customer interact with each other through multiple channels (e.g., directly and through intermediaries).

Indirect Channel: Distribution strategy in which the manufacturer and the end customer interact with each other through intermediaries.

Inventory Turnover: The number of times the inventory is replenished, typically calculated as the ratio of the annual revenues generated by a given offering to the average inventory.

Merchandisers: Indirect sales force that offers support to retailers for in-store activities, such as shelf location, pricing, and compliance with special programs.

Parallel Importing: The practice of importing products from a country in which the price is lower into a country in which the same product is priced higher. A hypothetical example of this practice would be importing drugs from Canada to the United States. In most cases, parallel importing is illegal in the United States.

Reverse Logistics: The process of reclaiming recyclable and reusable materials and returns for repair, remanufacturing, or disposal.

Same-Store Sales: A metric used in the retail industry comparing sales of stores that have been open for a year or more and have historical data to compare the current year's sales to the same timeframe last year. Same-store sales is a popular metric because it takes store closings and chain expansions out of the mix, indicating what portion of new sales has come from sales growth and what portion from the opening or closing of new stores.

Share of Shelf Space: Shelf space allocated to a given offering relative to the total shelf space in a given geographic area.

Shrinkage: A term used by retailers to describe theft of goods by customers and employees.

Vertical Marketing Systems: Centrally coordinated distribution channel.

Additional Readings

Anderson, Erin, Anne T. Coughlan, Louis W. Stern, and Adel I. El-Ansary (2006), *Marketing Channels* (7th ed.). Upper Saddle River, NJ: Prentice Hall.

Rolnicki, Kenneth (1998), *Managing Channels of Distribution*. New York, NY: Amacom.

Zoltners, Andris A., Prabhakant Sinha, and Sally Lorimer (2004), *Sales Force Design for Strategic Advantage*. Basingstoke, NH: Palgrave Macmillan.

Part Four

Applications

Chapter Sixteen

Managing Sales Growth

Sales growth is a key factor for achieving sustainable profitability. Understanding the key factors influencing sales volume and identifying strategies for effectively managing sales growth are important aspects of a company's strategic planning, and are the focus of this chapter. In particular, this chapter examines the two core strategies for increasing the sales volume of a company's offerings: managing product adoptions by new customers and managing product usage by current customers.

Managing Product Adoption

To identify the optimal strategy for increasing sales volume, a company first needs to understand the process by which its target customers adopt new products, then to identify the impediments to new product adoption in different stages of the process, and, finally, to develop an action plan to remove these impediments. These various aspects of managing product adoption are discussed in more detail in the following section.

The Product Adoption Process

From a customer's perspective, product adoption can be viewed as a multistage process in which each stage identifies a factor necessary for product adoption. In particular, six such factors can be distinguished: awareness, understanding, attractiveness, affordability, availability, and purchase intent. This view of product adoption implies that in order for customers to adopt an offering, they should (1) be aware of its availability, (2) understand its value proposition, (3) perceive the offering to be attractive, (4) perceive it to be affordable, (5) have access to the offering, and (6) intend to purchase it within a particular timeframe (Figure 1).[1]

Figure 1: The Product Adoption Process

The six key steps of product adoption can be summarized as follows:

- *Awareness* reflects customers' knowledge of the availability of the offering. Awareness can be generated by the company's direct communications to its target customers, by communications initiated by the company's collaborators (distribution partners, supplier partners, co-developers, and co-promoters), as well as by third-party communications, such as word-of-mouth, media coverage, and noncompensated endorsements.

- *Understanding* reflects customers' comprehension of the benefits and costs of the offering. Understanding the value of the offering goes beyond simply being aware of the existence of the offering; it must include comprehension of its benefits and costs. As in the case of creating awareness, understanding the value of the offering can be facilitated by the company's direct communications to its target customers, by communications initiated by the company's collaborators, and by third-party communications.

- *Attractiveness* reflects the utility customers expect to receive from the offering. This implies that consumers should not only be aware of the offering's existence and understand its benefits and costs, but should also find this offering's value proposition attractive. An offering's attractiveness is a function of two factors: its intrinsic value, which reflects the offering's innate ability to deliver value to its target customers in the absence of competitive offerings, and its competitive advantage, which reflects the offering's ability to deliver value superior to that of competitors' offerings. Thus, attractiveness reflects an offering's ability to satisfy a particular need of target customers better than competitors' offerings can.

- *Affordability* reflects customers' perceptions of the monetary cost of the offering with respect to their ability to pay for it. Thus, affordability implies that consumers not only find the offering attractive, but can also come up with the money to acquire it. Because affordability is a function of customers' financial resources, it often is the key impediment to product adoption in developing countries, as well as in financially strained demographics.

- *Availability* reflects the degree to which the offering is accessible by target customers. An offering's availability is a function of factors such as the density of the distribution channels catering to its target customers, as well as the availability of the offering in these channels on a day-to-day basis (e.g., absence of stock-outs).

- *Purchase intent* reflects customers' intention to purchase the offering within a particular timeframe. Thus, even though customers may find the company's offering attractive, affordable, and accessible, they may not necessarily have the intention to purchase it within the timeframe outlined by the company's sales goals.

- *Purchase* involves customers' actual acquisition of the offering. Purchase intent does not necessarily translate into an actual purchase: Numerous factors can either delay the intended action (e.g., anticipation of future price cuts) or void the purchase intent altogether (e.g., the introduction of a superior competitive offering).

Identifying and Closing Adoption Gaps

A useful approach to managing product adoption involves identifying and eliminating impediments at the different stages of the adoption process. One approach to removing such impediments begins with identifying the dispersion of customers across different stages of the adoption process. Consider the scenario illustrated in Figure 2 below.

Figure 2. Analyzing Product Adoption: The Decision Tree Approach

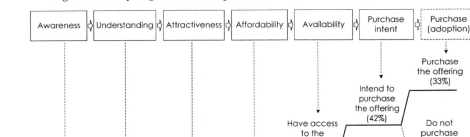

Here, 78% of all target customers are aware of the company's offering; 71% are both aware of the offering and understand its value; 63% are aware of the offering, understand its value, and find it attractive; 57% are aware of the offering, understand its value, and find it attractive and affordable; 49% are aware of the offering, understand its value, find it attractive, affordable, and have access to the offering; 42% are aware of the offering, understand its value, find it attractive, affordable, and available, and intend to purchase it within a given timeframe; and, finally, 33% actually purchase the offering within this timeframe. The dispersion of customers across different stages of the adoption process can be represented in the form of a decision tree whose branches indicate the state of target customers at each step of the adoption process.

The dispersion of customers across different stages of the adoption process can also be represented by a series of bars—a format that visualizes the potential hurdles in the adoption process (Figure 3). Here, the blank part of each bar corresponds to the share of potential customers who have not transitioned to the next stage of the adoption process, whereas the ratio of the blank part to the shaded part reflects the effectiveness of the company's actions at each step in acquiring new customers.

Figure 3: Analyzing Product Adoption: The Gap Approach

| All target customers | Aware of the offering's existence | Understand the offering's benefits | Perceive the offering to be attractive | Can afford the offering | Have access to the offering | Intend to purchase the offering | Purchased the offering |

Comparing the loss of potential customers at each step of the process offers a simple way to identify steps with a disproportionate drop in product adoption. These disproportionate drops in the product adoption process are also referred to as *adoption gaps*. To illustrate, consider the adoption chart in Figure 4. It indicates that the largest drops occur in steps 2 (communicating the benefits of the offering) and 3 (perceived attractiveness of the offering). The next largest drop in adoptions occurs at the point of forming intent to purchase the offering within the given timeframe (step 6).

Figure 4: Identifying Adoption Gaps

| All target customers | Aware of the offering's existence | Understand the offering's benefits | Perceive the offering to be attractive | Can afford the offering | Have access to the offering | Intend to purchase the offering | Purchased the offering |

The gap analysis can be used both to pinpoint the problem spots in product adoption and to identify specific *solutions* to close adoption gaps. Some of the most common solutions for closing performance gaps at the different stages of the adoption process are outlined below.

- A gap at *step 1* calls for increasing target customers' awareness of the offering. This can be achieved by optimizing company, collaborator, and third-party communications. In particular, optimizing company communications can be achieved by increasing the magnitude of communication expenditures and increasing the effectiveness and cost efficiency of these resources (e.g., by streamlining the message, developing a better creative solution, and using more effective media in a more cost-efficient manner). In addition to directly communicating the availability of the offering to target customers, the company can also involve some of its current collaborators to create awareness among target customers, as well as to identify new collaborators explicitly for the purpose of promoting the offering. Finally, the company may stimulate third-party communications that promote the offering (e.g., by encouraging product adoption by opinion leaders and facilitating the creation and functioning of early-adopter forums and user groups).

- A gap at *step 2* calls for increasing target customers' understanding of the true benefits and costs of the offering. As in the case of closing awareness gaps, a gap in customers' understanding of the offering's value can be closed by optimizing company, collaborator, and third-party communications. The key difference is that the focus of communications here is on improving the understanding of the value of the offering rather than simply creating awareness of its existence. In addition to using advertising, public relations, and personal communications, communicating the benefits of an offering can be effectively achieved by providing target customers with an option to experience the offering (e.g., using product samples and demos).

- A gap at *step 3* calls for improving the expected value of the offering. This typically can be achieved by reformulating/redesigning the offering to increase its perceived benefits and/or decrease its expected costs. This reformulation can involve permanent changes in the product, service, branding, and pricing aspects of the offering, as well as the use of incentives to improve the overall value proposition of the current offering.

- A gap at *step 4* indicates that target customers do not consider the offering to be affordable. For example, a customer may be aware of the existence of the Porsche GT, understand its benefits and costs, and find its value proposition attractive, yet not be able to afford its hefty price tag. One solution to increase sales volume in this case is to improve affordability of the offering. The intuitive solution is to lower the price or introduce price incentives targeting the desired customer segment. Lowering the price and introducing price incentives, however, while potentially increasing the sales volume, may eventually lead to a decline in sales revenues as well—a scenario that can occur when the marginal increase in the sales volume generated by the price cut cannot offset the decline in revenues associated with the drop in price. An alternative approach to circumvent the affordability barrier involves changing the perceived importance of the benefits provided by the offering so that customers reallocate additional resources to this offering in their budget planning.

- A gap at *step 5* indicates that the offering is not available to all target customers. To illustrate, an offering may be in short supply because a company underestimated its appeal to target customers or because of inadequate distribution coverage. The logical solution to increase sales volume in this case is to improve the offering's availability. This can be achieved by (1) ramping up production to meet demand, (2) improving the geographical coverage of the offering's distribution channels to offer its target customers better accessibility to the offering, and (3) improving channel operations to minimize logistical stock-outs.

- A gap at *step 6* indicates that target customers have no intention to purchase the offering within the timeframe set by the company. For example, a customer may have a general intention to buy a new car without having a specific timeframe in mind. The logical solution to increase sales volume in this case is to facilitate the formulation of purchase intent within the desired timeframe. Strategies to achieve this involve introducing time-sensitive incentives as well as making salient the immediate gratification from purchasing the offering.

- A gap at *step 7* indicates that target customers fail to act upon purchase intention. To illustrate, a consumer may fail to act upon the intent to purchase the offering because of unexpected budgetary constraints. To increase sales volume in this case, a company needs to improve the conversion of the purchase intent into purchase behavior. As in the case of facilitating the formation of purchase intent, the conversion of this intent into actual behavior can be facilitated by introducing time-sensitive incentives, as well as making salient the immediate gratification from purchasing the offering.

Managing Product Usage

The discussion so far has focused on increasing sales volume by concentrating on product adoption by new customers. In addition to increasing adoption by new customers, in many cases, an offering's sales volume can also be increased by influencing its usage by current customers. To identify the optimal product usage strategy for increasing sales volume, it is important to first understand factors that determine the process by which customers repurchase the offering, identify impediments to achieving the desired product usage, and develop an action plan to remove these impediments. These aspects of managing product usage are discussed in more detail in the following sections.

Understanding the Product Repurchase Process

From a customer's perspective, product repurchase can be viewed as a multistep process in which each step identifies a factor essential for repurchase. In particular, five key factors in product repurchase can be distinguished: satisfaction, usage frequency, usage quantity, and repurchase intent (Figure 5).

Figure 5: The Product Repurchase Process

The five key steps of product repurchase can be summarized as follows:

- *Satisfaction* reflects the degree to which customers find the offering attractive after having experienced it. Unlike the attractiveness stage in product adoption, which is based on customers' expectations of an offering's attractiveness, satisfaction reflects customers' postconsumption evaluation of the offering. Thus, satisfaction is a function of customers' experience of the benefits and costs of the offering.

- *Frequency* reflects the rate at which customers use the offering. For example, in the case of toothpaste, frequency refers to the number of times people use toothpaste to brush their teeth. The frequency of usage is a function of factors such as customers' satisfaction with the offering, their awareness of the offering and its optimal usage frequency, their understanding of the optimal usage rate, the affordability of the offering and its availability for repurchase, as well as customers' existing usage habits.

- *Quantity* reflects the amount of the offering customers consume on each usage occasion. This step is relevant for offerings where the quantity consumed on a given usage occasion is determined by customers. For example, in the case of toothpaste, quantity refers to the amount of toothpaste people use to brush their teeth.

  Based on the nature of the offering, two types of usage can be distinguished: volume-based usage and time-based usage. Volume-based usage reflects a scenario in which the usage quantity is determined by the actual amount of the item consumed on a given usage occasion (e.g., soft drinks, laundry detergent, toothpaste, and mobile phone service). In contrast, time-based usage reflects a scenario in which the product is offered in units, and each unit is used across multiple usage occasions (e.g., printer cartridges, water filters, and shaving blades). Here the usage quantity is determined by the number of occasions on which the item is used.

  Similar to the case of usage frequency, usage quantity is a function of factors such as customers' satisfaction with the offering, their awareness of the optimal usage rate, their understanding of the optimal usage rate, the affordability of the offering, its availability for repurchase, and customers' existing usage habits. In addition, usage quantity is also a function of the physical characteristics of the offering, such as packaging size and usage management features (e.g., dosage cup in laundry detergents).

- *Repurchase intent* reflects customers' intent to repurchase the offering within a particular timeframe. Thus, customers' satisfaction with the offering does not guarantee that they will necessarily form an intent to repurchase the company's offering; they may instead decide to purchase a competitor's offering. Even if customers remain loyal to the company, this does not necessarily imply that they will form an intention to repurchase the offering within the timeframe determined by the company's sales goals.

- *Repurchase* involves customers' actual reacquisition of the offering. Formulating intent to repurchase the offering in a given timeframe does not guarantee that customers will actually do so. A number of factors may either delay customers' acting on their intent (e.g., anticipation of future price cuts) or lead to customers deciding not to repurchase the product (e.g., introduction of a superior offering).

Identifying and Closing Usage Gaps

A functional approach to managing product usage calls for identifying and eliminating impediments at the different stages of the repurchase process. This can be achieved by identifying the dispersion of customers across different stages of the usage process (Figure 6).

Figure 6: Identifying Gaps in Product Repurchase

①	②	③	④	⑤

Purchased the offering | Satisfied with the offering | Use the offering frequently | Use adequate quantity per occasion | Intend to repurchase the offering | Repurchase the offering

Comparing the loss of potential customers at each stage of the repurchase process offers a simple way to identify stages in which there are disproportionate drops in product usage. These disproportionate drops are commonly referred to as *usage gaps*. In addition to pinpointing the hurdles in product repurchase, usage gap analysis also identifies specific *solutions* for closing these gaps. The most common solutions for closing usage gaps at the different stages of the repurchase process are outlined below.

- A gap at *step 1* calls for improving customer *satisfaction* with the offering. This can be achieved by improving actual product performance, for example by optimizing its design, functionality, and user friendliness.

- A gap at *step 2* calls for increasing customers' usage rate of the offering. This can be achieved by improving customers' satisfaction with the offering, their awareness of the optimal usage rate, and their understanding of its benefits by increasing the affordability of the offering and its availability for repurchase, and by changing customers' usage-rate habits. To illustrate, to increase sales volume from its current customers, Campbell Soup Company launched an advertising campaign to promote the use of its soup during summer. In the same vein, Arm & Hammer promotes baking soda not only for baking, but also as a household cleaner and deodorizer.

- A gap at *step 3* calls for increasing the *usage quantity* of the offering. This can be achieved by improving customers' satisfaction with the offering, their awareness of the optimal usage quantity and their understanding of its benefits; by increasing the affordability of the offering and its availability for repurchase; and by changing customers' existing usage-quantity habits. For example, to change consumers' usage habits, many shampoo companies have included the word "repeat" in usage instructions.

Usage quantity can also be managed by reformulating and/or redesigning the product in a way that will lead to greater consumption. One approach to achieve this goal involves increasing the size of the packaging in categories where increased package size typically leads to a greater usage quantity (e.g., laundry detergents as well as many food and beverage products). For example, PepsiCo's introduction of the larger, two-liter bottle in 1970 resulted in increased consumption of Pepsi products.

An alternative strategy involves designing the product in a way that ensures dispensing the optimal quantity per usage occasion. To illustrate, to increase the quantity of ketchup consumed at each usage occasion, Heinz introduced a plastic squeeze bottle, increased the size of the opening in the bottle neck, and designed the "upside-down bottle" in which ketchup is ready to be poured without having to wait for the contents to slide down to the opening of the bottle. Similarly, liquid laundry detergents often have caps that can be used to measure the optimal usage quantity, and solid detergents typically include measuring cups inside the box.

Using product design can also be effective in cases of time-based usage, where usage quantity is determined by the number of occasions on which the same item is used. For example, to encourage customers to replace their toothbrush, Gillette added blue indicator bristles on its Oral B toothbrush, which at a certain point faded halfway to alert users of the need to replace their brush. The new design was prominently featured in its advertising: "When the blue is gone, it's time to move on."

- A gap at *step 4* calls for facilitating the formulation of an *intent to repurchase the offering* within the desired timeframe. This can be achieved by creating awareness of the product's scarcity as well as by offering time-sensitive incentives encouraging customers to repurchase the offering within a specific timeframe. For example, printer manufacturers include toner-level indicators to alert users that the cartridge will soon need replacement. Similarly, to ensure that customers have milk in ready supply, the California Milk Processor Board launched the famous "Got Milk?" campaign in 1993, featuring scenarios in which customers consuming complementary products (e.g., chocolate-chip cookies and cereal) are deprived of milk.

- A gap at *step 5* calls for improving the conversion of repurchase intent into repurchase behavior. As in the case of facilitating the formation of repurchase intent, the conversion of this intent into actual behavior can be facilitated by creating awareness of the product's scarcity as well as by offering time-sensitive incentives encouraging customers to repurchase the offering within a specific timeframe. Ensuring an offering's availability at the time of purchase is also an important factor in encouraging the desired repurchase behavior. Another important and often overlooked aspect of managing the conversion of repurchase intent into behavior involves ensuring continuity in the product's appearance, functionality, and availability. Indeed, a dramatic change in an offering's marketing mix (e.g., packaging, branding, pricing, and distribution) can result in customers reevaluating their purchase intent, postponing their purchase decision, or even switching to a competitor's offering.

Summary

Sales growth is a key factor for achieving sustainable profitability. There are two core strategies for increasing the sales volume of a company's offerings: increasing product adoptions by new customers and increasing product usage by current customers.

Product adoption can be viewed as a multistage process comprising the following six key factors: awareness (knowledge of the existence of the offering), understanding (comprehension of the benefits and costs of the offering), attractiveness (utility customers expect to receive from the offering), affordability (customer perceptions of their ability to pay for the offering), availability (degree to which the offering is accessible by target customers), and purchase intent (intention to purchase the offering within a particular timeframe). A useful approach to managing product adoption involves identifying and eliminating impediments (adoption gaps) at the different stages of the adoption process.

In addition to increasing adoption by new customers, in many cases, an offering's sales volume can also be increased by influencing its usage (and, hence, repurchase frequency) by current customers. Product repurchase can be viewed as a multistage process comprising the following four factors: satisfaction (the degree to which customers find the offering attractive after having experienced it), usage frequency (rate at which customers use the offering), usage quantity (amount of the offering customers consume on each usage occasion), and repurchase intent (intent to repurchase the offering within a particular timeframe). A useful approach to managing product usage involves identifying and eliminating impediments (usage gaps) at the different stages of the repurchase process.

Relevant Concepts

Conversion Rate: The number of potential customers who have tried the product/service relative to the total number of customers aware of the product/service.

$$\text{Conversion rate} = \frac{\text{Current and former customers}}{\text{Potential customers aware of the offering}}$$

Customer Attrition Rate (Churn Rate): The number of customers who discontinue using a company's product or service during a specified time period relative to the average total number of customers over that same time period.

$$\text{Customer attrition rate} = \frac{\text{Number of customers who disadopt an offering during a specific period}}{\text{Total number of customers during that period}}$$

Market Size: Monetary value of an existing or potential market, typically measured on an annual basis. Market size is also used in reference to the number of customers comprising a particular market.

Pareto Principle: The 80/20 relationship discovered in the late 1800s by the economist Vilfredo Pareto.[2] Pareto established that 80% of the land in Italy was owned by 20% of the population. He later observed that 20% of the peapods in his garden yielded 80% of the peas that were harvested. The Pareto Principle, or the 80/20 Rule, has proven its validity in a number of other areas. In marketing, the most common illustration of the 80/20 rule is that 80% of revenues are often generated by 20% of customers (or products).

Penetration Rate: The number of customers who have tried the offering at least once relative to the total number of potential customers.

$$\text{Penetration rate} = \frac{\text{Current and former customers}}{\text{Potential customers}}$$

Retention Rate: The number of customers who have repurchased the offering during the current buying cycle (e.g., month, quarter, year) relative to the number of customers who have purchased the offering during the last cycle. Also used in reference to the number of customers who have repurchased the offering relative to the total number of customers who have tried the product at least once.

$$\text{Retention rate} = \frac{\text{Active customers during the current period}}{\text{Active customers during the last period}}$$

Additional Readings

Aaker, David A. (2007), *Strategic Market Management* (8th ed.). New York, NY: John Wiley & Sons.

Best, Roger J. (2004), *Market-Based Management: Strategies for Growing Customer Value and Profitability* (3rd ed.). Upper Saddle River, NJ: Prentice Hall.

Kumar, Nirmalya (2004), *Marketing as Strategy: The CEO's Agenda for Driving Growth and Innovation.* Boston, MA: Harvard Business School Press.

Notes

[1] Note that the sequence of these steps in the adoption process may vary across products and customers. The model presented in Figure 1 reflects the most common sequence.

[2] Koch, Richard (1998), *The 80/20 Principle: The Secret to Success by Achieving More with Less.* New York, NY: Doubleday.

Chapter Seventeen

Managing New Products

Companies launch new product offerings for a variety of reasons: to satisfy constantly changing consumer preferences, explore market opportunities, and respond to competitive threats. The key aspects of designing and managing new product offerings are the focus of this chapter.

Overview

The term "new products" has dual meaning: it is used in reference to products and services that are new to the company but not new to target customers (often referred to as "new-to-the-company" products), as well as to products and services that are new to the company and its target customers (often referred to as "new-to-the-world" products). New-to-the-company offerings usually involve using new processes to create the product, using new ways to communicate its benefits, and finding new distribution channels to deliver the product to target customers. The key in this case is that while these innovations are novel to the company, they have already been adopted by competitors and, hence, are already familiar to target customers. In contrast, new-to-the-world innovations are new not only to the company, but to target customers as well.

Depending on their novelty to target customers, new-to-the-world products can be either extensions of an existing category (often referred to as "slightly new" products) or can create their own category (often referred to as "really new" products). Slightly new products typically operate within the boundaries of an existing product category, target customers who are familiar with the offering's core value proposition, and compete with offerings from the same product category. To illustrate, slightly new products are different variants of an existing offering (e.g., different colors, flavors, tastes, sizes, designs, or packaging variations of an existing core product). In contrast, really new offerings typically create a new product category. Examples of really new products include Amazon.com (online retailing), eBay (consumer-to-consumer online auctions), Priceline.com (reverse-price auctions), TiVo (personal digital recorders), and SlingBox (TV-to-computer video streaming).

It is important to note that the boundaries between the slightly new and really new products are not well defined. In this context, it is more useful to think of the newness of the offering to target customers as a continuum, where minor variations to existing offerings are at one extreme and truly novel offerings that create their own category are at the other extreme.

The Concept of Product Life Cycle

Managing new products and services can be better understood when considered in the context of their entire life cycle. The product life cycle is a concept that describes the general trend of products and services as they progress through different stages in the marketplace.[1] It can be defined in terms of a product category (e.g., flat screen TVs), product class (e.g., LCD TVs), or particular product form (e.g., 42" LCD TVs). The concept of a product life cycle is based on four key assumptions: (1) products have a limited life, (2) they pass through distinct stages, (3) their profitability depends on the stage, and, as a result, (4) different stages require different marketing strategies. In this context, four key product life cycle stages are identified: introduction, growth, maturity, and decline.

During the introduction stage, product awareness is low and there are very few competitors; hence, the company's primary goal tends to be creating awareness and educating customers about the benefits of the product. As the product takes off during the growth stage, the number of competitors entering the market increases. In this context, the company's goal is likely to change from customer education to differentiation from the competition. At maturity, the number of competitors tends to peak, the market becomes saturated, and industry profitability starts to decline because of intensifying competition. Finally, the decline stage is characterized by declining demand for the product, relatively low profitability, and a decreasing number of competitors stemming from consolidation and exit from the market. The four stages of product life cycle and the corresponding market conditions at each stage are illustrated in Figure 1.

Figure 1. Product Life Cycle[2]

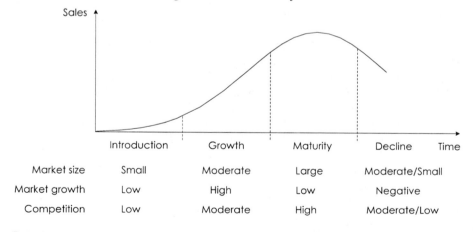

	Introduction	Growth	Maturity	Decline
Market size	Small	Moderate	Large	Moderate/Small
Market growth	Low	High	Low	Negative
Competition	Low	Moderate	High	Moderate/Low

It is important to note that the bell-shaped curve shown in Figure 1 is merely a stylized example of the product life cycle. In reality, many products and services follow different patterns that, for example, may include multiple peaks at different stages of the life cycle. In this context, the product-life-cycle curve is primarily a descriptive tool used to illustrate the general trend of products as they go through different stages in the market. It is not designed to predict the future market success of a particular product, nor exactly when it reaches the growth, maturity, and decline stage.

Understanding New Product Adoption

Understanding the process of new product adoption is essential for the company to be able to forecast demand for its offerings and optimize them in a way that facilitates their adoption by target customers.

Diffusion of innovations describes the process of adopting new ideas, products, services, and technologies. The process of diffusion of an innovation can be represented by an S-curve, which depicts the total number of adoptions at any given point in time. The pattern of the diffusion process can be defined by two key characteristics: (1) the size of the potential market, indicating the total number of users that will ultimately adopt the innovation, and (2) the speed of diffusion, which can be defined by the timeframe for reaching the inflection point—the point at which the rate of growth slows down and starts declining (the place where the shape of the diffusion curve turns from convex to concave). A typical S-shaped diffusion curve is shown in Figure 2.

Figure 2. The Typical S-Shaped Pattern of New Product Adoption

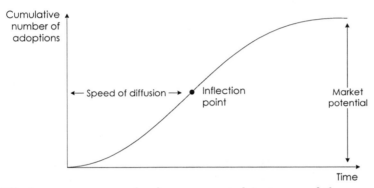

The diffusion process can also be represented in terms of the number of new (rather than cumulative) adoptions of the innovation at any given point in time. In this context, the process of adoption of innovation can be represented by a bell-shaped curve, whereby, after a relatively slow start, an increasing number of people adopt the innovation until it reaches a peak, then starts declining as the number of potential adopters decreases. Note that the noncumulative pattern of adoption illustrated in Figure 3 directly corresponds to the cumulative pattern given in Figure 2, with the key difference that Figure 3 illustrates the pattern of dispersion of new adoptions over time instead of the total number of current users of an innovation.

Figure 3. The Typical Bell-Shaped Pattern of New Product Adoption

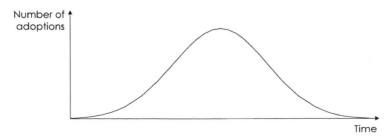

The bell-shaped diffusion pattern is based on the assumption that the adoption of an innovation can be represented by a normal distribution. This assumption, however, is not always a realistic one. Indeed, some innovations are adopted very rapidly, whereas others take a substantial amount of time to achieve their peak adoption period. Thus, an innovation may be adopted almost instantly by a large segment of the population and then diffused at a much slower rate until it is adopted by all target customers (Figure 4). While some innovations enjoy rapid adoption, others are adopted at a much slower rate (e.g., in the case where benefits are not readily apparent or the innovation is not heavily promoted by the company) and reach the point at which they are adopted by the majority of its target customers relatively late in the adoption process.

Figure 4. New Product Adoption: Fast and Slow Diffusion Scenarios

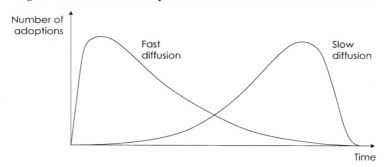

A popular interpretation of the bell-shaped curve of noncumulative product adoptions involves classifying customers into distinct categories based on their adoption pattern. The two most influential frameworks offering such classifications are the ones advanced by Everett Rogers and Geoffrey Moore, discussed at the end of this chapter.

Developing the Marketing Mix

The process of managing a new offering typically involves deciding on its product, service, brand, price, incentives, communication, and distribution characteristics. The key aspects of these decisions are outlined below.

Product Management

Product strategies vary as a function of the product's stage in its life cycle. Thus, at the introduction stage, companies typically offer a single product variant, targeted at the most likely adopters. As the product enters the growth stage, the number of customers adopting the product increases and so does the heterogeneity of these customers. To address the different needs of their current and potential customers, companies add product extensions designed to better meet the needs of various customer subsegments. The variety of product variants peaks at maturity and starts decreasing as the product enters its decline stage; profit margins shrink, and companies focus on best-seller products, phasing out products with insufficient volume to meet their profitability benchmarks.

The successful introduction of a new product/service is a function of several key factors: (1) its relative advantage (the relative benefits and costs) over the product it replaces, (2) transparency of the new offering's relative advantage (the degree to which the relative advantage of the new offering is readily observable and can be experienced by target customers), (3) compatibility of the new offering with customers' existing systems and processes, and (4) perceived risk stemming from the uncertainty associated with the product's performance (e.g., customer uncertainty about their own preferences, uncertainty about the product's future performance, and uncertainty about the magnitude of the risks associated with the new product).

An important aspect of new product decisions involves managing the evolution of the company's products over time. Thus, as products become obsolete, they are often replaced by a new generation of products that take advantage of market structure changes, such as changes in customer preferences, alterations in the competitive landscape, advances in technology, and changes in the regulatory environment. Thus, through innovation, companies can extend the life cycle of their individual products (Figure 5). To illustrate, consider Gillette's product development strategy leading to the introduction of Fusion, its eighth-generation wet-shaving razor. Gillette's original razor introduced in 1903 was replaced by the second-generation razor Trac II (1971), followed by Sensor (1990), SensorExcel (1995), MACH3 (1998), MACH3 Turbo (2002), M3 Power (2004), and Fusion (2006).

When developing a new generation of products, companies often develop strategies to make the earlier generation obsolete, a process often referred to as planned obsolescence. Planned obsolescence involves designing new products in a way that will make prior generations inferior (and, therefore, obsolete) on key dimensions such as functionality, compatibility, and style. To illustrate, to facilitate user migration to later versions of its operating system, Microsoft systematically terminates its support (e.g., software upgrades) for earlier versions. In addition, the added functionality of the new generations of its software often limits this software's backward compatibility; as a result, once the new software has been adopted by a critical mass of users, the earlier versions become obsolete because of their incompatibility. In the same vein, when designing new models, car manufactures often use styling to make previous models obsolete, thus encouraging customers to upgrade.

Figure 5. Extending Product Life Cycle through Innovation

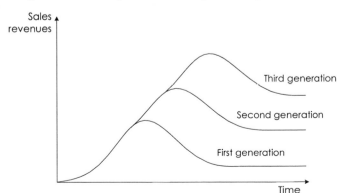

One important implication of planned obsolescence for new product design involves managing a new product's costs by optimizing its performance during its expected lifetime, a process often referred to as value engineering. For example, a company expecting its product to be obsolete within a given timeframe may optimize costs by designing the durability of product's components according to the expected product lifetime.

Brand Management

A key question in developing new offerings is that of branding. There are several options a company can choose: extend an existing brand to a new category (e.g., Heinz mustard), launch a new sub-brand under an existing umbrella brand (e.g., Apple iPhone), or create a new, free-standing brand (e.g., Nexium).

The primary reason to use an existing brand for a new offering is to leverage its customer equity. Indeed, using an existing brand is likely to facilitate the adoption of the offering by customers for whom the brand has positive equity in a cost-efficient and timely fashion. Using an established brand can also facilitate the company's ability to convince channel members to carry the new product. An important drawback of this strategy is that using an existing brand may limit the company's ability to attach a specific meaning to this brand in the context of the new product category (e.g., Heinz All-Natural Cleaning Vinegar, Harley-Davidson Cake Decorating Kit, and Kellogg Special K2 Protein Water). Brand extensions may also dilute the meaning associated with the original brand. Furthermore, poor performance of the new product can easily spill over and hurt the reputation of the entire brand.

Developing a strong new brand, on the other hand, typically requires significant resources and time. Launching a new brand is generally a better strategy in cases where the meaning associated with the existing brands in the company's portfolio is inconsistent with the image that the company needs to create for its new offering in order to optimize its value to target customers. Creating its own brand when pioneering a new category creates a unique opportunity for the company to associate its name with the entire category. To illustrate, brands like Google (information search), Amazon.com (e-commerce), eBay (online auctions), and Xerox (copying) have become virtual synonyms for the entire category. Thus, creating strong brand-category associations enables the company to recapture some of its marketing expenses in the form of brand equity.

Price Management

When launching a new offering, two core pricing strategies can be distinguished: skim pricing and penetration pricing.

Skim pricing involves setting a high initial price to "skim the cream" off the top of the market, represented by customers who value the offering's benefits and are not price sensitive. By setting high initial prices, skim pricing maximizes profit margins, usually at the expense of market share. Skimming tends to be more appropriate in cases where: (1) demand is relatively inelastic and lowering the price is not likely to substantially increase sales volume, (2) there is little or no competition for the target segment, (3) cost is not a direct function of volume—significant cost savings are not achieved as cumulative volume increases, (4) being the market pioneer is unlikely to result in a sustainable competitive advantage, and (5) the company lacks the capital expenditures required for volume production.

Penetration pricing involves setting relatively low prices in an attempt to gain higher sales volume, albeit at relatively low margins. Penetration pricing tends to be more appropriate in cases where: (1) the demand is relatively elastic—that is, lowering the price is likely to substantially increase sales volume, (2) the target segment becomes increasingly competitive, (3) cost is a function of volume and, as a result, significant cost savings are expected as cumulative volume increases, and (4) being the market pioneer is likely to result in a sustainable competitive advantage.

Incentives Management

Most new product/service incentives fall into one of three categories: incentives given to customers, incentives given to collaborators (e.g., channel members), and incentives given to company personnel.

Customer incentives (e.g., coupons, rebates, volume discounts, price reductions, premiums, rewards, and sweepstakes) are used by companies to achieve three primary goals: (1) to tailor the value of its new offering to the needs of different customer segments, (2) in response to a competitor's promotion, and (3) to better manage customers' rate of adoption of its new product. Thus, a company may offer different incentives to different customer segments based on the needs and resources of these customers and the strategic importance of these customers to the company (e.g., by giving substantial discounts to opinion leaders who could influence other potential buyers). Similarly, when introducing a new offering, companies often face competitive reaction, usually in the form of incentives given to potential buyers, and have to counter these incentives to make their offering appealing to target customers. Incentives are also used to manage the speed of adoption of the new offering by target customers. Thus, customers may form an intention to purchase a product without acting upon it (e.g., because of monetary and/or time constraints). In this case, by offering time-sensitive incentives, a company can encourage these customers to act upon their intent within a given timeframe. Incentives are often used to stimulate off-season sales (e.g., convertible cars introduced in the fall can use incentives to encourage forward buying).

Channel incentives are typically used for several reasons: (1) to gain shelf space for new products (e.g., through slotting allowances), (2) to encourage channel members to carry higher levels of inventory to avoid stock-outs (e.g., through stocking allowances, inventory financing, and volume discounts), (3) to encourage channel members to promote new products (e.g., through advertising and display allowances), and (4) to offset the impact of competitive promotions (e.g., through competitive price-matching incentives).

Company incentives involve various rewards aimed at the company's personnel, which can include the functional areas involved in developing and managing the new offering, such as management, engineers, and the sales force. Company incentives can involve monetary bonuses, recognition awards, contests, free goods and services, prizes, sweepstakes, and games.

Communication Management

The communications associated with a new offering typically pursue one or more of the following three goals: (1) create awareness of the new offering, (2) create a preference for the offering, and (3) incite an action (e.g., purchase the offering, contact the company for information).

The selection of a communication goal is typically a function of the offering's stage in its life cycle. Thus, because new products are, by definition, not familiar to target customers, the communication campaign at the early stages of new product introduction aims primarily at creating awareness among the early adopters, as well as among channel partners. As the product enters the growth stage, a company's communication goals shift to creating awareness of the product among the mass market while at the same time differentiating its offerings from those of competitors in response to increasing competition. As the product enters its maturity stage and the majority of customers are aware of the category benefits, communication focus shifts from creating awareness of the category benefits to differentiating the company's offering by highlighting its benefits vis-à-vis the competition. This emphasis on product differentiation continues as the product enters its decline stage; however, overall communication expenditures tend to decline.

Communications associated with a new offering are typically a function of two key factors: (1) communications initiated by the company and/or its collaborators and (2) communications initiated by a third party. Company/collaborator communications include activities such as advertising, press releases, event sponsoring, product placement, trade shows, free samples, free trials, sales force communications, and various other promotional incentives. In contrast, third-party communications include factors such as word of mouth, third-party media coverage (reviews, blogs, endorsements), and noncompensated endorsements.

From a chronological perspective, a company's own promotions typically precede third-party communications, whereby the release of a new product is accompanied by (and often preceded by) a targeted promotional campaign. Third-party communications are then generated by early adopters of the offering, who either deliberately or unintentionally make other potential buyers aware of the existence and the benefits of the offering (Figure 6). On many occasions, however, third-party communications precede the company's promotions. For example, Google, eBay, and Netscape relied primarily on third-party effects to build their initial customer base and started promoting their offering on a large scale only after achieving a certain level of growth.

In general, while third-party communications can facilitate the new product adoption process, they also can have a detrimental impact on product adoptions. Indeed, in cases where a new offering is perceived as unattractive, it can generate unfavorable third-party communications that may slow down the rate of the adoption process and decrease the overall market potential of the offering. To illustrate, helped by a massive advertising campaign, the movie "Hulk," released by Universal Pictures in 2003, became number one at the box office, with one of the highest grossing opening weekends of all time, only to be followed by a record 70% drop in ticket sales the second week. The drop stemmed from mixed reviews and negative word of mouth. In contrast, "My Big Fat Greek Wedding," released by IFC Films in 2002 with a relatively small advertising budget, was ranked twentieth at the box office its first week, steadily gained share from positive word of mouth and 20 weeks later, became the number two grossing movie.

Figure 6. Product Adoptions as a Function of Company, Collaborator, and Third-Party Communications

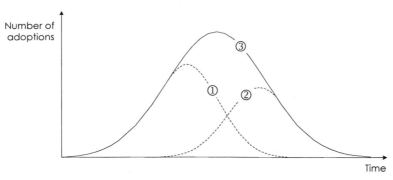

① Adoptions due to company and collaborator communications

② Adoptions due to third-party communications

③ Total adoptions

Managing promotional efforts in an effective and cost-efficient manner requires optimizing the impact of company, collaborator, and third-party communications. Thus, when the anticipated effects of third-party communications are likely to be strong (e.g., because of the shared consumption experience as in the case of movies and computer games), then an effective and cost-efficient communications strategy may involve an emphasis on third-party communications. In contrast, in cases where third-party communications are unlikely (e.g., because of the private nature of consumption or competitive issues in business-to-business markets), reliance on company and collaborator communications is crucial to ensure adoption.

Distribution Management

When designing the distribution aspect of its new offering, a company needs to decide on several key factors: channel structure (e.g., direct, indirect, or hybrid), channel ownership (e.g., ownership-based or contractual), channel type (e.g., specialized or broad), channel coverage (e.g., selective or intensive), and channel exclusivity (e.g., exclusive or not exclusive). More information on different distribution strategies is offered in Chapter 15.

As a general rule, the distribution strategy at a given point in a new product's life cycle is a function of the offering's overall strategy. Thus, in the case of offerings following a skimming strategy, distribution at the introduction stage tends to be more selective (e.g., specialty distributors), aiming to make the product available to early adopters. As the number of likely adopters increases, distribution becomes more intensive to include a broad range of distribution channels (e.g., mass merchandisers and volume resellers). In contrast, an offering following a market-penetration strategy is likely to pursue an intensive distribution strategy even at the early stages of its life cycle. As the popularity of the offering starts decreasing and it enters its decline stage, companies begin phasing out less profitable channels, focusing on those channels that are either likely to remain profitable or have strategic importance to the company (e.g., resulting from synergies with other offerings).

Summary

The term "new product" is used in reference to products and services that are new to the company but not new to target customers (often referred to as "new-to-the-company" products), as well as to products and services that are new to the company and its target customers (often referred to as "new-to-the-world" products).

Managing new products and services can be better understood when considered in the context of their entire life cycle. The concept of a product life cycle is based on four key assumptions: (1) products have a limited life, (2) they pass through distinct stages, (3) their profitability depends on the stage, and (4) different stages require different marketing strategies. In this context, four key product life cycle stages are identified: introduction, growth, maturity, and decline.

The process of new product adoption can be represented using an S-curve, which depicts the total number of adoptions at any given point in time. The diffusion process can also be represented in terms of the number of new (rather than cumulative) adoptions of the innovation at any given point in time. In this context, the process of adoption of innovation can be represented by a bell-shaped curve, whereby, after a relatively slow start, an increasing number of people adopt the innovation until it reaches a peak, then starts declining as the number of potential adopters decreases.

The process of managing a new offering typically involves deciding on its product, service, brand, price, incentives, communication, and distribution aspects.

Relevant Frameworks: Rogers' Model of Adoption of Innovations

The key premise underlying the Rogers model is that some consumers are inevitably more open to adaptation than others.[3] Based on the relative time of adoption of innovations, the Rogers model distinguishes five categories of customers (Figure 7): innovators (the first 2.5% of the adopters), early adopters (the 13.5% of the adopters following the innovators), early majority (the next 34% of adopters), late majority (the next 34%), and laggards (the remaining 16%).

Figure 7. Rogers' Categorization of Customers Based on the Time of Adoption of Innovation[4]

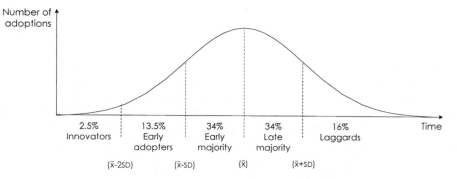

The respective percentage values associated with each category are based on the assumption that the process of adoption of innovations can be represented by a normal distribution, which is defined by two key parameters: its mean ($\bar{x}$) and its standard deviation (SD), a measure of the variation from the mean. In this context, the early and late majorities are defined as being one standard deviation from the mean (34%), whereas early adopters are defined as being two standard deviations from the mean. Note that this classification is not symmetric: There are three categories on the left of the mean and only two on the right. The reason is that the segment on the far left end is further divided into two categories: innovators and early adopters, which cumulatively add up to the size of the laggards segment on the right. The rationale for this division is that these two categories display distinct patterns of adoption behavior and, therefore, from a theoretical standpoint, need to be considered separately.

Despite its popularity, the Rogers model has a number of limitations. One of its key limitations is that it is essentially a classification model; although it identifies the five different categories of adopters of innovation, it does not explain the factors that determine this classification. Thus, for example, this model does not offer a decision rule to determine whether a particular individual will become an early adopter or a laggard. Another limitation is that individuals' classification into one of the five categories is linked to relatively stable personality traits, even though in reality, individuals who are innovators in one domain often may be laggards in another. Additional limitations can be traced back to some of its assumptions, such as the normally shaped distribution of adoption of innovation across the population and the preset percentage allocation of individuals into each of the five categories. As a result, the application of the Rogers' model is limited to a general description of the adoption of the innovation process and to classifying adopters into one of the five categories for descriptive purposes.

Relevant Frameworks: Moore's Model of Adoption of New Technologies

A popular application of Rogers' diffusion theory to technology products is Moore's[5] "chasm" model.[6] Moore argued that the adoption of technology-based innovations is discontinuous because different groups of adaptors have different adoption patterns and, therefore, require different marketing strategies. Moore's model identifies five distinct categories of customers based on their attitudes toward technology, which correspond to Rogers' five categories: technology enthusiasts (innovators), visionaries (early adopters), pragmatists (early majority), conservatives (late majority), and skeptics (laggards). These five categories of adopters can be described as follows:

- *Technology enthusiasts* (innovators) are fundamentally committed to new technology and derive utility from being the first to experience new technologies.

- *Visionaries* (early adopters) are among the first to apply new technologies to solve problems and exploit opportunities in the marketplace.

- *Pragmatists* (early majority) view technology innovation as a productivity tool. Unlike enthusiasts, they do not appreciate technology for its own sake. Unlike visionaries, they do not use technology innovations to change existing business models but rather to optimize the efficiency and effectiveness of existing business models.

- *Conservatives* (late majority) are generally pessimistic about their ability to significantly benefit from new technological innovations and are typically reluctant to adopt them.

- *Skeptics* (laggards) are critics of any innovative technology and are not likely to adopt such technologies even when they offer distinct benefits.

Unlike the Rogers model, which implies smooth and continuous progression across segments over the life of an offering, Moore's model assumes that the adoption of technology-based innovations follows a discontinuous pattern. This discontinuity in the adoption process is attributed to the fact that different groups of adaptors have different adoption patterns and, therefore, require different marketing strategies. Thus, once a technology has reached its market potential within a given segment, it may not naturally roll over to the next segment.

To illustrate, even though an innovation has been adopted by technology enthusiasts, it may never be widely accepted by the next segment, the visionaries. In this context, a company's biggest hurdle in promoting technology innovations is to bridge the gaps between different segments. According to Moore, the key gap between segments—typically referred to as a "chasm"—is the one between the early market (enthusiasts and visionaries) and the mainstream market (pragmatists, conservatives, and skeptics). In this context, the chasm describes the impediments to mainstream commercialization of technology innovations that prevent pioneers from gaining mainstream acceptance of their offerings (Figure 8). Thus, to be successful, an offering needs to "cross the chasm" between the early and the mainstream market.

Figure 8. Moore's Application of the Rogers Model to Technology Markets[7]

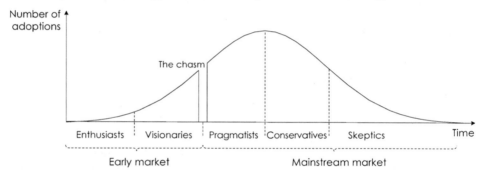

To avoid the perils of discontinuity of adoption of innovations, Moore's model suggests promoting innovations first to technology enthusiasts so that they help educate visionaries. Visionaries, in turn, are likely to serve as a reference for pragmatists, one of the two largest market segments. Leveraging its success with pragmatists, the company should be able to gain the know-how and achieve the economies of scale necessary to make the product reliable and inexpensive so that it meets the needs of conservatives. With respect to skeptics, referred to as "gadflies of high tech," the prescription is to let them be and not promote the innovation to them.

Despite the intuitive appeal of the idea that customers vary in terms of the speed and likelihood of adapting new technologies, Moore's model of technology adoption is subject to several important assumptions that limit the validity of its predictions. Dividing adopters into five distinct categories, as well as predefining the size of each category (e.g., enthusiasts/innovators are the first 2.5% of adapters), often involves an unrealistic assumption that does not apply to all high-tech innovations. Note that this assumption is not an issue for Rogers' model, which assumes continuous adoption across different segments. In contrast, because the presence of gaps between segments is the cornerstone assumption for Moore's model, the identification and size of each segment are crucial. To illustrate, the assumption that a pronounced discontinuity ("chasm") in the adoption process is likely to occur after 16% of customers (the "early market") have adopted the product is not likely to hold universally across different innovation types and industries. In the same vein, relative segment sizes are likely to be a function of the degree to which the technology appeals to the broader market. Indeed, certain types of innovations are likely to have much broader appeal than others and, as a result, the dynamics of their adoption patterns are likely to vary.

Additional Readings

Davidow, William H. (1986), *Marketing High Technology: An Insider's View*. New York, NY: Free Press.

Rogers, Everett M. (2003), *Diffusion of Innovations* (5th ed.). New York, NY: Free Press.

Schneider, Joan and Jeanne Yocum (2004), *New Product Launch: 10 Proven Strategies*. Deerfield, IL: Stagnito Communications.

Grieves, Michael (2006), *Product Lifecycle Management: Driving the Next Generation of Lean Thinking*. New York, NY: McGraw-Hill.

Kahn, Kenneth B. (2005), *The PDMA Handbook of New Product Development* (2nd ed.). Hoboken, NJ: John Wiley & Sons.

Notes

[1] Levitt, Theodore (1965), "Exploit the Product Life Cycle," *Harvard Business Review*, 43, (Nov/Dec), 81–94.

[2] Adapted from Ibid.

[3] Rogers, Everett M. (1962), *Diffusion of Innovations*. New York, NY: Free Press.

[4] Adapted from Ibid.

[5] Not to be confused with Intel's cofounder, Gordon E. Moore, widely known for "Moore's Law."

[6] Moore, Geoffrey A. (1991), *Crossing the Chasm*, New York, NY: HarperBusiness.

[7] Adapted from Ibid.

Chapter Eighteen

Managing Product Lines

The term "product line" is typically used in reference to a set of related offerings that function in a similar manner, are sold to the same target customers, or are distributed through the same channels. Product line management aims to optimize the value delivered by the individual offerings comprising a company's product line. The key aspects of this product-line-value-optimization process are the focus of this chapter.

The Big Picture

From a conceptual standpoint, product line management is similar to managing an individual offering and involves the same structural aspects: goal analysis, strategy analysis, tactical analysis, implementation, and control. The key difference is that in the case of product line management, the focus is on the coordination of each of these aspects across individual offerings. Thus, product line goal analysis relates the objectives of the individual offerings comprising a company's product line; product line strategy analysis identifies the relationship between the offerings' strategies; product line tactical analysis relates the relationship among the tactical aspects of these offerings; product line implementation analysis identifies the personnel and resource allocation across these offerings; and product line control analysis focuses on measures used to evaluate a company's progress toward its product line goals. The first three aspects of product line management—goal, strategy, and tactical management—are illustrated in Figure 1 and discussed in more detail in the following sections.

Figure 1. Product Line Management: The Big Picture

Offering A	Offering B	Offering C	
Goal	Goal	Goal	⇐ Product-line goal
Strategy	Strategy	Strategy	⇐ Product-line strategy
Tactics	Tactics	Tactics	⇐ Product-line tactics
Implementation	Implementation	Implementation	⇐ Product-line implementation
Control	Control	Control	⇐ Product-line control

Product Line Goals

Offerings comprising a company's product line often aim to achieve different goals. Thus, in addition to monetary goals such as profitability, revenue growth, and sales-volume growth, offerings in a company's product line can aim for certain nonmonetary goals, such as strengthening a company's and/or an offering's brand; providing synergies with other, more profitable offerings; preventing competitive entry; and/or establishing share dominance. Offerings comprising a company's product line also can vary in terms of their time horizon: Some offerings aim at providing an immediate impact, whereas others may have longer term goals. Finally, offerings may vary in the magnitude of the anticipated impact; some offerings are likely to have a greater profit, sales volume, or market share impact.

Product line goal management strives to coordinate the goals of individual offerings to optimize their joint performance. Only when considering the goals of an individual offering in the context of the company's entire product line can the true value of this offering be adequately managed. Thus, even though a particular offering may have relatively low direct profit potential, it may play an important role in the company's product line by offering synergies with other, more profitable offerings. To illustrate, laser printers, although not very profitable by themselves, are, nevertheless, an important component of HP's product line, driving the sales of other, more profitable offerings such as printer cartridges.

Product Line Strategy

Product line strategy analysis involves a comparative evaluation of the *market structure* of each individual offering (customers, company, collaborators, competitors, and context), as well as an assessment of the relative *value* of each offering to the relevant market parties: customers, the company, and its collaborators. These two aspects of strategy analysis are discussed in more detail below.

Market Structure

Because of the central role that customer needs play in identifying the company's competitors and collaborators, a starting point in product line market structure analysis entails identifying the customer segmentation underlying the logic of the company's product line. In this context, an important question that needs to be addressed by product line market structure analysis is whether the offerings comprising a company's product line target the same customer segments. In this context, two distinct product line strategies can be identified: (1) a multi-segment product-line strategy, in which offerings target different customer segments and (2) a single-segment product line strategy, in which offerings target the same customer segment.

Product lines targeting different customer segments are typically comprised of offerings featuring substantively different benefits (e.g., higher quality, higher price offerings vs. lower quality, lower price offerings). In contrast, product lines targeting the same customer segments are typically comprised of offerings featuring similar benefits aimed at satisfying the same underlying need (e.g., offerings differentiated by colors, flavors, or taste). The multi-segment and single-segment product lines, illustrated in the context of the company's segmentation and targeting strategy, are depicted in Figure 2.

Figure 2. Multi-Segment and Single-Segment Product Line Strategies: Customer Perspective

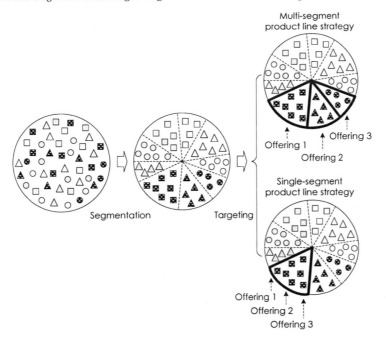

The multi-segment and single-segment strategies may further be represented in a matrix format as shown in Figure 3, which depicts two basic approaches to allocating a company's offerings (O_1, O_2, and O_3) across different target segments (S_1, S_2, and S_3). Note that here the underlying customer segmentation is already given, and the focus of analysis is on allocating individual offerings across the identified segments.

Figure 3. Multi-Segment and Single-Segment Product Line Strategies: Product Mix Perspective

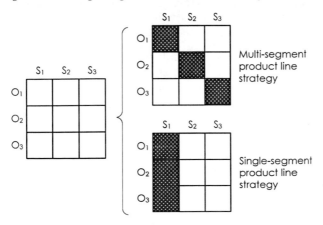

Identifying whether the offerings in a company's product line target the same customers is important because it determines the degree of similarity across their market structures. Thus, offerings targeting the same customer needs are likely to have similar market structures: They are also likely to have the same competitors and collaborators, be driven by the same core competencies and strategic assets of the company, and operate in the same marketing context. In contrast, offerings aimed at different segments are often characterized by different market structures: hey are likely to have different competitors and collaborators, require different competencies and assets from the company, and/or operate in a different marketing context. In general, the greater the similarity of offerings' market structures in a company's product line, the greater the overlap between the strategies of these offerings and the greater the potential for internal conflicts (e.g., profit cannibalization).

Value Proposition

Product line value management aims to ensure that the offerings comprising the product line, considered together, deliver superior value to target customers relative to the competition in a way that enables the company and its collaborators to achieve their strategic goals. Thus, product line value management has three key aspects: customer value management, collaborator value management, and company value management.

▸ Customer Value Proposition

Customer value management aims to optimize the value of each offering in a way that maximizes the value of the entire product line to target customers. It involves evaluating customer benefits and costs associated with multiple offerings in the company's portfolio. In terms of benefits, the presence of multiple offerings increases the probability of a match between a customer's needs and the benefits offered by the company's products and services. In terms of costs, extensive product portfolios, especially when not well differentiated, may complicate the logic of the company's offerings. The goal of customer value management is, therefore, to optimize the benefits and costs of each individual offering with respect to the value delivered by the entire product line.

A key aspect of customer value analysis involves the differentiation strategy underlying the company's product line. In this context, two common product line differentiation strategies can be identified: vertical differentiation and horizontal differentiation. These two strategies are discussed in more detail below.

Vertically differentiated offerings can be easily ordered in terms of the relative attractiveness of their benefits. Because better performance typically comes at a higher price, vertically differentiated product lines are readily differentiated on price as well. When extending its product line, a company can go upscale and/or downscale (Figure 4).

Figure 4. Vertically Differentiated Product Line

An *upscale extension* is characterized by a company's entry (either by developing its own offering or through acquisition) into a market to which it delivers a higher level of benefits at a higher price. Examples of upscale extensions include Volkswagen's entry into the sport/luxury sedan market with Jetta, Passat, and Phaeton; Fiat's entry into the racing car market with the acquisition of Ferrari; Gap's purchase of Banana Republic; Marriott's acquisition of Ritz-Carlton; and Black&Decker's launch of DeWalt. One of the main reasons for introducing an upscale extension is a company's desire to capture a more lucrative, typically higher margin, market.

In contrast, *downscale extensions* are characterized by a company's entry into a market to which it delivers a lower level of benefits at a lower price. Examples of downscale extensions include Intel's introduction of Celeron; United Airline's launch of Ted, and Gap's introduction of Old Navy stores. Downscale extensions are typically driven by the desire to capture larger customer segments, even though a move downscale is typically associated with lower profit margins. Downscale extensions are especially beneficial to companies operating in industries requiring high fixed-cost investments and in which economies of scale may be achieved, such as the airline and automotive industries.

A key challenge in managing the value of a vertically differentiated product line is creating meaningful differences across offerings while at the same time maximizing the competitiveness of each individual offering to target customers. In this context, there are two common mistakes. The first mistake is not sufficiently differentiating the offerings within the company's product line. This is likely to lead to cannibalization of the share of upscale offerings since a significant number of customers will ultimately gravitate toward the lower priced (and usually less profitable) offerings. The second mistake is differentiating the offerings too much, so that they fail to deliver superior value to their target customers. To illustrate, to avoid cannibalization, Intel overstretched its downscale extension Celeron, which resulted in inferior performance relative to its competitors AMD and Cyrix.

The simplest example of a vertically differentiated product line involves a set of two offerings, one of which delivers greater benefits at a higher price. These offerings are often referred to as "regular" vs. "premium," although the specific labels vary across companies and industries (e.g., economy vs. first-class airline service). Slightly more complex is tri-tier positioning, often referred to as "Good–Better–Best," in which the "best" offering delivers the highest level of benefits at the highest price, whereas the "good" offering delivers the lowest level of benefits at the lowest price (e.g., airline service: first, business, and economy class; Microsoft Office products: Microsoft Office Professional, Microsoft Office Home, and Microsoft Works; Figure 5).

Figure 5. "Good–Better–Best" Product Line Strategy

Horizontally differentiated offerings vary on benefits that tend to be subjective and, hence, do not imply a universal preference ordering. To illustrate, different types of soft drinks (regular, cherry, vanilla, diet, caffeine-free), different yogurt flavors, and different product colors comprise horizontally differentiated product lines. Note that although price may vary across horizontally differentiated offerings, it is nevertheless not the key differentiating factor (Figure 6).

Figure 6. Horizontally Differentiated Product Line (Price–Benefit Perspective)

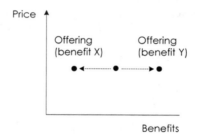

Because price is not the key distinguishing factor in the case of horizontally differentiated offerings, a more meaningful representation of the logic of the company's product line uses factors that represent the trade-offs required from customers. This representation is shown in Figure 7, in which customers have to trade off an offering's performance on two of the key benefits (e.g., power and battery life of a laptop computer, effectiveness and mildness of a laundry detergent, taste and nutrition of a meal).

Figure 7. Horizontally Differentiated Product Line (Benefit Trade-off Perspective)

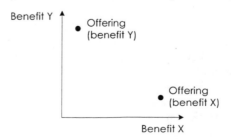

A key challenge in managing the value of a horizontally differentiated product line is creating meaningful differences across offerings without diluting the logic of the product line and complicating customer choice. Indeed, in the absence of meaningful differences in value delivered by the individual offerings in a company's product line, customers are likely to face difficulties deciding among these offerings, which, in turn, is likely to lead to delaying the choice and/or choosing a competitor's offering.

▶ Collaborator Value Proposition

Collaborator value management strives to optimize the benefits and costs associated with each individual offering in the company's product line in a way that maximizes the value of the entire product line to collaborators. To illustrate, consider the impact that extending a company's product line has on its channel partners. In terms of benefits, increasing the number of company offerings in a retailer's portfolio is likely to lead to greater customer satisfaction and an increase in sales revenues. Expanding a company's product line, however, inevitably leads to an increase in retailers' costs. Furthermore, when faced with a stagnant customer demand, expanding a company's product line may lead to cannibalization of retailer sales, with the new offering stealing share from the retailer's other offerings. The goal of collaborator value management, therefore, is to optimize the benefits and costs of each individual offering in order to maximize the value delivered to the company's collaborators by the entire product line. For example, to optimize profitability, retailers often choose to carry only the most profitable offerings from a company's product line, stocking slow-moving items only when incentivized by the manufacturer.

▶ Company Value Proposition

Company value management aims to optimize the value of individual offerings in a way that maximizes the value of the entire product line to the company. Company value management involves evaluating company benefits and costs associated with the presence of multiple offerings in the company's portfolio.

In terms of benefits, the presence of multiple offerings is likely to stimulate customer demand, thus leading to greater sales revenues. Product line extensions can also help to avoid channel conflicts that are likely to occur when distributors with different cost structures and profit margins have identical offerings (also referred to as horizontal channel conflicts). By creating channel-specific product variants, a company can minimize the potential for such conflicts. A comprehensive product line is also likely to prevent competitors from taking advantage of an existing market opportunity.

On the downside, increasing the number of offerings in a company's portfolio is usually associated with increasing product development, production, distribution, and/or management costs, which need to be offset by the revenues generated by the newly introduced offerings. There is also the potential danger that the new offerings will ultimately attract the company's current customers instead of stimulating new customer demand, thus cannibalizing sales of the company's existing offerings. Finally, while helping the company avoid horizontal channel conflicts, product line extensions often lead to vertical channel conflicts, which are driven by the difference in the profit-optimization strategies among the parties in the distribution chain. The nature of the conflict here is the gap between a manufacturer's desire that a retailer carry its entire product line and a retailer's desire to carry only the most profitable, noncompeting offerings from individual manufacturers. In this context, the goal of company value management is to optimize the benefits and costs of each individual offering in a way that maximizes value to the company from its entire product line.

Product Line Tactics

Managing product line tactics involves optimizing the marketing mix (i.e., product, service, brand, price, incentives, communication, and distribution) of individual offerings in a company's product line.

▸ Product and Service Management

From a product line perspective, product and service management aims to optimize the benefits delivered by the product and service aspects of an offering relative to those delivered by the other offerings comprising a company's product line. A key issue in product line management involves deciding on the degree of differentiation of the offerings in a company's product line. Because product and service benefits of an offering are among the key determinants of its value proposition, meaningful differentiation of these benefits is crucial for success. To illustrate, lack of clear differentiation of benefits delivered by the company's products and services can confuse customers, which, in turn, will decrease the probability that potential customers will buy any of the offerings in the company's product line.

▸ Brand Management

From a product line perspective, brand management focuses on issues concerning the branding of the individual offerings comprising the product line. In this context, a key issue involves determining whether different offerings in a company's product line should share the same brand, be positioned as sub-brands of a parent brand, or be positioned as new brands. The benefits of using the same brand for all offerings in a company's product line are straightforward: A single brand is not only cost-efficient but also can assure fast adoption of the new offering. The downside of a single-brand strategy is that applying the same brand to offerings delivering a variety of benefits to different customer segments could potentially weaken the brand by diluting its meaning to target customers. The product line aspect of brand enhancement and its dilution effects are better understood when considered in the context of vertically differentiated and horizontally differentiated offerings.

In the case of *vertically differentiated product lines*, brand enhancement is likely to occur when a product line is extended by adding a higher priced, higher performance offering carrying the same brand name. In this case, the newly added upscale offering is likely to raise the brand image, and with it the image of the overall product line. To illustrate, by introducing a line of premium, award-winning Gallo-branded wines, E. & J. Gallo Winery aimed in part to strengthen the image of the Gallo brand. In contrast, brand dilution is likely to occur when a product line is extended by adding a lower priced, lower performance offering carrying the same brand name. For example, in

1986 General Motors introduced a Chevrolet-based compact car branded as Cadillac Cimarron and, by doing so, weakened the image of its upscale Cadillac brand.

In the case of *horizontally differentiated product lines*, brand enhancement may occur by the increased brand exposure applied to related company offerings. For example, extending the Starbucks brand to bottled coffee drinks was likely to strengthen the brand's image by demonstrating its coffee-related expertise. In contrast, brand dilution is likely to occur when a single brand is extended to diverse product categories that are inconsistent with the meaning of the brand. To illustrate, the introduction of Cayenne, Porsche's SUV, was likely to dilute its traditional image as a pure sports car manufacturer. Similarly, Costco's strategy to use a single brand—Kirkland Signature—for all its store-branded products, from food and wine to appliances and clothes, limits its ability to attach a specific meaning to its brand.

▸ Price Management

Because price is a key component in setting an offering's value, optimizing the price across different offerings in a company's product line is an important aspect of product line value management. The key principle in product line price management is that the price of an offering should be consistent with its strategic role in a company's product line. In this context, an important consideration for vertically differentiated product lines is the possibility for cannibalization of the higher end offerings by the lower priced offerings. Here, the company's desire to make its lower end offerings superior to competitor offerings often clashes with the goal of optimizing profitability across the offerings in its product line. For example, Gap Warehouse, the forerunner to Old Navy, failed because, to avoid cannibalizing sales in Gap's core stores, it set relatively high prices, which in turn made it less attractive relative to its competitors. Product-line pricing can also be used to influence the demand for a company's offerings by virtue of customers' perceptions of the offerings' prices relative to one another. To illustrate, restaurants often price wine they are trying to dispose of as the second cheapest in its category because many customers who are not willing to spend much on wine are often embarrassed to select the least expensive one.

▸ Incentives Management

Because incentives rarely affect the core functional benefits of the offering, they are often used to channel customer demand to a particular offering in a company's product line. For example, by offering incentives, airlines can stimulate the demand on routes with excess capacity. In this context, managing product line incentives aims to optimize the impact of incentives applied to each individual offering with respect to the value delivered by the company's product line as a whole.

▸ Communication Management

An important aspect of product portfolio management is communicating the relative value of the offerings in a company's product line. The primary goal of these communications is to differentiate the offerings comprising the company's product line by highlighting their unique benefits and costs. The value-communications aspect of product line management is better understood when considered in the context of vertically differentiated and horizontally differentiated offerings. In the case of *verti-*

cally differentiated offerings with two or three price-tier levels, companies often use verbal descriptions, such as "regular" vs. "premium" and "good" vs. "better" vs. "best," to indicate the relative place of each offering. An alternative strategy, especially to communicate the relative positioning of offerings comprising more complex product lines, involves using numeric symbols, letters, and even various graphic shapes. In the case of vertically differentiated product lines, numbers are particularly useful because they inherently imply a certain ordering of the offerings (e.g., BMW 1-series, 3-series, 5-series, and 7-series). Another common example of using symbols to communicate the relative value of each offering in a company's product portfolio involves using star ratings to reflect benefits and dollar signs to reflect costs. To communicate the differences among *horizontally differentiated* offerings, companies use verbal descriptions when appropriate, such as "diet" ("light") vs. "regular," as well as letters, numbers, symbols, or their combination.

▸ Distribution Management

Distribution management aims to align the value-delivery strategies of individual offerings into a coordinated value-delivery strategy. The product line aspect of the value-delivery process often involves managing potential channel conflicts, which are driven by the difference in the profit optimization strategies among the various parties in the distribution chain. In this context, value-delivery management aims to optimize different aspects of the value-delivery process in a way that maximizes the value of the entire product line to all participants in the marketing exchange.

Summary

The term "product line" refers to a set of related offerings, which function in a similar manner, are sold to the same target customers, or are distributed through the same channels.

Product line management is conceptually similar to managing an individual offering and involves the same structural aspects: goal analysis, strategy analysis, tactical analysis, implementation, and control. The key difference is that, in the case of product line management, the focus is on the coordination of each of these aspects across individual offerings. Thus, product line goal analysis relates the objectives of the individual offerings comprising a company's product line; product line strategy analysis identifies the relationship between the offerings' strategies; product line tactical analysis relates the relationship among the tactical aspects of these offerings; product line implementation analysis identifies the personnel and resource allocation across these offerings; and product line control analysis focuses on measures used to evaluate a company's progress toward its product line goals.

Additional Readings

Cooper, Robert G., Scott J. Edgett, and Elko J. Kleinschmidt (2002), *Portfolio Management for New Products* (2nd ed.). Oxford: Perseus.

Lehmann, Donald R. and Russell S. Winer (2005), *Product Management* (4th ed.). Boston, MA: McGraw-Hill/Irwin.

McGrath, Michael E. (2001), *Product Strategy for High Technology Companies: Accelerating Your Business to Web Speed* (2nd ed.). New York, NY: McGraw-Hill.

Chapter Nineteen

Managing Product Portfolios

A company's product portfolio comprises the total mix of its individual offerings and can include multiple product lines. Unlike product lines comprising offerings that are functionally related (e.g., function in a similar matter, are sold to the same target customers, or are distributed through the same channels), the only common denominator for the offerings in a company's product portfolio is that they are managed by the same company.

Product portfolio management aims to optimize the value delivered by product lines and individual offerings managed by a particular company. In this context, decisions concerning a particular offering can be analyzed on three different levels: in the context of the overall product portfolio, in the context of its product line, and with respect to the specific marketing mix variables defining this offering (Figure 1).

Figure 1. The Hierarchy of Product Decisions

Managing a company's portfolio of products includes two basic types of decisions: (1) decisions involving the launch of new offerings and product lines, and (2) decisions involving the management of its existing offerings and product lines. The latter type of decisions involves issues such as allocating resources among existing offerings and product lines, deciding on the strategic direction of offerings and product lines (e.g., identifying target customers and collaborators, formulating an offering's value proposition, and developing a competitive strategy), and deciding to discontinue or divest a particular offering/product line.

Product portfolio management typically goes beyond analyzing a particular offering by focusing on sets of offerings managed by distinct strategic business units. A strategic business unit (SBU) is an operating company unit with a discrete set of offerings sold to an identifiable group of customers, and in competition with a well-defined set of competitors. Managing product portfolios typically involves allocating resources across different SBUs in order to optimize the company's overall performance.

In general, product portfolio management focuses on two types of factors: (1) opportunities presented by a particular industry or market and (2) the company's resources, which determine its ability to take advantage of the identified opportunities (Figure 2). Here, market opportunities are typically defined in terms of overall market/industry attractiveness factors, such as its size, growth, and profitability. A company's resources, on the other hand, reflect its competitive position in the marketplace and are often measured in terms of factors such as strategic assets, core competencies, and market share.

Figure 2. The Opportunity–Resources Product Portfolio Matrix

Based on market attractiveness and a company's resources, four basic scenarios can be identified:

- The *high-attractiveness/superior-resources* scenario (Scenario 1) refers to an attractive market that a company has the resources to exploit. This is the optimal scenario, and companies typically invest in business units operating in these conditions.

- The *high-attractiveness/low-resources* scenario (Scenario 2) refers to a market that is attractive, but for which the company does not have adequate resources to succeed. Because of the attractiveness of market conditions, companies often selectively invest in developing the resources required to achieve success.

- The *low-attractiveness/superior-resources* scenario (Scenario 3) refers to a market that is relatively less attractive but for which the company has the adequate resources to succeed. Because of the limited market potential, companies often reinvest part of the revenues from business units operating under these conditions in areas with greater market potential (Scenarios 1 and 2).

- The *low-attractiveness/low-resources* scenario (Scenario 4) refers to a relatively less attractive market for which the company does not have adequate resources. This is the least favorable scenario and companies often tend to either reposition their businesses into other markets offering greater opportunities (Scenario 2) or to divest the business to companies with a better fit.

Most companies aim to position their business units in the high-attractiveness/ superior-resources cell of the opportunity–resources matrix. The general strategy to achieve that is fairly intuitive. A company can move from unattractive to attractive markets (moving from Scenarios 3 and 4 to Scenarios 1 and 2) by developing offerings that will successfully compete in these markets. Similarly, a company can increase its competitive position in a given market (moving from Scenarios 2 and 4 to Scenarios 1 and 3) by developing or acquiring the resources (strategic assets and core competencies) vital for achieving success in this market.

Because the principles for making resource allocation decisions across different business units are very similar across industries, many companies have developed generalized strategies for making such decisions. These generalized strategies are often integrated into formal product portfolio models that offer guidance on how to allocate resources across multiple strategic business units.

A key aspect in developing product portfolio models involves identifying the metrics underlying the performance of a given business unit. Depending on the assumption of the model, these metrics can include factors such as: return on investment, market share, and industry growth rate. One of the earliest and most popular algorithms for identifying the overall performance of a strategic business unit of a company is the DuPont model, which quantifies the profitability of a given SBU as a function of three key factors: net profit margin, asset turnover, and an equity multiplier (Appendix 1).

The most widely used approach to product portfolio analysis that came into common use in the 1960s is the model developed by the Boston Consulting Group (BCG). This approach, commonly known as the BCG matrix, emphasizes two main criteria in evaluating a company's product portfolio: the market growth rate and the product's relative market share (Appendix 2). A more comprehensive, albeit more complex, model was developed jointly by General Electric and McKinsey and is commonly known as the GE matrix (Appendix 3).

Summary

A company's product portfolio comprises the total mix of its individual offerings and can include multiple product lines. Unlike product lines, which comprise offerings that are functionally related (e.g., function in a similar matter, are sold to the same target customers, or are distributed through the same channels), the only common denominator for the offerings in a company's product portfolio is that they are managed by the same company. In this context, product portfolio management aims to optimize the value delivered by product lines and individual offerings managed by a particular company.

Managing a company's portfolio of products includes two basic types of decisions: (1) decisions involving the launch of new offerings and product lines, and (2) decisions involving the management of its existing offerings and product lines. Decisions of the latter type involve issues such as allocating resources among existing offerings and product lines, deciding on the strategic direction of a company's offerings and product lines, and deciding to discontinue or divest a particular offering/product line.

Product portfolio management focuses on two types of factors: (1) opportunities presented by a particular industry or market and (2) the company's resources that determine its ability to take advantage of the identified opportunities. Here, market opportunities are typically defined in terms of overall market/industry attractiveness factors such as its size, growth, and profitability. A company's resources, on the other hand, reflect its competitive position in the marketplace and are often measured in terms of factors such as strategic assets, core competencies, and market share. These two factors comprise the Opportunity–Resources Product Portfolio Matrix.

Relevant Frameworks: The DuPont Model

The DuPont model is a management model based on analyzing profitability of a company using performance management tools such as return on investment and asset turnover. It was developed by F. Donaldson Brown, an engineer from the DuPont company. Its first large-scale application involved restructuring the General Motors Corporation, of which DuPont was the majority shareholder. Following General Motors' success, the model gained prominence among major U.S. corporations and remained one of the dominant forms of financial analysis until the 1970s. The popularity of the DuPont model can be attributed to its simplicity and ability to link company performance to financial results.

The DuPont model of management allows large companies to allocate resources across different business units competing for funding. The traditional DuPont model relies on three key components to calculate return on equity: net profit margin, asset turnover, and an equity multiplier.

- *Net profit margin* is the profit generated by the company relative to its revenues and is typically calculated by dividing the company's net income by its overall revenues.

- *Asset turnover* reflects the sales revenues generated by the company relative to its assets and is typically calculated by dividing the company's sales revenues by its assets. Asset turnover is used by the DuPont model to allow comparing companies that are using different business models. In most cases, asset turnover is often inversely correlated with profit margins (high-margin, low-volume vs. low-margin, high-volume).

- The *equity multiplier* is a measure of a company's financial leverage and is calculated as the ratio of a company's assets to shareholders' equity. The equity multiplier is used to account for the potential impact of a company's debt when calculating its return on equity.

In this context, a company's return on equity (ROE) can be calculated as follows:

$$\text{ROE} = \text{Return on assets} \cdot \text{Equity multiplier} = \text{Net profit margin} \cdot \text{Asset turnover} \cdot \text{Equity multiplier}$$

The DuPont model has several popular applications: (1) it provides managers with a basic understanding of the factors that contribute to the company's success and suggests strategies for managing the company's overall performance; (2) it provides quantifiable benchmarks that can be used for evaluating a company's performance over time; and (3) it can also be used as an indicator of a company's overall performance for valuation purposes.

The DuPont model of management, and in particular the ROE metric, has been used as the basis for many product-portfolio models (e.g., the BCG and GE matrixes), which depict a company's strategic business units on two dimensions: their position relative to the competition and the growth rate of the markets they serve.

Relevant Frameworks: BCG Product-Portfolio Matrix

The BCG product-portfolio model is based on the notion that to be successful, a company should have a portfolio of products with different market shares and different growth rates. The portfolio composition is viewed as a function of balancing cash flows between high-growth and low-growth products. In this context, the main goal of the BCG product portfolio model is to guide the cash allocation decisions across different strategic business units of a company.

The BCG model is based on two key assumptions. The first is that profit margins are a function of market share, such that high market share leads to high margins. This assumption is derived from the experience curve effect and, in particular, from the notion that increasing the scale of production leads to a lower cost structure and, hence, to higher profit margins.[1] The second assumption is that profit margins are a function of the growth of the industry in which the company operates and that different stages of growth require different cash management strategies. In particular, high-growth businesses require cash investment, whereas low-growth businesses tend to generate cash in excess of what needs to be reinvested to maintain share. These two assumptions are reflected in the fact that market share and market growth are the two key components of evaluating the performance of a given strategic business unit.

Using the BCG matrix entails two major steps: classification and action. The *classification phase* calls for categorizing all SBUs into four types: question marks, stars, cash cows, and dogs. This categorization is based on each SBU's performance on two factors: (1) relative market share (share relative to the largest competitor) and (2) market growth. For example, a relative market share of 0.4 means that the SBU has 40% of the market leader's share, and a relative market share of 2.0 means that the SBU is the leader and has twice the share of the next largest competitor (Figure 3). For presentation purposes, the relative market share is drawn on a logarithmic scale. Market growth rate is drawn on a normal scale, with 10% annual market growth often used as the reference point. The circles depict the revenue contribution of individual SBUs, such that each circle's area is proportional to the SBU's dollar sales.

Figure 3. BCG Matrix Step 1 (classification)[2]

The *action phase* identifies the role to be assigned to each SBU (Figure 4). There are four basic strategies to achieve an efficient resource allocation: (1) hold (preserve market share, usually applied to stars); (2) build (increase market share and forgo near-term earnings, usually applied to question marks); (3) harvest (increase cash flow and forego building market share, usually applied to cash cows); and (4) divest (sell or liquidate, usually applied to dogs).

Figure 4. BCG Matrix: Step 2 (action)[3]

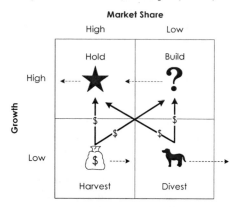

The BCG model has numerous limitations. First, its main objective is to guide a company's resource allocation across different SBUs; as a result, it is not designed to assist with strategic decisions of a single SBU. Second, it considers market share and market growth to be the only relevant cash allocation factors (factors such as cost, competitive reaction, synergies between SBUs, and various macroeconomic factors are not part of the model). Third, it assumes that higher market share means higher cash-generating ability and higher profitability from economies of scale, learning curve/experience effects, monopoly power, etc., even though these factors may not apply to all industries. Fourth, market share and market growth are ambiguous and difficult to quantify. To illustrate, the same SBU can be classified as a question mark, a star, a cash cow, or a dog when alternative operational definitions of the matrix dimensions are involved. Finally, the use of the BCG matrix can have important self-fulfilling organizational implications: Labeling an SBU as a dog will lead to minimizing the cash allocated to this unit, which is likely to decrease its performance and turn the unit into a "real" dog.

Overall, the BCG model offers a simple strategy for evaluating the relative performance of a company's strategic business units and making cash allocation recommendations. Its recommendations, however, are based on highly restrictive assumptions (e.g., market share and industry growth rate are the only relevant performance factors), and its application is subject to multiple interpretations (e.g., defining the industry in which the firm competes). While the general idea—classifying a company's strategic business units based on their relative performance and the attractiveness of the industry in which they compete—is a viable approach, the use of the BCG model in its original form in today's business world is rather limited.

Relevant Frameworks: GE Product-Portfolio Matrix

The GE (General Electric) product-portfolio model can be viewed as a more comprehensive version of the BCG model. Similar to the BCG model, it classifies business units into different categories based on their performance on two key business dimensions: market attractiveness and business strength. However, unlike the BCG matrix, in which the dimensions are identified by a single factor (industry growth and market share), the GE matrix uses composite measures comprised of different factors. Thus, market attractiveness is calculated as a weighted average of factors such as market size, market growth, historical profit margin, stage in the life cycle, competitive intensity (number of competitors, competitive structure, differentiation, entry barriers, substitutes), technological requirements, inflationary vulnerability, investment intensity, and various context factors (e.g., social, political, and legal). In the same vein, business position is calculated as a weighted average of factors such as market share, share growth, product differentiation, brand image, relative cost position, capacity utilization, technological and R&D performance, patents, distribution network, marketing effectiveness, access to supplies, and managerial personnel.

Because each of the two dimensions has three levels (low, medium, high), different strategic business units are classified into nine different types (rather than four, as in the BCG matrix). Each SBU is denoted with a circle representing the relative size of the market and the SBU's share of that market. The recommendations derived from the GE matrix are similar to that of the BCG approach, with the four key strategies further refined to match the 3 × 3 design of the GE matrix (Figure 5).

The GE approach requires relatively complex analysis, which tends to limit its usability as a standardized approach. Similar to the BCG matrix, the GE approach suffers from subjectivity in evaluating different performance benchmarks (e.g., product differentiation, stage in the life cycle, brand image) and does not incorporate multi-period competitive strategies.

Overall, the GE approach offsets many of the shortcomings of the BCG model, mainly its single-factor approach to identifying the key business factors that account for the overall profitability of a strategic business unit. The comprehensiveness of the GE approach, however, comes at the expense of simplicity, which is one of the most attractive features of the BCG matrix. Because of its complexity, the GE approach is often used as a guideline for analyzing different strategic business units rather than as a quantifiable normative model.

Figure 5. GE Product-Portfolio Matrix

Additional Readings

Cooper, Robert G., Scott J. Edgett, and Elko J. Kleinschmidt (2002), *Portfolio Management for New Products* (2nd ed.). Oxford: Perseus.

Stern, Carl W. and George Jr. Stalk (1998), *Perspectives on Strategy: From the Boston Consulting Group*. New York, NY: Wiley.

Lynch, Richard L. (2006), *Corporate Strategy* (4th ed.). New York, NY: Prentice Hall.

Notes

[1] Stern, Carl W. and George Stalk (1998), *Perspectives on Strategy: From the Boston Consulting Group*. New York, NY: John Wiley & Sons.

[2] Adapted from Ibid.

[3] Adapted from Ibid.

Chapter Twenty

Market Forecasting

Market forecasting is important for making new product launch and market exit decisions, for resource allocation decisions that determine the level of support for a given offering, for setting goals and performance benchmarks, and for developing the strategy of a particular offering. The key issues involved in market forecasting are the focus of this chapter.

Types of Forecasting

There are two common types of market estimates: market potential forecast and sales forecast. *Market potential forecast* is an estimate of the total sales volume that ultimately could be achieved by all companies in a given market. Forecasting market potential, often referred to as market sizing, is typically used to make market entry and exit decisions, resource allocation decisions, as well as to set goals and evaluate performance. Market potential estimates are also used as inputs in market and sales forecasts.

Unlike market potential forecasts, which indicate the sales volume that ultimately could be achieved in a particular market, sales forecasts impose a specific timeframe for achieving the sales volume. Thus, *sales forecast* is an estimate of the total sales volume attainable within a given timeframe. Similar to the estimates of market potential, market and sales forecasts typically are used to make entry and exit decisions, allocate resources, plan production capacity, and evaluate the impact of various marketing mix variables on sales.

Forecasting Methods

There are several general categories of demand forecasting methods. On a most general level, two types of methods can be identified: methods that involve collecting *primary data* (data collected especially for the purposes of demand forecasting) and methods that involve analyzing *secondary data* (existing data). Primary-data forecasting methods can be further divided into two categories: *expert-judgment forecasts* and *customer-research forecasts*. These forecasting methods are discussed in more detail below.

Expert-Judgment Forecasts

Expert-judgment forecasts rely on experts' opinions to estimate market demand. Depending on the nature of the expert's background, there are three main categories of forecasts.

Executive forecast is a top-down approach in which the forecast is based on the aggregated opinion of a company's executives and senior managers.

Sales force forecast is a bottom-up approach in which the forecast is based on the aggregated opinion of a company's sales force and sales managers.

Industry forecast is based on the aggregated opinion of industry experts, such as industry analysts, executives, managers, and sales forces from competitive companies.

Because most expert-judgment forecasts are based on aggregating the opinions of multiple experts, an important issue concerns the process of aggregating individual judgments to arrive at the final estimate. A popular method for eliciting group expert judgments is the *Delphi method,* named after the site of the most revered oracle in ancient Greece, the Temple of Apollo in Delphi. The Delphi method involves multiple rounds of anonymous collection of expert opinions. The primary goal of the Delphi method is to ensure an accurate forecast from a group of experts by controlling for many of the potential decision biases, such as social conformity (agreeing with the majority), status (e.g., seniority within the organization), confirmation bias (ignoring new information that is inconsistent with the original forecast), and other related effects (e.g., experts' ability to eloquently articulate their forecast). To achieve this degree of control, individual forecasts are collected by a moderator who ensures anonymity of the expert opinions. Each forecast typically consists of two parts: the forecast and its rationale. In the Delphi method, after each round of forecast elicitation, the moderator provides the experts with the anonymous forecasts and their rationale, and gives them the option to revise their opinion. This process is repeated until a consensus is reached. In cases where consensus is unlikely after several rounds, the individual forecasts are typically aggregated into an overall estimate (e.g., by averaging the individual numeric forecasts).

To facilitate the use of the expert knowledge that has been gained, it is often made available in the form of *expert systems*, which are computer applications that contain market-related knowledge of one or more experts. Unlike other forms of expert judgment, expert systems translate human expertise into rules that enable the system to diagnose situations without the presence of a human expert.

Customer-Research Forecasts

The customer-research approach to market forecasting examines customers' reaction to the offering at different stages of the product development process. The two most popular forms of customer-based forecasting are concept testing and market testing.

Concept testing is the process of evaluating consumer response to a particular offering prior to its introduction to the market. Concept testing can be based on a description of the offering or, alternatively, can also involve evaluating fully functional prototypes. One approach to concept testing involves using a sample representation of the target customer segment (e.g., a focus group) with the purpose of revealing insights, ideas, and observations related to the key aspects of the offering. Another methodology involves estimating the probability of the offering's purchase by target customers based on a description of its main benefits and costs. Because it is based on customers' estimates of their future behavior, concept testing provides only rough estimates of sales volume.

Market testing relies on test markets to estimate market potential and/or future sales volume. It is often used as the litmus test for a go or no-go decision in launching a new product, as well as for testing specific aspects of the offering's marketing mix (product attributes, branding, price, incentives, communication, and distribution strategy). Test markets aim to replicate all relevant aspects of the environment in which the company's offering would be launched (e.g., offering-related advertising and incentives, competitive offerings, point-of-purchase environment, etc.) so that the test market outcome can be extrapolated to more general (e.g., national) sales forecasts. To ensure greater validity for the results, multiple test markets are often used, typically located in different geographic areas. Because of its relatively high costs, market testing is normally used only for products that successfully pass the concept testing stage.

Secondary Data Forecasts

Forecast methods involving already existing (secondary) data can be divided into three categories based on whether the available data pertains to (1) the offering that is the object of the forecast, (2) a related offering, or (3) an entire product category. These three forecasting methods are discussed in more detail below.

Offering-specific forecasting involves using past data from the sales of the same offering for which the demand is being forecast. A popular approach relies on past sales data to identify trends, then extrapolating these trends to a sales forecast. A variety of time-series statistical approaches could be employed for this type of analysis, such as linear trend analysis, moving-average analysis, and exponential smoothing. Another popular approach involves identifying the relationships between the offering's sales and a variety of internal factors (e.g., the offering's price, incentives, and communications) and external factors (e.g., competitors' price, incentives, and communications). Different forms of regression are often used to identify the nature of these relationships.

Forecasting by analogy involves forecasting an offering's performance by comparing its adoption cycle to a functionally similar product for which sales data are available. This approach is useful for new-to-the-world products (e.g., TiVo, SlingBox, and Segway Human Transporter) for which adoption data is not available, or for nontraditional marketing activities involving existing products (e.g., drastic price change, novel incentives, nontraditional communications campaign) for which the market reaction is unknown. The key assumption of analogy-based forecasts is that the pattern of adoption of the new product (e.g., speed and depth of market penetration) follows a similar pattern to that of the analogous product. To illustrate, consider the adoption pattern illustrated in Figure 1. If the diffusion of a new-to-the-world product is assumed to follow the same pattern (i.e., these products are analogous), then the existing data can be used to predict future sales volume. Using the above example, in 10 years the demand for the new offering would be approximately 420,000.

Figure 1. Forecasting by Analogy: An Example

Category-based forecasting involves utilizing available product-category data to estimate a particular product's performance. One category-based forecasting approach to quantifying the sales potential of a given category involves estimating the Category Development Index (CDI). CDI involves evaluating the degree to which sales in a given category have captured the total market potential in a particular geographical area based on the population of that area and average consumption per user nationally. To estimate the market potential of an existing product, CDI is compared with the Brand Development Index (or BDI), which reflects the degree to which sales of a given brand have captured the total market potential in a particular market. Comparing these two indexes reveals a brand's performance relative to the category. Thus, a combination of high BDI and low CDI indicates that the brand is doing better than the competitive offerings in a given market, whereas a combination of low BDI and high CDI indicates that the brand is doing worse than the competitive offerings.

The Big Picture

To avoid common biases and arrive at more accurate estimates, forecast *assumptions* must be clearly articulated and supported by empirical data and logical reasoning. Thus, an assumption should not be simply a footnote in the spreadsheet outlining the forecast; instead, it should be the starting point of the forecast. Forecasts based on assumptions that cannot be readily supported by empirical data or logical reasoning should be tested for the degree to which they are sensitive to changes in the underlying assumptions. Common assumptions in demand forecasting involve estimating the total market potential, the rate of adoption of the category (for new-to-the-world products) and the company's offering, the rate of competitive entries into the category, and the degree of competitive intensity. For example, Webvan, an online grocery delivery business, overestimated the speed with which its target customers would adopt the new service and was bankrupt before many of its target customers had even tried the service.

Because most forecasting methods use a variety of assumptions, a more accurate forecast can be achieved by using *multiple methods*. The goal is to achieve converging estimates when using a diverse set of methods (e.g., expert judgment, consumer research, and secondary data analyses).

Summary

There are several general categories of demand forecasting methods. On the most general level, two types of methods can be identified: methods that involve collecting primary data (data collected especially for the purposes of demand forecasting) and methods that involve analyzing secondary data (existing data).

Primary-data forecasting comprises two types of methods: expert-judgment forecasts and customer-research forecasts. Expert-judgment forecasts rely on experts' opinions to estimate market demand. Depending on the nature of the expert's background, there are three main categories of forecasts: executive forecasts, sales force forecasts, and industry forecasts. The customer-research approach to market forecasting examines customers' reaction to the offering at different stages of the product development process. The two most popular forms of customer-based forecasting are concept testing and market testing.

Forecast methods involving already existing (secondary) data can be divided into three categories based on whether the available data pertains to (1) the offering that is the object of the forecast (offering-specific forecasting), (2) a related offering (forecasting by analogy), or (3) an entire product category (category-based forecasting).

To avoid common biases and arrive at more accurate estimates, forecast assumptions must be clearly articulated and supported by empirical data and logical reasoning. Assumptions should not be simply footnotes in the spreadsheet outlining the forecast; instead, they should be the starting point of the forecast. Forecasts based on assumptions that cannot be readily supported by empirical data or logical reasoning should be tested for the degree to which they are sensitive to changes in the underlying assumptions. The accuracy of forecasts can be improved by testing for estimate convergence using multiple forecast methods.

Relevant Concepts

Brand Development Index (BDI): A measure of the degree to which sales of a given brand have captured the total market potential in a particular geographical area based on the population of that area and average consumption per user nationally. BDI quantifies the sales potential of a given brand in a particular market. Comparing BDI with the related concept, CDI (Category Development Index), reveals a brand's performance relative to the category (competitive offerings). Thus, a combination of high BDI and low CDI indicates that the brand is doing better than the competitive offerings in a given market, whereas a combination of low BDI and high CDI indicates that the brand is doing worse than the competitive offerings.

$$BDI = \frac{\text{Percent of a brand's total U.S. sales in market X}}{\text{Percent of the total U.S. population in market X}} \cdot 100$$

Category Development Index (CDI): A measure of the degree to which sales in a given category have captured the total market potential in a particular geographical area based on the population of that area and average consumption per user nationally.

In other words, CDI quantifies the sales potential of a given category in a particular market.

$$CDI = \frac{\text{Percent of a category's total U.S. sales in market X}}{\text{Percent of the total U.S. population in market X}} \cdot 100$$

Product Preferences: A measure of the degree to which the product/service appeals to current and potential customers. Preferences can be measured in absolute terms (i.e., independent from the other products and services in the marketplace) or relative to other offerings (e.g., the degree to which the company's products and services are better than competitors'). Preferences typically comprise two dimensions: the valence of preferences (e.g., positive vs. negative) and the strength of preferences (e.g., strong vs. weak). Product and service preferences can be measured using a variety of techniques, such as questionnaires, conjoint analysis, and perceptual maps.

Product Satisfaction: A measure of customers' experience with the product. Unlike product-preference metrics that can be measured prior to purchase as well as post purchase, satisfaction requires consumers to have actual experience with the product or service. Satisfaction is typically measured using a five-point or a seven-point scale (e.g., very dissatisfied, somewhat dissatisfied, neither satisfied nor dissatisfied, somewhat satisfied, and very satisfied).

Purchase Intent: Self-reported likelihood of purchasing a company's products or services. A popular approach to estimating the purchase likelihood involves using a five-point scale with the following anchors: "definitely would buy," "probably would buy," "might or might not buy," "probably would not buy," "definitely would not buy." To account for an overestimation bias, whereby respondents tend to overestimate the probability of actually purchasing the surveyed product, the stated purchase probabilities are typically corrected. A common methodology for correcting this overestimation bias involves using generalized industry estimates. To illustrate, with consumer packaged goods, these responses are sometimes corrected as follows: "Definitely would buy" responses are reduced by 20% (which implies that only 80% of those stating that they will definitely buy the product will end up actually buying it); "probably would buy" responses are reduced by 70% (which implies that only 30% of those stating that they will probably buy the product will end up actually buying it); responses falling into the three remaining categories are considered to be no-purchase responses.

Additional Readings

Aaker, David A., V. Kumar, and George S. Day (2006), *Marketing Research* (9th ed.). New York, NY: John Wiley & Sons.

Kahn, Kenneth B. (2006), *New Product Forecasting: An Applied Approach*. Armonk, NY: M.E. Sharpe Inc.

Lilien, Gary L. and Arvind Rangaswamy (2006), *Marketing Engineering: Computer-Assisted Marketing Analysis and Planning* (2nd ed.). Upper Saddle River, NJ: Prentice Hall.

Part Five

References

Chapter Twenty One

Writing a Strategic Marketing Plan

The strategic marketing plan delineates the key aspects of managing the value of a company's offering, its product lines, and/or the entire company. The basic aspects of developing a strategic marketing plan are the focus of this chapter.

Writing a marketing plan is often confused with strategic planning, partially because strategic planning is often driven by the need to generate a marketing plan. Strategic planning and writing a marketing plan, however, are two fundamentally different activities. Strategic planning is the process of identifying a goal and developing a course of action to achieve this goal. Writing a marketing plan captures on paper the identified goal and the decided-upon course of action.

There is no unique approach for writing a strategic marketing plan; companies use diverse formats to structure them. Despite their differences, however, most marketing plans share many common elements. Thus, a typical marketing plan is comprised of an executive summary; situation overview; an outline of the company's goal(s), strategy, tactics, implementation, and controls (G-STIC); and a set of relevant exhibits. This common structure is shown in Figure 1 and outlined in more detail below.

Figure 1. The Marketing Plan

A typical strategic marketing plan starts with an executive summary, which delineates the key aspects of the company's goal and the proposed course of action. The executive summary is then followed by an overview of the current situation (usually based on SWOT analysis). The situation overview is followed by an outline of the goals identifying the focus and performance benchmarks to be achieved by the company. The goal analysis is followed by a description of the company's strategy, which involves identifying the key aspects of market structure and outlining the offering's value to the company, its customers, and collaborators. The strategy analysis is followed by a description of marketing tactics, and, in particular, the processes of creating, communicating, and delivering value. The tactical analysis is followed by an implementation plan that identifies the processes and people involved in translating the planned strategy and tactics into reality. The control section of the marketing plan outlines a policy for evaluating the company's performance and monitoring the market environment to ensure adequate progress toward the set goal. Finally, the exhibit section of the marketing plan includes all relevant background materials (e.g., tables, figures, and financial calculations).

A streamlined approach for developing an actionable marketing plan derived from the value-driven marketing framework outlined in this book is given in Appendix 1. In addition, several alternative approaches to writing a marketing plan are illustrated in Appendix 2. Note that the marketing plans outlined in Appendices 1 and 2 do not explicitly focus on managing portfolios of offerings. When a company's activities involve several related offerings, its marketing plan should include, in addition to analysis of each individual offering, an analysis of the relationship among individual offerings that focuses on product line factors, such as product line goals, synergies across offerings, and potential cannibalization issues.

Appendix 1: The Strategic Marketing Plan

▸ Executive Summary

Provide a brief overview of the company's goal and the proposed course of action.

▸ Situation Overview

Evaluate the market in which the company operates and its competitive position. This analysis typically involves identifying the strengths, weaknesses, opportunities, and threats facing the company.

▸ Goal

Identify the key goal(s) to be achieved by the offering. Define the focus of the goal (e.g., net income, profit margins, and earnings per share) and the key benchmarks to be achieved (e.g., quantify the net income to be achieved and identify the timeframe for achieving it).

▸ Strategy

Customer value analysis

- Identify customers targeted by the offering. Describe their underlying needs and distinguishing characteristics (profile).
- Identify the competitive offerings that provide similar benefits to the target customers.
- Identify the relevant context factors (e.g., social, technological, economic, political, and legal) that are likely to influence customer needs and preferences.
- Define the offering's value proposition and positioning strategy.

Collaborator value analysis

- Identify the key collaborators (e.g., suppliers, channel members, and marketing partners) and their strategic goals.
- Identify the competitive offerings that provide similar benefits to these collaborators.
- Identify the relevant context factors (e.g., social, technological, economic, political, and legal) that are likely to influence collaborators' goals.
- Define the offering's value proposition and positioning strategy to collaborators.

Company value analysis

- Identify the strategic business unit directly responsible for the offering and its key stakeholders (e.g., investors and shareholders).
- Identify the competitors that serve the company's target customers. Identify the company's strategic assets and core competencies vis-à-vis those of its competitors.
- Identify the relevant context factors (e.g., social, technological, economic, political, and legal) that are likely to influence company's goals.
- Define the offering's value proposition and positioning strategy to company stakeholders and personnel.

▸ Tactics

- *Product:* Identify relevant product attributes and corresponding benefits delivered to customers by the company and its collaborators.
- *Service:* Identify relevant service attributes and corresponding benefits delivered to customers by the company and its collaborators.
- *Brand:* Identify the key branding elements (e.g., name, logo, symbol, character, and slogan) and brand associations.
- *Price:* Identify the price(s) at which the offering is provided to customers and collaborators.
- *Incentives:* Define the incentives received by customers (e.g., price reductions, coupons, rebates, premiums, and rewards), collaborators (e.g., trade allowances, volume discounts, price reductions), and relevant company personnel and stakeholders (e.g., sales bonuses, rewards, and contests).
- *Communications:* Define the manner in which various aspects of the offering (product, service, brand, price, incentives) are communicated to target customers, collaborators, and relevant company personnel and stakeholders.
- *Distribution:* Define the manner in which various aspects of the offering (product, service, brand, price, incentives) are delivered to target customers, collaborators, and relevant company personnel and stakeholders.

▸ Implementation

Processes

Outline the business processes involved in implementing the company's strategy and tactics. Develop a financial plan and an implementation timeline.

People

Identify the human resources involved in developing and implementing the offering. Define the key functional areas (e.g., research and development, manufacturing, marketing, and sales), identify the key managers and employees, and develop strategies for securing and developing key personnel.

▸ Control

Company Performance

Identify the key criteria for evaluating the company's performance and progress toward its goals.

Changes in the Environment

Identify metrics for evaluating the environment in which the company operates and develop a policy for making adjustments to the plan to accommodate changes in the business environment.

▸ Exhibits

Include tables, figures, and appendixes offering additional information that delineates and/or supports specific aspects of the marketing plan. Exhibits can include market structure data (e.g., industry overview, company overview, and customer trend analyses), financial calculations (e.g., break-even analysis, net present value analysis, best/worst case scenario analysis, customer value analysis), details pertaining to specific marketing variables (e.g., product and service specifications, communication plan, and distribution structure), implementation (e.g., process specifications and personnel overview), and control (e.g., performance metrics and environmental analysis) aspects of the marketing plan.

Appendix 2: Additional Marketing Plan Designs

▶ Marketing Plan A[1]

1. Executive summary and table of contents
2. Current marketing situation
3. Opportunity and issue analysis
4. Objectives
5. Marketing strategy
6. Action programs
7. Financial projections
8. Controls

▶ Marketing Plan B[2]

1. Executive summary
2. Situation analysis
    - Market summary (demographics, needs, trends, growth)
    - SWOT analysis
    - Competition
    - Product offering
    - Keys to success
    - Critical issues
3. Marketing strategy
    - Mission
    - Marketing objectives
    - Financial objectives
    - Target markets
    - Positioning
    - Strategies
    - Marketing mix
    - Marketing research
4. Financials
    - Break-even analysis
    - Sales forecast
    - Expense forecast
5. Controls
    - Implementation
    - Marketing organization
    - Contingency planning

▶ Marketing Plan C[3]

1. Executive summary
2. Company description
3. Strategic focus and plan
   - Mission
   - Goals
   - Core competencies and sustainable competitive advantage
4. Situation analysis
   - SWOT
   - Industry analysis
   - Competition analysis
   - Company analysis
   - Customer analysis
5. Product-market focus
   - Marketing and product objectives
   - Target markets
   - Points of difference
   - Positioning
6. Marketing program
   - Product strategy
   - Price strategy
   - Promotion strategy
   - Distribution strategy
7. Financial data and projections
8. Implementation plan
9. Evaluation and control
10. Appendices

▶ Marketing Plan D[4]

1. Executive summary
2. Introduction
3. Situational analysis
   - The situational environs
     - Demand
     - Social and cultural factors
     - Demographics
     - Economic conditions
     - Technology
     - Politics
     - Laws and regulations

- The neutral environs
  - Financial environment
  - Government environment
  - Media environment
  - Special interest environment
- The competitor environs
- The company environs
4. The target market
5. Problems and opportunities
6. Marketing objectives
7. Marketing strategy
8. Marketing tactics
9. Implementation and control
10. Summary
11. Appendices

▶ **Marketing Plan E**[5]

1. Executive summary
2. Situation analysis
   - Category/competitor definition
   - Category analysis
     - Aggregate market factors
       - Category size
       - Category growth
       - Stage in product life cycle
       - Sales cyclicity
       - Seasonality
       - Profits
     - Category factors
       - Threat of new entrants/exits
       - Bargaining power of buyers
       - Bargaining power of suppliers
       - Pressure from substitutes
       - Category capacity
       - Current category rivalry
     - Environmental factors
       - Technological
       - Political
       - Economic
       - Regulatory
       - Social

- Company and competitor analysis
  - Product features matrix
  - Objectives
  - Strategies
  - Marketing mix
  - Profits
  - Value chain
  - Differential advantage/resource analysis
    - Ability to conceive and design new products
    - Ability to produce /manufacture or deliver the service
    - Ability to market
    - Ability to finance
    - Ability to manage
    - Will to succeed in this category
  - Expected future strategies
- Customer analysis
  - Who are the customers?
  - What do they buy and how do they use it?
  - Where do they buy?
  - When do they buy?
  - How do they choose?
  - Why they prefer a product
  - How they respond to marketing programs
  - Will they buy it again?
  - Long-term value of customers
  - Segmentation
- Planning assumptions
  - Market potential
  - Category and product sales forecasts
  - Other assumptions

3. Objectives
   - Corporate objectives (if appropriate)
   - Divisional objectives (if appropriate)
   - Marketing objective(s)
     - Volume and profit
     - Timeframe
     - Secondary objectives (e.g., brand equity, customer, new product)
     - Program (marketing mix)

4. Product /brand strategy
   - Customer target(s)
   - Competitor target(s)
   - Product/service features
   - Core strategy
     - Value proposition
     - Product positioning
5. Supporting marketing programs
   - Integrated marketing communications plan
   - Advertising
   - Promotion
   - Sales
   - Price
   - Channels
   - Customer management activities
   - Website
   - Marketing research
   - Partnerships/joint ventures
6. Financial documents
   - Budgets
   - Pro forma statements
7. Monitors and controls
   - Marketing metrics
   - Secondary data
   - Primary data
8. Contingency plans

▶ Marketing Plan F[6]

1. Executive summary
2. Agenda
3. State of the business
   - Vision and product positioning
   - Recent results
   - Business challenge
4. Objectives
5. Strategic initiatives
6. Tactics
7. Financial implications
8. Milestones
9. Executive summary

Notes

[1] Adapted from Philip Kotler (2003), *A Framework for Marketing Management*, 2nd ed., Prentice Hall.

[2] Adapted from Philip Kotler and Kevin Lane Keller (2008), *Marketing Management*, 13th ed., Prentice Hall.

[3] Adapted from Roger A. Kerin and Robert A. Peterson (2000), *Strategic Marketing Problems*, 9th ed., Prentice Hall.

[4] Adapted from William A. Cohen (2001), *The Marketing Plan*, 3rd ed., John Wiley & Sons.

[5] Adapted from Donald Lehman and Russell Winer (2004), *Analysis for Marketing Planning*, 6th ed., McGraw-Hill/Irwin: New York, NY.

[6] Adapted from Tim Calkins (2008), *Breakthrough Marketing Plans*, Palgrave Macmillan.

Chapter Twenty Two

Essential Financial Concepts in Marketing

Break-Even Analysis: Analysis aimed at identifying the break-even point at which the benefits and costs associated with a particular action are equal, and beyond which profit occurs. The four most common types of break-even analyses are: (1) break-even of a fixed-cost investment, (2) break-even of a price cut, (3) break-even of a variable cost increase, and (4) cannibalization break-even analysis.

Break-Even Analysis of a Fixed Cost Investment: Analysis aimed at identifying the sales volume at which a company neither makes a profit nor incurs a loss after making a fixed cost investment (see Appendix 2 for more details).

Break-Even Analysis of a Price Cut: Analysis aimed at identifying the increase in the sales volume needed for the price cut to have no impact on profitability (see Appendix 3 for more details).

Break-Even Analysis of a Variable Cost Increase: Analysis aimed at identifying the increase in the sales volume needed for the increase in variable costs to have no impact on profitability (see Appendix 4 for more details).

Break-Even Analysis of Cannibalization: Analysis aimed at identifying the ratio of the cannibalized sales volume of an existing offering to the sales volume generated by a new offering at which a company neither makes a profit nor incurs a loss (see Appendix 5 for more details).

Compound Annual Growth Rate (CAGR): The year-to-year growth rate of an investment over a specified period of time.

Contribution Margin ($): When expressed in monetary terms ($), contribution margin typically refers to the difference between total revenues and total variable costs. Contribution margin can also be calculated on a per-unit basis as the difference between the unit selling price and the unit variable cost. The per-unit margin, expressed in monetary terms ($), is also referred to as contribution (i.e., the dollar amount that each unit sold "contributes" to the payment of fixed costs).

$$\text{Margin}_{\text{Total}}(\$) = \text{Revenue}_{\text{Total}} - \text{Variable costs}_{\text{Total}}$$

$$\text{Margin}_{\text{Unit}}(\$) = \text{Price}_{\text{Unit}} - \text{Variable costs}_{\text{Unit}}$$

Contribution Margin (%): When expressed in percentages (%), contribution margin typically refers to the ratio of the difference between total revenues and total variable costs to total revenues. Contribution margin can also be expressed as the ratio of unit contribution to unit selling price.

$$\text{Margin (\%)} = \frac{\text{Revenue}_{\text{Total}} - \text{Variable cost}_{\text{Total}}}{\text{Revenue}_{\text{Total}}} = \frac{\text{Price}_{\text{Unit}} - \text{Variable costs}_{\text{Unit}}}{\text{Price}_{\text{Unit}}}$$

Cost of Goods Sold (COGS): Expenses directly related to creating the goods or services being sold. Cost of goods sold can have a variable (e.g., cost of raw materials, cost of turning raw materials into goods) and a fixed component (e.g., depreciation of equipment).

Economic Value Analysis: The process of translating the nonmonetary (i.e., functional and psychological) aspects of an offering's value proposition into financial terms (see Appendix 6).

Fixed Costs: Expenses that do not fluctuate with output volume within a relevant period (see Appendix 1 for more details).

Goodwill: Accounting term referring to a company's intangible assets. Goodwill is recorded on a company's books when it acquires another company, and pays a premium over the listed book value of its assets. The excess paid is categorized as goodwill, added to the acquiring company's balance sheet as an asset, and then depreciated over time (usually 15 years). The Internal Revenue Code defines goodwill as the value of a trade or business attributable to the expectancy of continued customer patronage. Such value results from several factors, including quality product lines and stable employees.

Gross (Profit) Margin: The ratio of gross profit to gross revenues (sometimes also used as a synonym for gross profit). Gross margin analysis is a useful tool because it implicitly includes unit selling prices of products or services, unit costs, and unit volume. Note, however, the difference between gross margin and contribution margin: Contribution margin includes all variable costs; in contrast, gross margin includes some, but often not all, variable costs, a number of which can be part of the operating margin.

$$\text{Gross margin} = \frac{\text{Gross profit}}{\text{Gross revenue}} = \frac{\text{Gross revenue - Cost of goods sold}}{\text{Gross revenue}}$$

Gross Profit: The difference between total sales revenue and total cost of goods sold. Gross profit can be also calculated on a per unit basis as the difference between unit selling price and unit cost of goods sold. For example, if a company sells 100 units, each priced at \$1 and each costing the company \$.30 to manufacture, then the unit gross profit is \$.70, the total gross profit is \$70, and the unit and total gross margins are 70%.

$$\text{Gross profit}_{\text{Total}} = \text{Gross revenues}_{\text{Total}} - \text{Cost of goods sold}_{\text{Total}}$$

$$\text{Gross profit}_{\text{Unit}} = \text{Price}_{\text{Unit}} - \text{Cost of goods sold}_{\text{Unit}}$$

Income Statement: Financial document showing a company's income and expenses over a given period (see Appendix 7).

Internal Rate of Return (IRR): The annualized effective compounded return rate that can be earned on the invested capital (i.e., the yield on the investment).

Margin: Margins reflect the difference between two factors and are typically expressed either in monetary terms or percentages. There are two types of margins: (1) contribution margins, which reflect the relationship between variable and fixed costs and (2) income margins, which reflect the relationships between a company's gross profit, income, and gross revenues.

Marginal Cost: The cost of producing one extra unit.

Market Share: An offering's share of the total sales of all offerings within the product category in which the brand competes. Market share is determined by dividing an offering's sales volume by the total category sales volume. Sales can be defined in terms of revenues or on a unit basis (e.g., number of items sold or number of customers served).

$$\text{Market share} = \frac{\text{An offering's sales in market X}}{\text{Total sales in market X}}$$

Markup: See *Trade Margin*.

Net Earnings: See *Net Income*.

Net Income: Gross revenues minus all costs and expenses (e.g., cost of goods sold, operating expenses, depreciation, interest, and taxes) in a given period of time.

$$\text{Net income} = \text{Gross revenues - Total costs}$$

Net Margin: The ratio of net income to gross revenues.

$$\text{Net margin} = \frac{\text{Net income}}{\text{Gross revenues}}$$

Operating Expenses: The primary costs, other than cost of goods sold, incurred to generate revenues (e.g., sales, marketing, R&D, general and administrative expenses).

Operating Income: Gross profit minus operating expenses. Operating income reflects the firm's profitability from current operations without regard to the interest charges accruing from the firm's capital structure.

$$\text{Operating income} = \text{Gross profit - Operating expenses}$$

Operating Margin: The ratio of operating income to gross revenues.

$$\text{Operating margin} = \frac{\text{Operating income}}{\text{Gross revenues}}$$

Return on Investment (ROI): Net income as a percentage of the investment required to generate this income. Conceptually similar metrics are Return on Assets (ROA), Return on Net Assets (RONA), and Return on Capital (ROC).

$$\text{ROI} = \frac{\text{Gain from an investment - Cost of investment}}{\text{Cost of investment}}$$

Return on Marketing Investment (ROMI): A measure of the efficiency of a company's marketing expenditures. Most often calculated in terms of incremental net income, sales revenues, market share, or contribution margin. ROMI can also be calculated with respect to the overall marketing expenditures or to a specific marketing mix variable (e.g., branding, incentives, and communications).

$$\text{ROMI} = \frac{\text{Incremental net income generated by the marketing investment}}{\text{Cost of the marketing investment}}$$

Return on Sales (ROS): Net income as a percentage of sales revenues.

$$\text{ROS} = \frac{\text{Net income}}{\text{Sales revenue}}$$

Total Costs: The sum of the fixed and variable costs (see Appendix 1 for more details).

Trade Margin: The difference between unit selling price and unit cost at each level of a marketing channel (see Appendix 8). A trade margin is frequently referred to as a markup by channel members and is often expressed as a percentage. Trade margins are typically determined on the basis of selling price, but practices vary among firms and industries.

Variable Costs: Expenses that fluctuate in direct proportion to the output volume of units produced (see Appendix 1 for more details).

Variable Profit: The difference between gross revenues and variable costs.

Appendix 1: Fixed, Variable, and Total Costs

Cost accounting identifies three basic types of costs: fixed costs, variable costs, and total costs.

Fixed costs are expenses that do not fluctuate with output volume within a relevant period. Typical examples of fixed costs include research and development expenses, mass media advertising expenses, rent, interest on debt, insurance, plant and equipment expenses, and salary of permanent full-time workers. Note that even though their absolute size remains unchanged regardless of output volume, fixed costs become progressively smaller per unit of output as volume increases, a decrease that results from the larger number of output units over which fixed costs are allocated.

In contrast, *variable costs* are expenses that fluctuate in direct proportion to the output volume of units produced. To illustrate, expenses incurred by consumer incentives (e.g., coupons, price discounts, and rebates) are commonly viewed as variable marketing costs. Other expenses, such as channel incentives (e.g., promotional allowances) and sales force compensation, can be classified as either fixed or variable costs depending on their structure (e.g., performance-based compensation vs. fixed salary).

Finally, the term *total costs* refers to the sum of the fixed and variable costs. The relationship between fixed, variable, and total costs is shown in Figure 1.

Figure 1: The Relationship between Fixed, Variable, and Total Costs

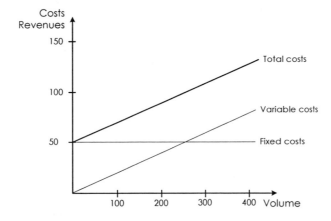

It is important to note that deciding which costs are fixed and which costs are variable depends on the time horizon. For example, in the short run, the salaries of permanent full-time employees will be considered fixed costs because they do not depend on output volume. In the longer run, however, a company may adjust the number and/or salaries of permanent employees based on the demand for its products or services—a scenario in which these costs would be considered variable rather than fixed. Thus, in the long run, all costs would be considered variable.

Appendix 2: Break-Even Analysis of a Fixed Cost Investment

Break-even analysis of a fixed-cost investment identifies the unit or dollar sales volume at which the company is able to recoup a particular investment, such as research and development expenses, product improvement costs, and/or the costs of an advertising campaign. The break-even volume of a fixed-cost investment (BEV_{FC}) is the ratio of the size of the fixed-cost investment to the unit margin.

$$BEV_{FC} = \frac{\text{Fixed cost investment}}{\text{Unit margin}}$$

Because the unit margin can be expressed as the difference between unit selling price and unit variable costs, break-even volume is also often given as:

$$BEV_{FC} = \frac{\text{Fixed-cost investment}}{\text{Unit selling price - Unit variable cost}}$$

The break-even analysis of a fixed-cost investment can be illustrated as shown in Figure 2.

Figure 2: Break-Even of a Fixed Cost Investment

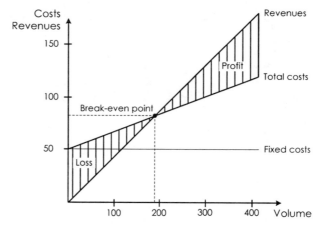

To illustrate, consider an offering priced at $100 with variable costs of $50 and fixed costs of $50M. In this case,

$$BEV_{FC} = \frac{\text{Fixed cost investment}}{\text{Unit margin}} = \frac{\$50M}{\$100 - \$50} = 1,000,000$$

This implies that in order for a $50M fixed-cost investment to break even, sales volume should reach 1,000,000 items.

In addition to the break-even analysis of a fixed-cost investment associated with launching a new offering, a company may need to calculate the break-even volume of a change (most often an increase) in its current fixed-cost investment. Typical problems to which this type of analysis could be applied are estimating the incremental increase in sales necessary to cover the costs of an R&D project, the costs of an advertising campaign, and even the costs of increasing the compensation package of senior executives. The break-even analysis of such increase in the fixed-cost investment is shown in Figure 3.

Figure 3: Break-Even of an Increase in a Fixed-Cost Investment

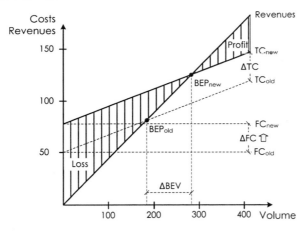

To illustrate, consider the impact of an increase in fixed costs from $50M to $60M for a product priced at $100 with variable costs of $50. In this case,

$$BEV_{\Delta FC} = \frac{\text{Increase in the fixed-cost investment}}{\text{Unit margin}} = \frac{\$60M - \$50M}{\$100 - \$50} = 200{,}000$$

This implies that in order for the $10M fixed-cost investment to break even, sales volume should increase by 200,000 items.

Appendix 3: Break-Even Analysis of a Price Cut

The impact of a price cut on profitability is twofold. On one hand, lowering price tends to increase the volume of units sold, thus increasing total revenues. On the other hand, lowering price decreases unit margin, thus lowering total revenues. In this context, break-even analysis estimates the increase in sales volume that needs to be achieved in order for a price cut to have a neutral impact on profitability. The break-even analysis of a price cut is shown in Figure 4.

Figure 4: Break-Even of a Decrease in Revenues (Resulting from a Price Cut)

To break even, lost profits resulting from a lower margin after a price cut must be equal to the additional profits generated by the incremental volume from the lower price. Thus, to have a neutral or positive impact on the company's bottom line, the additional profits generated from the incremental volume resulting from a lower price must be equal to or greater than the lost profits that result from a lower margin.

$$\text{Profit}_{\text{NewPrice}} \geq \text{Profit}_{\text{OldPrice}}$$

Given that profit is a function of unit volume and unit margin, the above equation can be modified as follows:

$$\text{Volume}_{\text{NewPrice}} \cdot \text{Margin}_{\text{NewPrice}} \geq \text{Volume}_{\text{OldPrice}} \cdot \text{Margin}_{\text{OldPrice}} \quad (1)$$

Now, the above equation can be restructured as follows:

$$\text{Volume}_{\text{NewPrice}} \geq \frac{\text{Margin}_{\text{OldPrice}}}{\text{Margin}_{\text{NewPrice}}} \cdot \text{Volume}_{\text{OldPrice}}$$

Hence, the sales volume that needs to be achieved for a price cut to break even is:

$$\text{BEV}_{\text{PC}} = \frac{\text{Margin}_{\text{OldPrice}}}{\text{Margin}_{\text{NewPrice}}} \cdot \text{Volume}_{\text{OldPrice}}$$

In addition to calculating the break-even volume of a price cut, it may be useful to calculate the rate at which sales volume must increase in order for a price cut to be profitable.

In this context, the break-even rate of a price cut (BER_{PC}) can be derived from equation (1) as follows:

$$\frac{Volume_{NewPrice}}{Volume_{OldPrice}} \geq \frac{Margin_{OldPrice}}{Margin_{NewPrice}}$$

$$\frac{Volume_{NewPrice}}{Volume_{OldPrice}} - 1 \geq \frac{Margin_{OldPrice}}{Margin_{NewPrice}} - 1$$

$$\frac{Volume_{NewPrice} - Volume_{OldPrice}}{Volume_{OldPrice}} \geq \frac{Margin_{OldPrice}}{Margin_{NewPrice}} - 1$$

Note that the left side of the equation reflects the increase in volume resulting from a price cut as a percentage of the initial volume before the price cut. Hence, the Break-Even Rate (BER_{PC}) at which sales should increase so that a price cut has a neutral impact on profitability is:

$$BER_{PC} = \frac{Margin_{OldPrice}}{Margin_{NewPrice}} - 1$$

To illustrate, consider the impact of a price cut from \$100 to \$75 for a product with a variable cost of \$50. In this case, $Margin_{OldPrice} = \$100 - \$50 = \$50$ and $Margin_{NewPrice} = \$75 - \$50 = \$25$. Therefore, the break-even volume can be calculated as follows:

$$BEV_{PC} = \frac{Margin_{OldPrice}}{Margin_{NewPrice}} \cdot Volume_{OldPrice} = \frac{\$50}{\$25} \cdot Volume_{OldPrice} = 2 \cdot Volume_{OldPrice}$$

This essentially means that for the price cut to break even, sales volume should double at the lower price. It is noteworthy that relatively small changes in sales price can require what may appear to be a disproportionately greater increase in sales volume. Indeed, in the example above, a 25% decrease in price requires a doubling of sales volume.

Alternatively, one may calculate the rate at which the current volume should increase so that the price cut has neutral impact on profitability.

$$BER_{PC} = \frac{Margin_{OldPrice}}{Margin_{NewPrice}} - 1 = \frac{\$50}{\$25} - 1 = 1$$

The above calculation means that, for the price cut to break even, sales volume should increase by a factor of 1, or by 100%.

Appendix 4: Break-Even Analysis of a Variable Cost Increase

Break-even analysis of a variable cost increase identifies the sales volume at which a company neither makes a profit nor incurs a loss after increasing the variable costs associated with a particular offering. Typical problems to which this type of analysis can be applied are estimating the incremental increase in sales necessary to cover an increase in the cost of goods sold, estimating the costs associated with increasing an item-specific level of service, and estimating the costs associated with running item-specific incentives (e.g., premiums). The break-even analysis of a variable-cost increase is shown in Figure 5.

Figure 5: Break-Even of a Variable Cost Increase

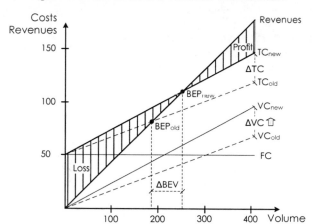

The basic principle of calculating the break-even point of an increase in an offering's variable costs is similar to that of estimating the break-even point of a price cut. The key difference in this case is that a decrease in the margin generated by the new offering is a result of an increase in the offering's costs rather than a decrease in revenues. Thus, the break-even volume of a variable-cost increase can be calculated as follows:

$$BEV_{VC} = \frac{Margin_{OldVC}}{Margin_{NewVC}} \cdot Volume_{OldVC}$$

Similarly, the break-even rate of an increase in variable costs can be calculated as follows:

$$BER_{VC} = \frac{Margin_{OldVC}}{Margin_{NewVC}} - 1$$

To illustrate, consider the impact of an increase in variable costs from \$50 to \$60 for a product priced at \$100. In this case, $Margin_{OldVC}$ = \$100 − \$50 = \$50 and $Margin_{NewVC}$ = \$100 − \$60 = \$40. Therefore, the break-even volume of a variable cost increase can be calculated as follows:

$$BEV_{VC} = \frac{Margin_{OldVC}}{Margin_{NewVC}} \cdot Volume_{OldVC} = \frac{\$50}{\$40} \cdot Volume_{OldVC} = 1.25 \cdot Volume_{OldVC}$$

Thus, for the variable cost increase to break even, sales volume should increase by a factor of 1.25, or by 125%.

Alternatively, one could calculate the rate at which the current volume should increase so that the increase in variable costs has neutral impact on profitability.

$$\text{BER}_{VC} = \frac{\text{Margin}_{\text{OldVC}}}{\text{Margin}_{\text{NewVC}}} - 1 = \frac{\$50}{\$40} - 1 = 0.25$$

The above calculation implies that, for the increase in variable costs to break even, sales volume should increase by a factor of .25, or by 25%.

Appendix 5: Break-Even Analysis of Cannibalization

The primary goal of extending a company's product line by launching a new offering is to increase the company's sales revenues by growing demand for the overall category and/or by stealing share from competitors. A typical side effect of such product line extensions is that, in addition to stealing share from competitors, the new offering also takes away share from a company's current offerings, a process commonly referred to as cannibalization (Figure 6).

Figure 6: Impact of Launching a New Offering on the Sales Volume of an Existing Offering

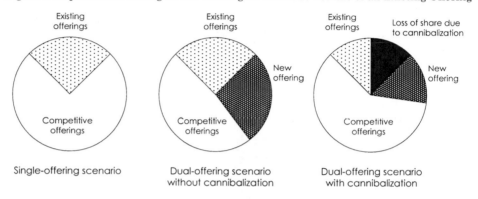

In this context, the break-even rate of a potential cannibalization of sales of an existing offering from a product line extension identifies the ratio of the cannibalized sales volume of the existing offering to the sales volume generated by the new offering at which a company neither makes a profit nor incurs a loss. Thus, the break-even rate of cannibalization indicates the maximum proportion of the sales volume of the new offering that could come from the company's existing offering(s) without incurring a loss. The break-even rate of cannibalization can be derived as follows:

To avoid loss of profit across all offerings, profit from the new product must be equal to or greater than the lost profits from cannibalization (the dark-shaded area in the above chart).

$$\text{Profit}_{\text{NewOffering}} \geq \text{LostProfit}_{\text{OldOffering}}$$

Given that profit is a function of unit volume and unit margin, the above equation can be modified as follows:

$$\text{Volume}_{\text{NewOffering}} \cdot \text{Margin}_{\text{NewOffering}} \geq \text{LostVolume}_{\text{OldOffering}} \cdot \text{Margin}_{\text{OldOffering}} \quad (1)$$

Now, equation (1) can be restructured as follows:

$$\frac{\text{LostVolume}_{\text{OldOffering}}}{\text{Volume}_{\text{NewOffering}}} = \frac{\text{Margin}_{\text{NewOffering}}}{\text{Margin}_{\text{OldOffering}}}$$

Note that the left part of the equation is the ratio of sales volume of the old offering that was lost because of cannibalization of the sales volume of the new offering, which is exactly the definition of the break-even rate of cannibalization (BER$_C$). Hence:

$$\text{BER}_C = \frac{\text{Margin}_{\text{NewOffering}}}{\text{Margin}_{\text{OldOffering}}}$$

For example, consider a company launching a new product priced at $70 with variable costs of $60, which may cannibalize the sales of an existing product priced at $100 and that also has variable costs of $60. In this case, $\text{Margin}_{\text{NewOffering}} = \$70 - \$60 = \$10$ and $\text{Margin}_{\text{OldOffering}} = \$100 - \$60 = \$40$. Therefore, the break-even rate of cannibalization can be calculated as follows:

$$\text{BER}_C = \frac{\text{Margin}_{\text{NewOffering}}}{\text{Margin}_{\text{OldOffering}}} = \frac{\$10}{\$40} = 0.25$$

The break-even rate of cannibalization in this case is 0.25 or 25%, which means that to be profitable to the company, no more than 25% of the sales volume of the new offering should come from the current offering, which in turn implies that at least 75% of sales volume should come from competitors' offerings and/or from increasing the overall size of the market.

Appendix 6: Economic Value Analysis

The concept of economic value analysis (EVA) is predicated on the idea that the monetary value of an offering should be estimated not only based on its purchase price but also on the overall value it delivers to target customers. In this context, EVA involves monetizing the nonmonetary aspects of an offering's value proposition. Building on the notion that an offering's value proposition has three distinct dimensions: functional, monetary, and psychological, EVA implies translating functional and psychological value into financial terms (Figure 7).

Figure 7. The Concept of Economic Value Analysis

Economic value analysis is typically used to evaluate the monetary value of an offering in two cases: (1) to identify the intrinsic value of an offering to its target customers (i.e., in the absence of competition) and (2) to identify an offering's monetary value relative to that of the competition. These two approaches are discussed in more detail below.

Identifying the intrinsic monetary value of an offering is particularly useful when developing a primary demand strategy that aims to gain share by attracting customers who are unfamiliar with this type of product. In this context, the monetary value of an offering is calculated as the difference between the monetary equivalent of its functional, monetary, and psychological benefits and its functional, monetary, and psychological costs (Figure 8).

Figure 8. Economic Value as a Function of an Offering's Benefits and Costs

In addition to representing economic value as a function of the difference between benefits and costs, it can be represented as the relative advantage of an offering vis-à-vis its competitors. Defining the monetary value of an offering relative to the competition is particularly useful when developing a steal-share strategy that aims to gain share by attracting competitors' customers. In this context, an offering's economic advantage can be represented as the difference in the monetary value of the company's offering relative to its competitors (Figure 9).

Figure 9. Economic Value of the Relative Advantage of an Offering

In business-to-business markets, the economic advantage of an offering is often calculated as the difference in the total costs of ownership of the offerings. This type of economic value analysis is especially useful to relate the price and nonprice aspects of the offering. To illustrate, consider the two offerings depicted in Figure 10. Although Offering Y is priced higher than Offering X, when all relevant costs (downtime, replacement, maintenance, usage, financing, inventory, and installation costs) are considered, the total cost of the higher priced Offering Y ends up being lower than that of the lower priced Offering X.

Figure 10. Economic Value as a Function of the Differences in the Total Costs

Calculating the economic value as a function of the difference in the total costs of an offering can be illustrated by the following example. Consider a farm equipment manufacturer selling a tractor priced at $180,000. Imagine that its price is $25,000 higher than functionally similar offerings from its competitors. Although this company's tractor is more durable, reliable, and has a longer warranty and faster response to service calls, justifying the $25,000 price difference is not a trivial task for its sales force. One approach to sales is to identify the monetary value of the functional differences between the company's tractor and its competitors, which involves estimating the incremental value of the benefits of the company's offering to the customer vis-à-vis its competitors.

This approach is illustrated in Table 1, which indicates that the customer value of the functional benefits delivered by the company's offering is $41,000, significantly greater than the $25,000 price difference between the offerings. This analysis shows that the company's offering is *underpriced* by $16,000 relative to the competition.

Table 1. Economic Value Analysis: An Example

Value ($)	Benefit
$6,000	Greater durability (2 extra years of product usage)
$14,000	Greater reliability (2 fewer breakdowns per year × 10 years × downtime costs to the company)
$9,500	Longer warranty (2 years extra warranty × 3 service calls per year × value of replacement parts)
$11,500	Faster response to service calls (3 service calls per year × 10 years × 4-hour faster response × hourly downtime costs)
$41,000	Total monetary value of the competitive advantage

Appendix 7: Income Statement: An Overview

The income statement is a financial document showing a company's income and expenses over a given period. It typically identifies revenues, costs, operating expenses, operating income, and earnings (Figure 12).

Figure 12: An Example of Revenues, Costs, and Margins as Shown in a Company's Income Statement

Gross Revenues	
Product sales	$ 12,000
Services	3,000
Total (Gross) Revenues	15,000
Cost of Goods Sold	
Product costs	4,000
Services costs	1,500
Depreciation	500
Total Cost of Goods Sold	6,000
Gross Profit	9,000
Gross Margin	60%
Operating Expenses	
Sales and Marketing	5,000
General and Administrative	1,000
Research and Development	1,500
Total Operating Expenses	7,500
Operating Income	1,500
Operating Margin	10%
Interest payments on loans	500
Earnings before taxes	1,000
Provision for taxes	250
Net Income (Earnings)	750
Net (Profit) Margin	5%

Appendix 8: Distribution Channel Margin Analysis

A useful approach to analyzing margins of the individual members of a distribution channel involves mapping the channel structure to identify margins for each channel member (Figure 13).

Figure 13: An Example of Distribution Channel Margins

Note that margins are almost universally calculated based on sales revenue (e.g., sales price) rather than based on cost (e.g., purchase price). To illustrate, the margin for an item purchased for $10 (cost) and sold for $15 (revenue) can be calculated as follows:

$$\text{Margin} = \frac{\text{Revenue - Cost}}{\text{Revenue}} = \frac{\text{Selling price - Purchase price}}{\text{Selling price}} = \frac{\$15 - \$10}{\$15} = 0.33$$

Chapter Twenty Three

Essential Marketing Metrics

The effectiveness of a company's marketing activities is a function of the degree to which these activities enable to the company to reach its strategic goals. Monitoring a company's progress toward its goals is typically achieved using performance benchmarks commonly referred to as marketing metrics. Here, the term "metric" refers to a criterion used to evaluate the past, current, and/or future performance of a company, product line, or a particular offering. The key marketing metrics are usually delineated in a company's strategic goal(s). To illustrate, the goal of increasing net income by a certain amount within a given timeframe identifies net income as the key performance metric.

Marketing metrics vary in the degree to which their components are readily observable and can be uniquely derived from those components. For example, net income is uniquely defined as the difference between gross revenue and the total costs. In contrast, in the case of other metrics such as brand power, brand equity, and customer equity, there is no commonly agreed-upon formula to derive these metrics. Instead, the derivation of these metrics is contingent on the use of particular theoretical models believed to represent the underlying phenomenon.

Marketing metrics also vary in their level of generality. Some reflect more fundamental aspects of a company's business activities, whereas others capture the company's performance in the context of relatively more specific business activities. Accordingly, marketing metrics can be divided into two categories: (1) *strategic metrics,* which reflect a company's progress toward achieving its strategic goal(s), and (2) *tactical metrics,* which focus on specific marketing mix variables, including product, service, brand, price, incentives, communications, and distribution. These two types of metrics are discussed in more detail below.

Strategic Performance Metrics

Strategic marketing metrics reflect a company's overall performance with respect to its ability to achieve its strategic goals. Two types of performance metrics can be identified: (1) financial metrics, such as net income, gross margins, and return on investment and (2) nonfinancial metrics, such as conversion, retention, and penetration rates.

Financial Performance Metrics

Compound Annual Growth Rate (CAGR): The year-to-year growth rate of an investment over a specified period of time (Chapter 22).

Contribution Margin ($): When expressed in monetary terms (e.g., in dollars), contribution margin typically refers to the difference between total revenues and total variable costs. Contribution margin can also be calculated on a per-unit basis as the difference between the unit selling price and the unit variable cost (Chapter 22).

Contribution Margin (%): When expressed in percentages (%), contribution margin typically refers to the ratio of the difference between total revenues and total variable costs to total revenues. Contribution margin also can be expressed as the ratio of unit contribution to unit selling price (Chapter 22).

Customer Equity: The lifetime monetary value of a company's customers. Customer equity (also referred to as customer lifetime value) can also be calculated on a per-customer basis by estimating the direct monetary impact of a customer during his/her tenure with the company (Chapter 22).

Gross Margin: The ratio of gross profit to gross revenues (Chapter 22).

Internal Rate of Return (IRR): The annualized effective compounded return rate that can be earned on the invested capital (Chapter 22).

Market Share: An offering's share of the total sales of all offerings within the product category in which the brand competes. Market share is determined by dividing an offering's sales volume by the total category sales volume. Sales can be defined in terms of revenues or on a unit basis (Chapter 22).

Net Income: Gross revenues minus all costs and expenses (e.g., cost of goods sold, operating expenses, depreciation, interest, and taxes) in a given period of time (Chapter 22).

Net Margin: The ratio of net income to gross revenues (Chapter 22).

Operating Income: Gross profit minus operating expenses. Operating income reflects the firm's profitability from current operations without regard to the interest charges accruing from the firm's capital structure (Chapter 22).

Operating Margin: The ratio of operating income to gross revenues (Chapter 22).

Return on Investment (ROI): Net income as a percentage of the investment required to generate this income. Conceptually similar metrics are Return on Assets (ROA), Return on Net Assets (RONA), and Return on Capital (ROC; Chapter 22).

Return on Marketing Investment (ROMI): A measure of the efficiency of a company's marketing expenditures. Most often calculated in terms of incremental net income, sales revenues, market share, or contribution margin. ROMI can also be calculated with respect to the overall marketing expenditures or to a specific marketing mix variable (Chapter 22).

Return on Sales (ROS): Net income as a percentage of sales revenues (Chapter 22).

Nonfinancial Performance Metrics

Brand Development Index (BDI): A measure of the degree to which sales of a given brand have captured the total market potential in a particular geographical area based on the population of that area and average consumption per user nationally (Chapter 19).

Category Development Index (CDI): A measure of the degree to which sales in a given category have captured the total market potential in a particular geographical area based on the population of that area and average consumption per user nationally (Chapter 19).

Conversion Rate: The number of potential customers who have tried the product/service relative to the total number of customers aware of the product/service (Chapter 16).

Cost per Customer: The average cost of acquiring a new customer (Chapter 16).

Customer Attrition Rate (Churn Rate): The number of customers who discontinue using a company's product or service during a specified time period relative to the average total number of customers over that same time period (Chapter 16).

Net Promoter Score: A popular metric designed to measure customers' satisfaction by using as a proxy their willingness to generate word of mouth about the company and/or its products (Chapter 14).

Penetration Rate: The number of customers who have tried the offering at least once relative to the total number of potential customers (Chapter 16).

Retention Rate: The number of customers who have repurchased the offering during the current buying cycle (e.g., month, quarter, year) relative to the number of customers who have purchased the offering during the last cycle. Also used in reference to the number of customers who have repurchased the offering relative to the total number of customers who have tried the product at least once (Chapter 16).

Tactical Metrics

Tactical metrics describe an offering's performance with respect to one or more marketing mix variables, including product, service, brand, price, incentives, communications, and distribution. Some of the key metrics are identified below.

Product and Service Metrics

Product/Service Preferences: A measure reflecting the degree to which the product/service appeals to current and potential customers (Chapter 17).

Product/Service Satisfaction: A measure reflecting customers' experience with the product. Unlike product-preference metrics that can be measured prior to purchase as well as post purchase, satisfaction requires consumers to have actual experience with the product or service (Chapter 17).

Purchase Intent: Self-reported likelihood of purchasing a company's products or services (Chapter 17).

Brand Metrics

Brand Power: A brand's ability to differentiate the offering from the competition and create customer value through meaningful associations. Unlike brand equity, which reflects the value of the brand to the company, brand power reflects the value of the brand among current and potential customers (Chapter 11).

Brand Equity: The net present value of the financial benefits derived from the brand. Brand equity is a function of brand power, as well as a number of additional factors reflecting the company's utilization of the strength of its brand (Chapter 11).

Price Metrics

Price Elasticity: The percentage change in quantity sold relative to the percentage change in price for a given product or service (Chapter 12).

Cross-Price Elasticity: The percentage change in quantity sold of a given offering caused by a percentage change in the price of another offering (Chapter 12).

Incentives Metrics

Incentives Ratio: Percentage of sales that involves an incentive relative to the company's total sales (Chapter 13).

Pass-through Incentives Ratio: Percentage of the incentives provided to customers by a given channel (e.g., a retailer) relative to the incentives provided to that channel (Chapter 13).

Communication Metrics

Awareness: The number of potential customers who are aware of the offering (Chapter 14).

Awareness Rate: The number of potential customers who are aware of the offering, relative to the total number of potential customers (Chapter 14).

Top-of-Mind Awareness: The first brand identified by respondents when asked to list brands in a given product category (Chapter 14).

Cost per Point (CPP): A measure representing the cost of a communications campaign. CPP is the media cost of reaching one percent (one rating point) of a particular demographic (Chapter 14).

Cost per Thousand (CPM): A measure used to represent the cost of a communications campaign. CPM is the cost of reaching 1,000 individuals or households with an advertising message in a given medium (Chapter 14).

Gross Rating Point (GRP): A measure of the total volume of advertising delivery to the target audience. GRP is equal to the percent of the population reached times the frequency of exposure (Chapter 14).

Reach: The size of the audience that has been exposed to a particular advertisement at least once in a given period (Chapter 14).

Share of Voice: A company's communications expenditures relative to those of the entire product category (Chapter 14).

Target Rating Point (TRP): A measure of the total volume of advertising delivery to the target audience. TRP is similar to GRP, but its calculation involves using only the target audience (rather than the total audience) as the base (Chapter 14).

Total Impressions: The number of times each recipient has been exposed to the message (Chapter 14).

Distribution Metrics

All-Commodity Volume (ACV): A measure of an offering's availability, typically calculated as the total annual volume of the company's offering in a given geographic area relative to the total sales volume of the retailers in that geographic area across all product categories (hence, the term "all-commodity volume"). Also refers to the gross sales in a specific geographic area (i.e., total sales of all stores; Chapter 15).

Inventory Turnover: The number of times the inventory is replenished, typically calculated as the ratio of the annual revenues generated by a given offering to the average inventory (Chapter 15).

Same-Store Sales: A metric used in the retail industry comparing sales of stores that have been open for a year or more and have historical data to compare the current year's sales to the same timeframe last year (Chapter 15).

Share of Shelf Space: Shelf space allocated to a given offering relative to the total shelf space in a given geographic area (Chapter 15).

Additional Readings

Paul W. Farris, Neil T. Bendle, Phillip E. Pfeifer, and David J. Reibstein (2006), *Marketing Metrics: 50+ Metrics Every Executive Should Master*. Philadelphia, PA: Wharton School Publishing.

Douglas W. Hubbard (2007), *How to Measure Anything: Finding the Value of "Intangibles" in Business*. New York, NY: John Wiley & Sons.

John Davis (2006), *Measuring Marketing: 103 Key Metrics Every Marketer Needs*. New York, NY: John Wiley & Sons.

James D. Lenskold (2003), *Marketing ROI: The Path to Campaign, Customer, and Corporate Profitability*. New York, NY: McGraw-Hill.

Index

Terms listed in this index are grouped in four categories: (1) marketing concepts, (2) financial concepts, (3) marketing frameworks, and (4) companies, products, and brands.

Marketing Concepts

Financial Concepts

Marketing Frameworks

Companies, Products, and Brands

Printed in the United States
118618LV00008B/117-280/P

9 780979 003929